# GERALD OF WALES

# GERALD OF WALES

## New Perspectives on a Medieval Writer and Critic

Edited by
Georgia Henley and A. Joseph McMullen

UNIVERSITY OF WALES PRESS

2018

*www.uwp.co.uk*
*British Library CIP Data*

A catalogue record for this book is available from the British Library

ISBN    978-1-78683-163-7 (hardback)
        978-1-78683-164-4 (paperback)
e-ISBN  978-1-78683-165-1

Designed and typeset by Chris Bell, cbdesign
Printed by CPI Antony Rowe, Melksham

# Contents

# Acknowledgements

The editors are very grateful to Harvard University's Department of Celtic Languages and Literatures, the Standing Committee on Medieval Studies, the Friends of Harvard Celtic Studies, the Provostial Fund Committee for the Arts and Humanities, and *Sententiae: The Harvard Undergraduate Journal of Medieval Studies*, for their generous support of the conference which first united this group of scholars under one roof in April 2015. We owe a debt of gratitude to the faculty, staff and students of Harvard's Department of Celtic Languages and Literatures, especially Professor Catherine McKenna, Mary Violette and Steven Duede, for their very kind assistance. We thank the conference attendees and speakers who do not appear in this volume but who nevertheless shaped it with their enthusiastic participation and comments: Christopher Berard, Ann and Charlie Heymann, Stephen Jones, Lindsey Panxhi, Joel Pattison, Diarmuid Scully, Victoria Shirley, and many others. We are grateful to our anonymous reviewer and to the staff at University of Wales Press (particularly Bethan Phillips, Elin Lewis, Sarah Lewis and Dafydd Jones) for their careful attention and guidance, and to Paul Russell for his gracious assistance. We thank the College of Liberal Arts and Sciences Dean's Office at the University of Connecticut and the Friends of Harvard Celtic Studies for their generous support of the colour images in the volume.

✣

# Abbreviations

| | |
|---|---|
| *Catalogus* | *Catalogus brevior librorum suorum* ('A Catalogue of his Shorter Works'), in J. S. Brewer (ed.), *Giraldi Cambrensis Opera*, 8/1 (London, 1861) |
| *De invectionibus* | ('On Shameful Attacks'), in W. S. Davies (ed.), 'The Book of Invectives of Giraldus Cambrensis', *Y Cymmrodor*, 30 (1920), 1–248 |
| *De iure* | *De iure et statu Menevensis ecclesiae* ('On the Rights and Status of the Church of St Davids'), in J. S. Brewer (ed.), *Giraldi Cambrensis Opera*, 8/3 (London, 1863) |
| *De principis instructione* | ('Instruction for a Ruler'), in G. F. Warner (ed.), *Giraldi Cambrensis Opera*, 8/8 (London, 1891) |
| *De rebus* | *De rebus a se gestis* ('On The Things He Has Achieved'), in J. S. Brewer (ed.), *Giraldi Cambrensis Opera*, 8/1 (London, 1861) |
| *Descriptio* | *Descriptio Kambriae* ('Description of Wales'), in J. F. Dimock (ed.), *Giraldi Cambrensis Opera*, 8/6 (London, 1868) |
| *Epistola ad capitulum* | *Epistola ad capitulum Herefordense* ('Letter to the Chapter at Hereford'), in J. S. Brewer (ed.), *Giraldi Cambrensis Opera*, 8/1 (London, 1861) |
| *Expugnatio* | *Expugnatio Hibernica* ('Conquest of Ireland'), in A. B. Scott and F. X. Martin (ed. and trans.), *Expugnatio Hibernica: The Conquest of Ireland, by Giraldus Cambrensis* (Dublin, 1978) |

| | |
|---|---|
| *Gemma ecclesiastica* | ('The Jewel of the Church'), in J. S. Brewer (ed.), *Giraldi Cambrensis Opera*, 8/2 (London, 1862) |
| *Itinerarium* | *Itinerarium Kambriae* ('Journey Through Wales'), in J. F. Dimock (ed.), *Giraldi Cambrensis Opera*, 8/6 (London, 1868) |
| *Retractationes* | ('Retractions'), J. S. Brewer (ed.), *Giraldi Cambrensis Opera*, 8/1 (London, 1861) |
| *Speculum duorum* | ('A Mirror of Two Men'), in Yves Lefèvre and R. B. C. Huygens (eds), Brian Dawson (trans.) and Michael Richter (gen. ed.), *Giraldus Cambrensis: Speculum Duorum, or A Mirror of Two Men, Preserved in the Vatican Library in Rome, Cod. Reg. Lat. 470* (Cardiff, 1974) |
| *Speculum ecclesiae* | ('A Mirror of the Church'), in J. S. Brewer (ed.), *Giraldi Cambrensis Opera*, 8/4 (London, 1873) |
| *Symbolum electorum* | ('A Collection of Choice Works'), in J. S. Brewer (ed.), *Giraldi Cambrensis Opera*, 8/1 (London, 1861) |
| *Topographia* | *Topographia Hibernica* ('Topography of Ireland'), in J. F. Dimock (ed.), *Giraldi Cambrensis Opera*, 8/5 (London, 1867) |
| *Vita Davidis* | *Vita Sancti Davidis* ('The Life of St David'), in J. S. Brewer (ed.), *Giraldi Cambrensis Opera*, 8/3 (London, 1863) |
| *Vita Ethelberti* | *Vita Sancti Ethelberti* ('The Life of St Ethelbert'), in M. R. James (ed.), 'Two Lives of St. Ethelbert, King and Martyr', *English Historical Review*, 32 (1917), 214–44 |
| *Vita Galfridi* | *Vita Galfridi Archiepiscopi Eboracensis* ('Life of Geoffrey, Archbishop of York'), in J. S. Brewer (ed.), *Giraldi Cambrensis Opera*, 8/4 (London, 1873) |
| *Vita Hugonis* | *Vita Sancti Hugonis* ('The Life of St Hugh'), in Richard M. Loomis (ed. and trans.), *The Life of St. Hugh of Avalon, Bishop of Lincoln 1186–2000* (New York, 1985) |
| *Vita Remigii* | *Vita Sancti Remigii* ('The Life of St Remigius'), in J. F. Dimock (ed.), *Giraldi Cambrensis Opera*, 8/7 (London, 1877) |

# Illustrations

# Notes on Contributors

**Robert Bartlett** is the Wardlaw Professor of Mediaeval History Emeritus at the University of St Andrews. He is the author of *Gerald of Wales, 1146–1223* (Oxford, 1982). He is also known for the critically acclaimed *The Making of Europe: Conquest, Colonization and Cultural Change, 950–1350* (Princeton, 1993) as well as his extensive research on medieval cults of saints and English history from the Norman Conquest to the fourteenth century. His most recent works include a survey of Christian saints' cults *Why Can the Dead Do Such Great Things? Saints and Worshippers from the Martyrs to the Reformation* (Princeton, 2013) and the Wiles Lectures, *The Natural and the Supernatural in the Middle Ages* (Cambridge, 2008).

**Michael Faletra** is Professor of English and Humanities at Reed College in Portland, Oregon, where he teaches the literatures of medieval Britain. He has translated Geoffrey of Monmouth's *History of the Kings of Britain* for Broadview Press and recently published *Wales and the Medieval Colonial Imagination* with Palgrave Macmillan. He is at work on a larger project on the making of meaning in the works of Gerald of Wales.

**Ben Guy** is a Junior Research Fellow at Robinson College, Cambridge. In 2016 he completed a PhD thesis in the Department of Anglo-Saxon, Norse and Celtic at the University of Cambridge, entitled 'Medieval Welsh Genealogy: Texts, Contexts and Transmission'. He has published articles on Welsh historical writing and medieval Welsh manuscripts.

**Georgia Henley** is a Postdoctoral Scholar in English and the Center for Spatial and Textual Analysis, Stanford University. In 2017 she completed a PhD in Celtic

Languages and Literatures from Harvard University. Her research focuses on historical literature and textual transmission in medieval Wales and the March.

**Peter Jones** is a Visiting Scholar at the Pembroke Center, Brown University. From 2014–16 he was an Andrew W. Mellon Postdoctoral Fellow at the Jackman Humanities Institute, University of Toronto. He received a PhD in History from New York University in 2014. Peter has just completed a book manuscript on the role of laughter in twelfth-century culture, politics and theology. His current research focuses on the political humour of medieval saints, and he is also working on a project on revolutionary movements in twelfth-century Europe.

**Brendan Kane** specialises in early modern Irish history and British history. He is the author of *The Politics and Culture of Honour in Britain and Ireland, 1541–1641* (Cambridge, 2010/14) and co-editor, with Valerie McGowan-Doyle, of the edited collection *Elizabeth I and Ireland* (Cambridge, 2014). Currently he is completing a book on knowledge production and legitimacy in early modern Ireland, and directing (with Tom Scheinfeldt) a multi-institutional, collaborative digital humanities project '*Léamh*: Learn Early Modern Irish (a digital guide to Irish Gaelic, *c*.1200–1650)'.

**Suzanne LaVere** received her PhD in history from Northwestern University, and is an Associate Professor at Indiana University-Purdue University Fort Wayne. Her first book, *Out of the Cloister: Scholastic Exegesis of the Song of Songs, 1100–1250*, was published by Brill in 2016. She is currently working on a book project examining writings on pastoral care and church reform in the long twelfth century.

**A. Joseph McMullen** is an Assistant Professor of English at Centenary University. He received a PhD in English and Celtic Literatures and Languages from Harvard University in 2015. His work is broadly concerned with medieval literary landscapes and connections between Anglo-Saxon England and early medieval Ireland.

**Simon Meecham-Jones** is an Affiliated Lecturer for the English faculty at the University of Cambridge. His research interests include twelfth-century Latin lyric poetry, fourteenth-century Middle English poetry, the representation of Wales and the Welsh people in English medieval culture and language contact, particularly code-switching. He has begun an investigation of code-switching in *Sir Gawain and the Green Knight* and is currently completing a study of Geoffrey Chaucer entitled *Chaucer and Imagination*.

**Owain Nash** studied History and Politics at University College, Oxford, from where he transferred to Bristol University for an MA in History. His MA thesis discusses the characterisation of language in the Aberdeen Bestiary. After achieving a rank of distinction he began a PhD, also at Bristol University. His PhD dissertation concerns twelfth-century colonial narratives, especially those of Gerald of Wales, Walter Map and Gervase of Tilbury, in relation to contemporary theories of the body.

**Huw Pryce** is Professor of Welsh History at Bangor University. He has published extensively on the history of medieval Wales and also on Welsh historiography. His publications include *Native Law and the Church in Medieval Wales* (Oxford, 1993), an edition of the documents of the Welsh princes, *The Acts of Welsh Rulers 1120–1283* (Cardiff, 2005) and *J. E. Lloyd and the Creation of Welsh History: Renewing a Nation's Past* (Cardiff, 2011). He is co-editor of *The Welsh History Review* and one of the editors of the monograph series Studies in Celtic History.

**Peter Raleigh** is a PhD candidate at the University of North Carolina, Chapel Hill, whose dissertation research is concerned with medieval historiography and narrative images of the English kings. Before beginning his PhD, he completed an MA in the History of the Crusades at Cardiff University.

**Catherine Rooney** studied for a BA, MPhil and PhD in the Department of Anglo-Saxon, Norse and Celtic at the University of Cambridge. Her PhD was a palaeographical study of 'The Manuscripts of the Works of Gerald of Wales' which she received in 2005.

**Joshua Byron Smith** is an Assistant Professor of English at the University of Arkansas. He is the author of *Walter Map and the Matter of Britain* (University of Pennsylvania Press, 2017).

**Caoimhe Whelan** is a Postdoctoral Fellow at the Department of History at Trinity College, Dublin, working on a project funded by the Irish Research Council exploring the earliest English writing in Ireland. She is particularly interested in vernacular historiography, and her doctoral studies at Trinity College, Dublin focused on the late medieval English translation of Gerald of Wales's *Expugnatio Hibernica*. This research was funded by the Irish Research Council and she received the Daniel O'Connell Award for research in Irish history from the council.

# Gerald of Wales: Interpretation and Innovation in Medieval Britain

Georgia Henley and A. Joseph McMullen
*Stanford University and Centenary University*

T HE APPEAL OF GERALD OF WALES (*c.*1146–*c.*1223) as a writer and critic lies in his unique perspective and unrelentingly self-expressive voice. Committed to describing the present day as he saw it, he left behind a collection of works valued not only for its range, enthusiasm and inquisitiveness, but also (and most often) for its unique observations on Irish and Welsh culture. Best known for his innovative works on Ireland and Wales and for his ill-fated struggle to become the archbishop of the Welsh diocese of St Davids, Gerald has been utilised by historians, Celticists and linguists alike as a valuable source of information about the twelfth-century Insular world, including Angevin court life, ecclesiastical reform and clerical conduct, the Norman conquest of Ireland, southern Welsh politics, English saints' lives, natural history, and a host of other topics discussed in his characteristically energetic voice. Gerald also imparted a great deal more biographical information and self-reflection than most of the contemporaries to whom he is compared (Walter Map, Geoffrey of Monmouth and, less often, John of Salisbury), providing us with a rich impression of his evolving personality and career goals across a long life, which spanned the turbulent decades from King Stephen's reign to the early years of Henry III and touched upon many of the major figures of twelfth-century Britain.

The present volume takes a new approach to his life and works. While much of the scholarship concerning Gerald to date has (with a few important exceptions) focused on his popular works on Ireland and Wales, the essays in this volume bring attention to some of his lesser-known works, including the *Gemma ecclesiastica*, *Vita Sancti Hugonis*, *Vita Ethelberti* and the *Speculum Ecclesiae*, as well as *The History of Llanthony Priory*, newly ascribed to him. Some of these essays offer new perspectives on his works on Ireland and Wales, detailing his use of Welsh genealogies and other sources, as well as his intellectual influences, while others examine instances of his reception in Wales and Ireland. Overall, the volume articulates a defence of Gerald's rhetorical skill, purpose and narrative style, and, in doing so, comes closer to understanding his intentions and goals.

Throughout his life, Gerald was surrounded by a variety of influences and was able to operate in several political spheres. He was born *c.*1146 at Manorbier Castle in Pembrokeshire into an aristocratic Marcher family of mixed Norman and Welsh ancestry. His father was William de Barri, son of Gerald of Windsor, who had served as the constable of Pembroke Castle under leading Norman magnate Arnulf de Montgomery.[1] His mother was Angharad; his grandmother was the Welsh princess Nest, the only legitimate daughter of Rhys ap Tewdwr, who was widely regarded at the time of his death in 1093 as the last king of Deheubarth (a kingdom in southern Wales).[2] The youngest of four brothers, Gerald was ushered into an ecclesiastical career under the tutelage of his maternal uncle, David fitz Gerald, bishop of St Davids (1148–76).[3] Educated in his early years at the Benedictine abbey of St Peter's, Gloucester, he travelled to Paris for additional learning (*c.*1165–74), where he came into contact with some of the great scholastic teachers of the twelfth century and received the best education available in his day.[4] Equipped with this advanced training, he returned to Britain, where his uncle David rewarded him for collecting tithes throughout the diocese of St Davids with the archdeaconry of Brecon.[5] Shrugging off a thwarted attempt to succeed his uncle into the bishopric in 1176, he returned to Paris to study and teach canon law and theology from *c.*1176–9.[6] Once back in England, he spent five more years studying theology, possibly at Lincoln.[7] He then found employment as a clerk for Henry II and his young son John, and spent ten years in royal service, including one year in Ireland (1185).[8] It was during these years that he penned his popular early works, the *Topographia* and *Expugnatio Hibernica*, and the *Itinerarium* and *Descriptio Kambriae*, which he revised and lengthened in subsequent years. Following an abrupt retirement from court life *c.*1194, he seems to have travelled to Lincoln; by 1199, his earnest fight to become the bishop of St Davids brings his life back into critical focus.[9] His election by the St Davids chapter was refused by King John, probably because his ties to the southern Welsh nobility made his elevation too dangerous for the Crown to consider, bruised as it was by the FitzGeralds' activities in Ireland.[10] Following four unsuccessful appeals to the pope, Gerald resigned his archdeaconry in 1203 and retired to Lincoln in defeat, where he wrote detailed accounts of his failed elections.[11] His late works are tinged by bitterness, frustrated ambition and a tendency to see betrayal in everything; he seems to have focused much of his ire on a wayward nephew under his supervision.[12] Gerald died *c*.1223, leaving behind a legacy that is broadly acknowledged by scholars of medieval Britain and Ireland alike.

Despite his contributions to our understanding of late twelfth-century history, society and Latinity in Britain and Ireland, Gerald remains somewhat of an enigma to modern scholars. By comparison to other twelfth-century Latin writers from Britain, such as William of Malmesbury, Henry of Huntingdon and Geoffrey of Monmouth, his life and works have received very little individual attention, with Bartlett's groundbreaking 1982 monograph representing the only book-length assessment of him to date. His journey from young and promising royal clerk, befit for high-level ecclesiastical appointment, to embittered old man, retiring to Lincoln with thwarted ambitions, is a compelling one, yet never fully explained in his own words. He does not account for his retirement from royal service *c*.1194, his evolving loyalties to the Welsh people, nor his exact reasons for seeking the independent status of the diocese of St Davids. For an author who wrote so much about himself, much about him remains ambiguous.

Exacerbating the difficulty of understanding the influences, motivations and goals that underpin his diverse writings and tumultuous life is a long-standing tendency among scholars to focus primarily on his Welsh and Irish works, the *Topographia Hibernica* ('Topography of Ireland', first issued *c*.1187), the *Expugnatio Hibernica* ('Conquest of Ireland', *c*.1189), the *Itinerarium Kambriae* ('Journey Through Wales', 1191) and the *Descriptio Kambriae* ('Description of Wales', 1194) – understandably so, as their blending of ethnography, history, miracle and marvel represents Gerald's most innovative and captivating achievement.[13] These strikingly original compositions provide a detailed view of societies on the margins of the Anglo-Norman empire from the point of view of an informed outsider, exemplifying many of the assumptions about barbarity, civility and ecclesiastical reform that broadly characterise the Anglo-Norman relationship with its Celtic neighbours in this period. These important works have had lasting effects on our understanding of British cultural relations in the medieval period, informing both medieval and modern historiographical narratives. Yet, as this volume demonstrates, a broader and more extensive view of his collected works has the ability to contextualise this achievement within a more complex, nuanced frame.

To date, scholarly attention to Gerald has been broad, and several trends are observable. From the late nineteenth to mid-twentieth centuries, Gerald's observations on Welsh society and culture were an important source for historical interpretations of medieval Wales. His Welsh works were claimed as native histories written by a champion of Welsh independence.[14] Recent studies have been more tempered, viewing Gerald within his own historical context and as a complex product of Marcher society, exhibiting conflicted views about his identity.[15] Bartlett's *Gerald of Wales, 1146–1223* (Oxford, 1982) represented a great leap forward in the study of Gerald's life, works and influences, viewing his output within its historical and political context, and demonstrating how intellectual trends of historiography, naturalism and humanism run throughout his work. By comparison to his positive reception by Welsh historians, in Ireland his works have historically and in the modern period received considerable vitriol, probably because his prejudiced portrayal of the Irish played a role in the propaganda used during the Tudor conquest of Ireland and left lasting damage.[16] The stark contrast between Gerald's reception in Ireland and his reception in Wales attest to his complexities and highlight the importance of understanding him as a writer and rhetorician.[17]

Recent critical attention to Gerald's works has been devoted to untangling his perceptions of and experiences with his hybrid ethnic identity.[18] Born into a Pembrokeshire Marcher family intermarried with south Welsh royalty, he does not fit into the easy binaries of 'Welsh' and 'English', and critics who grapple with his ethnicity must confront his seemingly contradictory views on the Welsh and his ill-defined place in Welsh and Anglo-Norman society. While his privileged position as a Marcher aristocrat with Welsh familial connections gave him an independent view into several cultures, as well as the ability to explain native Welsh society in detail to outsiders, it also made him an unsettling threat to royal authority in Wales, and seems to explain why he never received the ecclesiastical preferment he so desired in the late 1190s. Yet he was never quite Welsh either, preferring to distance himself from the society and customs of *pura Wallia*. It may be this tense insider/outsider status that has made him such a compelling figure for modern critics, as it seems to have heightened both his observational skills and his ambitions, granting us a unique view into aspects of medieval British and Irish society and culture.

While details from his works are frequently cherry-picked for inclusion in broader studies of medieval Ireland and Britain, little attention tends to be devoted to Gerald himself. Despite his influence on our understanding of a number of topics, a substantial part of his corpus – his religious, political, hagiographical, autobiographical and polemical writings – remains almost untouched by scholars. Yet his extant works on these topics add up to nineteen in total, vastly outweighing his Irish and Welsh compositions in both length and breadth.[19] His extant corpus include the *Gemma ecclesiastica* ('The Jewel of the Church'), an instructive manual on clerical reforms; the *Speculum duorum* ('A Mirror of Two Men'), in which Gerald charges his nephew, Giraldus fitz Philip, and his nephew's tutor, William Capella, with misusing the income from the archdeaconry of Brecon; and *De principis instructione* ('Instruction for a Ruler'), a critique of the Angevin kings John and Henry II, the first book of which is in the 'mirror for princes' genre, instructing a prince on proper moral qualities, while the second and third books criticise Henry II for his poor judgement.[20] Gerald's corpus also includes detailed narratives of his struggle for election to the bishopric of St Davids and the issue of its metropolitan status (*De iure et statu Menevensis ecclesiae*, 'On the Rights and Status of the Church of St Davids'; *De invectionibus*, 'On Shameful Attacks'; and a portion of his autobiography, *De rebus a se gestis*, 'On the Things He Has Achieved').[21] His letters, poems, prefaces and other writings are collected in *Symbolum electorum*, 'A Collection of Choice Works'. He also leaves behind *Retractationes* ('Retractions'), a brief admission that his criticisms of Hubert Walter, one of his main opponents in the St Davids issue, were exaggerated, as well as four saints' lives: the Lives of Remigius, Hugh of Avalon, Geoffrey Plantagenet and St David (a purported Life of Caradog is now lost). Because of the strength of their invective and political riskiness, several of these texts were circulated anonymously, including the *Vita Galfridi* and the *De iure*, and portions of *De principis instructione* were delayed until after King John had died.[22] Gerald was aware that he was a controversial figure in his own time.

These assembled works constitute a remarkable amount of extant writing and an unusual amount of autobiographical content and opinion. They touch upon many aspects of twelfth-century Anglo-Norman life, including secular and ecclesiastical politics, society and cultural mores. They also display a range of influences and sources that provide evidence for the availability of classical Latin works in twelfth-century Britain. Yet this portion of Gerald's corpus, with the exception of the materials relating to the St Davids case, has received so little critical attention that it represents almost a no man's land in Giraldian scholarship.[23] This lack of attention is most likely due to the inherent difficulty of interpreting these works: they are not narrative-driven in the same way as his Welsh and Irish works are; they deal with less popular, sometimes personal topics, and they do not impart the kind of historical information that has been favoured by scholars in the past. The narrative structure of this part of his corpus comprises a blend of personal opinion, anecdote and jeremiad overlaid by quotations that can come across as bewildering to all but the most expert medievalist readers. These lesser-known works are, simply put, less accessible than his compositions on Ireland and Wales.[24]

It is the intention of the present volume, therefore, to bring to prominence some of these lesser-known, lesser-studied works and discuss them in
concert with his more familiar works. Close attention to these works, as the
essays in this volume demonstrate, brings to light new and important evidence
for Gerald's rhetorical strategies, political interests, use of source material and
far-flung influences. A fuller understanding of these interests and influences
qualifies those details from his better-studied works which have become such
an important part of the historical record.

In addition to focusing the attentions of a group of researchers, for the first
time, on Gerald's lesser-known works, this volume also reassesses his status as
a writer. Drawing inspiration from previous studies by Bartlett and Pryce, the
essays in this volume, in reading Gerald on his own terms, find that he is a thoroughly self-conscious and careful crafter of argument, deliberate in his use of
sources and intended impact. Collectively, the essays in this volume suggest that
Gerald's narrative style was not disordered, careless or mercurial, as has been
previously suggested, but rather meticulous and thorough. This more nuanced
understanding of his rhetorical methods, motivations and influences helps us
evaluate the details in his works, as his portrayal of events is never beyond the
reach of these factors. By interpreting Gerald as a self-conscious and purposeful
writer, a more accurate picture of his achievement within the context of the
intellectual, literary and political mores of medieval Britain becomes possible.
Additionally, this approach allows for a more accurate view of the position and
status of Gerald's work in relation to other extant Latin texts of the twelfth century. His Latin style, having been shaped by Continental themes and scholastic
influences, was brought home and moulded into something regionally focused
and innovative.

The present volume began life as a conference at Harvard University, 'New
Perspectives on Gerald of Wales', held on 10–11 April 2015, which sought to
draw attention to Gerald's lesser-studied works and give this important medieval writer the undivided attention of a group of experts for the first time. Our
approach was timely: recent, foundational work on the complete manuscripts
of his works by Catherine Rooney, as well as new studies of his ethnographic
interests and the vernacular reception of his texts, have opened up new avenues
for research, and several new editions of Gerald's works are forthcoming.[25] In
fact, the present volume will complement another new publication on Gerald,
Robert Bartlett's forthcoming study of *De principis instructione*, which provides
a comprehensive and much-needed study of one of Gerald's lesser-known
works. The 2015 conference revealed something that this book makes clear:
that Gerald's writings touch upon almost every aspect of twelfth-century British society and history. Because of his diverse interests and the unusually large
corpus of surviving texts, his works benefit particularly from a group of experts

collaborating on a wide-ranging analysis and approaching the material from a variety of directions. Analysing his lesser-studied works not only informs our understanding of his rhetorical and political positions, but also draws attention to just how deliberate, complex and grounded in contemporary themes his writings were. At the same time, our analysis highlights Gerald's departure from contemporary mores through moments of innovation.

The volume is divided into four thematic parts, intended to group the essays into approximate temporal categories. It moves from the 'past', discussing how Gerald viewed and interpreted the historical past, to the 'present', examining first how Gerald operated as a writer, rhetorician and producer of texts and manuscripts, and secondly, how he brought together his diverse influences and experiences to participate in contemporary discourse; and, finally, the 'future', detailing Gerald's reception by subsequent generations of intellectuals and translators.

The first section of the volume, 'Appropriating the Past', assesses Gerald's perception and use of the past. As Huw Pryce argues in 'Gerald of Wales and the Welsh Past' – an expansive essay that traces Gerald's complicated relationship with Welsh history – Gerald was a selective historian who shaped the past to serve his own interests in the present, whether for exemplary or propagandistic purposes. Pryce discusses the *Descriptio Kambriae* and *Itinerarium Kambriae* as historical texts which set out origin legends concerning both the Welsh as a people and their saints and ecclesiastical traditions. The essay then delves into one of the major preoccupations of Gerald's life, the alleged metropolitan status of the church of St Davids. Drawing on Geoffrey of Monmouth, oral tradition and other written sources, Gerald adapted sources on the purported early history of St Davids to craft his own understanding of Welsh history. Pryce sheds new light particularly on two lists intended to demonstrate episcopal succession at St Davids found in separate recensions of the *Itinerarium Kambriae*. These lists, Pryce argues, were part of Gerald's case for the metropolitan status of St Davids, and indicate his willingness to use the past for his own pursuits in the present.

The other articles in this section expand Pryce's conclusions in two different directions: 'traditional' Welsh learning and the Anglo-Saxon past. Ben Guy's 'Gerald and Welsh Genealogical Learning' reassesses the evidence for Gerald's use of texts produced in Wales, particularly as sources for the genealogies in the *Itinerarium Kambriae* and the *Descriptio Kambriae*. Guy argues that Gerald had access to two Welsh genealogical texts: a version of the Latin *De situ Brecheniauc* ('Concerning the Establishment of Brycheiniog'), probably at Brecon Priory, and a vernacular version of the patrilineal genealogy of Rhodri Mawr. Gerald makes use of the former in the *Itinerarium* when discussing Brychan, the purported founder of Brycheiniog (Brecknockshire), and the latter in the *Descriptio* when naming the descendants of Rhodri Mawr. Both of these genealogical texts were recent creations, indicating that Gerald accessed up-to-date Welsh genealogies in written rather than oral form. In 'Gerald of Wales, Walter Map and the Anglo-Saxon History of Lydbury North', Joshua Byron Smith examines how the Anglo-Saxon past could be invoked and invented for the purposes of the present. Gerald and Walter Map, both canons of Hereford, wrote separate, roughly contemporaneous accounts of how the Hereford bishopric came to possess the important estate of Lydbury North. While Walter's account in *De nugis curialium* attaches the legend to Eadric Streona, a great landowner and holdout against William the Conqueror, Gerald frames his story around Offa, a famous Anglo-Saxon king, in his *Vita Ethelberti*. While their thematic similarities have led scholars to assume that Gerald plagiarised Walter, Smith demonstrates that Gerald is not guilty of plagiarism; instead, these stories are notable for their similar use of the Anglo-Saxon past to authorise Hereford's possession of Lydbury North. The articles in this section reveal Gerald's penchant for shaping the past to fit his own interests, his comprehension of the power of history, and his willingness to adapt any 'historical' source – from Geoffrey of Monmouth to Welsh genealogies.

Smith's article ends with an exhortation to consider the example of Lydbury North as a better model for thinking about Gerald as a writer working in a particular courtly and ecclesiastical milieu. It is impractical and, indeed, impossible to divorce Gerald's 'historical' works from his own contemporary ambitions – these works are never solely about the past, but speak to present and future concerns. The next section of this collection considers 'Gerald the Writer: Manuscripts and Authorship', offering essays on his writing process, habits of revision, style and rhetoric. It begins with an essay that not only adds a new text to Gerald's already impressive corpus, but potentially identifies this text as Gerald's final work: in 'Gerald of Wales and the *History of Llanthony Priory*', Robert Bartlett discusses Gerald's relationship to this little-known text, long suspected to be a product of Gerald's pen but never fully evaluated as such. The *History* provides an origin story for Llanthony Prima, an Augustinian house in Monmouthshire, before recounting the sequence of priors and changing fortunes of the priory down to the late twelfth century, including the abandonment of the site for a time and the founding of Llanthony Secunda in Gloucestershire, which soon superseded it in wealth. Bartlett demonstrates, based on close analyses of Latin style, verbal allusions, quotations and similarities in sentiment to Gerald's known writings, that *The History of Llanthony Priory* can indeed be ascribed to Gerald's authorship. He evaluates this work in the context of Gerald's other writings, viewing it as an important contribution to our knowledge of Gerald's Welsh interests, his involvement in Welsh politics and his relationship with the princes of Deheubarth and the Cistercian order.

Moving on from the questions of authorship which help characterise and define Gerald's Latin style, Catherine Rooney makes a case for Gerald's involvement in the production of the earliest manuscripts of his works in her contribution 'The Early Manuscripts of Gerald of Wales'. Stemming from the work of her groundbreaking doctoral dissertation, which discussed 100 manuscripts containing Gerald's works, twenty-five of which had not been previously identified, this essay explores the twenty-two that are datable to his lifetime. Rooney examines the physical evidence of these early manuscripts, including script, illustrations, composition, layout and textual apparatus, in order to argue that nine of these manuscripts are connected paleographically and that another four were produced in the same place as those nine. Rooney argues that the most likely source of such a large group of manuscripts datable to the author's lifetime is Gerald himself, and draws on other evidence (marginal additions and insertions, illustrations, maps and a sophisticated system of reading aids) to solidify these claims. If over half of these early manuscripts can be linked to Gerald, further investigations into the manuscripts could yield even more information about his practices as a writer and his supervision of his works in circulation and production.

One criterion in Rooney's analysis is the presence of marginal alterations that 'advance' the texts in these manuscripts from one redaction to the next. The process of revision was central to Gerald's works, which he tirelessly amended and altered over the course of, sometimes, several different redactions. Michael Faletra outlines this very phenomenon in his 'Giraldian Beavers: Revision and the Making of Meaning in Gerald's Early Works' by evaluating Gerald's preoccupation with describing the Welsh beaver in his writings on Ireland and Wales. Faletra explains how Gerald drafted his account of beavers and their habits in the first version of the *Topographia Hibernica*, revised it in subsequent versions and then developed the material further in both the *Itinerarium Kambriae* and *Descriptio Kambriae*. He demonstrates that Gerald crafted the material to fit the specific agenda and narrative context of each work, in particular noting how he distances himself, on the one hand, from a strictly naturalistic account of the beaver, and, on the other hand, from the narrowly overdetermined modes of reading dictated by the bestiary tradition. Faletra concludes by reading the beaver as just one of many examples which showcase Gerald's understanding of the polysemic nature of zoological, cultural and historical phenomena.

Having covered style, manuscript context and revision, the section then turns to Gerald's rhetoric and distinctive voice in Simon Meecham-Jones's 'Style, Truth and Irony: Listening to the Voice of Gerald of Wales's Writings'. Responding to a variety of critics' attempts to define Gerald's voice (a voice which, indeed, pursued different principles and priorities over the years as he adjusted to new audiences), Meecham-Jones proposes that all of Gerald's writings should be understood through his highly developed sense of himself as a rhetorician trained in the classical tradition. He explores how Gerald developed a procedure favouring the precedent of Quintilian, rather than Cicero, as a model for advancing original premises without risking breaches of ecclesiastical orthodoxy. Examining Gerald's use of allegory, metaphor and quotation from scriptural, patristic and classical texts to add authority to his arguments, Meecham-Jones sees rhetoric where previous scholars saw 'waywardness'. He characterises Gerald's misquotations as, potentially, attempts to extract ironic humour from the inability of words to prevent their own misappropriation – much in the 'Goliardic' style of satirical verse espoused by writers such as Walter of Châtillon and Peter of Blois.

Following these analyses of Gerald's practices as a writer, our third section turns to his application of these methods in the popular discourses of the day – considering 'Gerald the Thinker: Religion and Worldview'. As Meecham-Jones describes Gerald's rhetorical style as laden with 'ironic humour', Peter J. A. Jones demonstrates how this humour was essential to Gerald's political and spiritual projects in 'Gerald of Wales's Sense of Humour'. Jones explains that, within Gerald's lifetime, humour acquired a new range of meaning and moral implications, finding a new place in both the royal court and the church. He examines how Gerald joked in both of these spheres: using spiritual humour to attack the hypocrisy of Cistercian monks and promote the moral reform of the clergy, while taking up political humour in critiques of courtly politics and political figures. Jones explores the full range of Gerald's philosophy of laughter, considering his sense of humour as a window into the moral and political universe of the late twelfth and early thirteenth centuries. In his recognition of humour as a powerful vehicle for reform and criticism, Gerald melded comic persuasion with ecclesiastical reform.

The same tension between political and ecclesiastical noted by Jones in Gerald's sense of humour is expanded upon by Peter Raleigh in '*Fere tirannicus*: Royal Tyranny and the Construction of Episcopal Sanctity in Gerald of Wales's *Vita Sancti Hugonis*'. This essay examines how Gerald negotiated the conflict between royal and ecclesiastical authority through a close reading of the understudied *Vita Sancti Hugonis*. In particular, Raleigh positions Thomas Becket's career and murder as a crucial thematic element which shapes and inflects the *Vita*, providing Gerald's narrative of royal-ecclesiastical conflict with much of its urgency and dramatic weight, and offering a model for episcopal sanctity against which Hugh is repeatedly juxtaposed. He argues further that Gerald's references to Becket situate the *Vita Sancti Hugonis* within a wider implied narrative of English church history in which the incorrigibly wrathful and violent Angevin kings are timeless antagonists, placing the *Vita Sancti Hugonis* within a discourse of kingship and royal critique which runs throughout Gerald's *oeuvre*.

In '"A Priest Is Not a Free Person": Condemning Clerical Sins and Upholding Higher Moral Standards in the *Gemma ecclesiastica*', Suzanne LaVere examines another of Gerald's ecclesiastical works for evidence of his concerns with the practical and moral issues facing clergy. Gerald addresses clerical failings most thoroughly in the *Gemma ecclesiastica*, pointing out the sins of the secular clergy and advising them how to improve and fulfil their role as mediators between God and the laity. LaVere's essay addresses the specific areas where Gerald seemed to feel the problems among clergy were most dire, categorising these issues into fleshly sins (lust and incontinence), intellectual sins (ignorance or slavish devotion to philosophy) and material sins (greed and excessive ambition). She also examines his proposed solutions and instructions for how priests can attain the lofty standards he sets out for them. This essay offers our best glimpse at Gerald the ecclesiastical reformist: a skilful rhetorician who took up the pen in an attempt to disseminate his ideas for change.

Owain Nash explores the cosmology and natural theory underlying Giraldian works in 'Elements of Identity: Gerald, the Humours and National Characteristics'. Whereas LaVere focuses on Gerald's plans to reform the sinful body, Nash examines how the body became out of sync to begin with and, further, how a fixed natural theory allowed for future prediction. He explains that a sophisticated cosmological theory of the natural world, showing signs of influence from classical models, existed in Gerald's works, especially of the human body as a microcosm made up of the four elemental humours. After tracing Gerald's theories of the physical universe and the body, Nash argues that the abstract, theoretical cosmology present in Gerald's writings must be read alongside his naturalistic ethnography, where Gerald makes use of his comprehension of natural theory to make sweeping judgements about various peoples. Ultimately, he shows how Gerald's ethnographic legacy can be enhanced by examining his descriptions of different cultures from a bodily perspective.

Given Gerald's far-reaching influence as a writer, thinker and critic, it should come as no surprise that posterity remembered him well. The fourth group of chapters, entitled 'Reception in England, Ireland and Wales', considers the various futures of Gerald's writing as it was transmitted into the vernacular languages of Ireland and Britain, attesting to the long life and popularity of his works and their various resonances within these cultures. In 'Gerald's Circulation and Reception in Wales: The Case of *Claddedigaeth Arthur*', Georgia Henley examines how a few chapters of Gerald's prose were excerpted, translated into Middle Welsh and selected for a fourteenth-century manuscript containing wisdom literature, fables, hagiography and visionary literature (rather than 'historical' texts). This excerpt, his account of the discovery and exhumation of the grave of Arthur and Guinevere at Glastonbury Abbey in 1190 or 1191, was adapted from the *Speculum ecclesiae* and *De principis instructione*. As the only known translation of Gerald's writings into Middle Welsh, Henley discusses possible motives for translation, the Welsh text's likely milieu and its placement within the context of Welsh prose translations before turning to broader questions about the circulation of Gerald's works in Wales.

In 'The Transmission of the *Expugnatio Hibernica* in Fifteenth-century Ireland', Caoimhe Whelan turns to Gerald's reception in late medieval Ireland. Whelan examines and contextualises the continued interest in the *Expugnatio Hibernica* in the late Middle Ages, and explores a rendition of the history undertaken in Ireland, a colonial sphere situated at the periphery of the English world. The translation and transformation of this narrative into fifteenth-century Hiberno-Middle English provides a fascinating glimpse of how twelfth-century histories could be reused and imbued with new meanings. Alongside its incorporation into numerous historical accounts, the continued use of certain aspects of Gerald's narrative in various political and legal arguments underlined its relevance in the late medieval world. This translation in particular offered a community history for the English colonists which amplified the original moral and religious agenda of the invasion as expressed by Gerald, building on these earlier claims to establish more firmly the English king's rights to Ireland.

The final essay in this volume, Brendan Kane's 'Did the Tudors Read Giraldus? Gerald of Wales and Early Modern Polemical Historiography', reconsiders Gerald's influence on early modern Irish and English polemical historiography. Over the sixteenth and early seventeenth centuries, English and Irish authors raided Gerald's writings – especially the *Expugnatio* – to buttress competing claims for political authority in Ireland. And yet, as Kane explains, Gerald's work is glaringly absent from the hundreds of policy tracts and treatises that comprised the documents of state dealing directly with how to govern Ireland and the Irish. Kane questions previous scholarship, which assumed a heavy Giraldian debt in early modern political thought, and suggests additional sources that might have influenced these writings. While Kane does not discount Gerald's influence in the period – and, indeed, offers new avenues for exploring his reception – he presents this 'curious fact' as a case study in the broader question of understanding the relationship between letters and politics in early modern English-Irish relations.

The widened perspective offered by this volume, which draws together specialists from a variety of disciplines, provides a more diverse picture of Gerald's influences, thinking and works than has previously been attempted. The diversity of influences, sources, discursive methods and contemporary events in which Gerald was involved underscores his value to our understanding of Insular society and history in the Middle Ages, and also, more broadly, to medieval Latinate culture overall. By placing him in the context of these interpretations and innovations, this volume interprets Gerald as a highly educated and skilled Latin writer, with strong connections to Continental culture, scholasticism and humanism, along with a keenly developed sense of rhetoric, contemporary politics and style. These qualities, though honed by approximately thirteen years in Paris, were emboldened by Gerald's origins in the semi-independent society of the Welsh March, resulting in a unique perspective that was to benefit and discomfit him throughout his life. As the chapters on the reception of Gerald's works in Wales and Ireland attest, his works resonated throughout the Middle Ages and into the early modern period, and he set a precedent for understanding medieval Welsh and Irish culture that still finds traction today. By broadening our critical views to include his entire corpus, we demonstrate that his writings are not only valuable to the study of Welsh and Irish history and society, but also necessary for any study of twelfth-century Latin prose writing and the intellectual, religious and political debates in which it was engaged. We anticipate that future work on these topics will be stimulated and encouraged by the present collection.

## Notes

1   *De rebus*, i.1, p. 21.

2   For Rhys ap Tewdwr and Deheubarth, see Robert S. Babcock, 'Rhys ap Tewdwr, King of Deheubarth', *Anglo-Norman Studies*, 14 (1994), 21–36; his death is reported in these terms in *Brut y Tywysogion*, Red Book of Hergest version: Thomas Jones (ed. and trans.), *Brut y Tywysogyon, or, The Chronicle of the Princes, Red Book of Hergest Version* (1st edition, Cardiff, 1955), p. 33; and in the Chronicle of John of Worcester: P. McGurk (ed. and trans.), *The Chronicle of John of Worcester, Volume III: The Annals from 1067 to 1140 with the Gloucester Interpolations and the Continuation to 1141* (Oxford, 1998), pp. 64–5. Through his maternal line Gerald was related to the nobility of Deheubarth, including the Lord Rhys ap Gruffudd. For Gerald's own words on his homeland, his family's history and Welsh connections, see *Itinerarium*, ii.12, pp. 89–91; *De rebus*, i.1, p. 21; ii.9, pp. 58–9.

3   *De rebus*, i.2, p. 22.

4   *De rebus*, i.2, p. 23; Robert Bartlett, *Gerald of Wales, 1146–1223* (Oxford, 1982), p. 3; for discussion of Parisian schools in the twelfth century see Stephen C. Ferruolo, *The Origins of the University: The Schools of Paris and their Critics, 1100–1215* (Stanford, 1985); also John J. Hagen (trans.), *The Jewel of the Church: A Translation of Gemma ecclesiastica by Giraldus Cambrensis* (Leiden, 1979), pp. xxxi–xxxiv. The dates of Gerald's tenure in Paris are uncertain, and critics have proposed various time frames; he says he was in Paris when Philip Augustus was born in 1165 (*De principis instructione*, iii.15, p. 292).

5   *De rebus*, i.4, pp. 27–9.

6   *De rebus*, i.9–11, pp. 41–4; ii.1, pp. 45–6.

7   John W. Baldwin, *Masters, Princes, and Merchants: The Social Views of Peter the Chanter and his Circle*, 2/1 (Princeton, 1970), 42 suggests that his theological study in this period took place at Lincoln under the tutelage of William de Montibus.

8   *De rebus*, ii.9, p. 57; ii.21, pp. 80–1. He also visited his brother in Ireland *c*.1183.

9   For extensive background and discussion of Gerald's fraught election to the bishopric, see Michael Richter, *Giraldus Cambrensis: The Growth of the Welsh Nation* (2nd edition, Aberystwyth, 1976), pp. 87–124; *De iure, De invectionibus, De rebus*, iii.4–19, pp. 94–122.

10  Bartlett, *Gerald*, pp. 50–1; expressed by Gerald in *De iure*, vii, pp. 340–1.

11  *De iure, De invectionibus, De rebus*, iii.4–19, pp. 94–122.

12  The subject of *Speculum duorum*, issued *c*.1216; see Yves Lefèvre and R. B. C. Huygens (eds), Brian Dawson (trans.) and Michael Richter (gen. ed.), *Giraldus Cambrensis: Speculum Duorum, or A Mirror of Two Men, Preserved in the Vatican Library in Rome, Cod. Reg. Lat. 470* (Cardiff, 1974), pp. xx–xxi.

13  For rationales for these dates, see Bartlett, *Gerald*, p. 213 (*Topographia*), narrowed to Gerald's recitation of a version of the *Topographia* at Oxford in 1187, *De rebus*, ii.16, pp. 72–3; A. B. Scott and F. X. Martin (eds and trans.), *Expugnatio Hibernica: The Conquest of Ireland, by Giraldus Cambrensis* (Dublin, 1978), pp. xvi–xvii (*Expugnatio*); Thorpe, *Gerald*, p. 38, n. 16 (*Itinerarium*); J. F. Dimock (ed.),

*Giraldi Cambrensis Opera*, 8/6 (London, 1868), pp. xxxix–xlii (*Itinerarium* and *Descriptio*).

14 Henry Owen, *Gerald the Welshman* (2nd edition, London, 1904); J. Conway Davies, 'Giraldus Cambrensis, 1146–1223', *Archaeologia Cambrensis*, 9 (1946–7), 85–108, 256–80; Thomas Jones, *Gerallt Gymro: Gerald the Welshman* (Cardiff, 1947) and 'The Wales of Gerald', in A. J. Roderick (ed.), *Wales Through the Ages* (Llandybïe, 1959), pp. 105–12; J. F. Rees, *Studies in Welsh History: Collected Papers, Lectures, and Reviews* (Cardiff, 1947); Glanmor Williams, 'An Old Man Remembers: Gerald the Welshman', *Morgannwg*, 32 (1988), 7–20.

15 Julia C. Crick, 'The British Past and the Welsh Future: Gerald of Wales, Geoffrey of Monmouth and Arthur of Britain', *Celtica*, 23 (1999), 60–75; Richter, *Giraldus Cambrensis*; Huw Pryce, 'In Search of a Medieval Society: Deheubarth in the Writings of Gerald of Wales', *Welsh History Review*, 12 (1987), 265–81; Michael A. Faletra, *Wales and the Medieval Colonial Imagination: The Matters of Britain in the Twelfth Century* (New York, 2014).

16 For Elizabethan reception of Gerald, see, for example, John Brannigan, '"A particular vice of that people": Giraldus Cambrensis and the Discourse of English Colonialism', *Irish Studies Review*, 6 (1998), 121–30; Hiram Morgan, 'Giraldus Cambrensis and the Tudor Conquest of Ireland', in Hiram Morgan (ed.), *Political Ideology in Ireland, 1541–1641* (Dublin, 1999), pp. 22–44.

17 Attention has also been paid to Gerald by art historians and geographers interested in the vibrant marginalia in the early manuscripts of his work and the information he imparts about geography and natural history: see Michelle P. Brown, 'Marvels of the West: Giraldus Cambrensis and the Role of the Author in the Development of Marginal Illustration', *English Manuscript Studies 1100–1700*, 10 (2002), 34–59; John Barry, 'A Wild Goose Chase: Giraldus Cambrensis and Natural History', in Gerhard Petersmann and Veronkia Oberparleiter (eds), *The Role of Latin in Early Modern Europe: Texts and Contexts*, Grazer Beiträge, Supplementband 9 (Salzburg-Horn, 2005), pp. 154–60; Jason Harris, 'Giraldus as Natural Historian: Transformations and Reception', in Kathleen Cawsey and Jason Harris (eds), *Transmission and Transformation in the Middle Ages: Texts and Contexts* (Dublin, 2007), pp. 77–97.

18 Herbert Hughes, 'Giraldus de Barri: An Early Ambassador for Wales', *Brycheiniog*, 38 (2006), 35–48, at 35, 37; Richter, *Giraldus Cambrensis*, p. 2; Jeffrey Jerome Cohen, *Hybridity, Identity, and Monstrosity in Medieval Britain: On Difficult Middles* (New York, 2006), pp. 78–82, 94–5, 99–104; Faletra, *Wales*, pp. 135–9, 156–7; cf. John Gillingham, '"Slaves of the Normans"? Gerald de Barri and Regnal Solidarity in Early Thirteenth-Century England', in Pauline Stafford, Janet L. Nelson and Jane Martindale (eds), *Law, Laity and Solidarities: Essays in Honour of Susan Reynolds* (Manchester, 2001), pp. 160–71.

19 Four additional works are known to be lost: a *Cronographia metrica*, *Mundi nascentis discriptiunculus et Cosmographia*, which he says he wrote in his youth; *Mappa Kambriae; Vita Sancti Caradoci*; and *De fidei fructu fideique defectu*; he mentions these works in *Epistola ad capitulum*, pp. 414–16, and *Catalogus*, pp. 421–3.

20 For an expansive introduction to *De principis instructione*, see Robert Bartlett's forthcoming volume from Oxford University Press (2018).

21 *De rebus* exists in fragmentary form in one manuscript, London, British Library, Cotton MS Tiberius B. xiii, and while only eighteen chapters of the book survive, 236 chapter headings are extant; for discussion, see J. S. Brewer (ed.), *Giraldi Cambrensis Opera*, 8/1 (London, 1861), pp. lxxxviii–lxxxix.

22 For discussion, see Bartlett, *Gerald*, pp. 63–5, 69–77.

23 Important exceptions to this desideratum are the published translations of the *Gemma ecclesiastica* by Hagen (trans.), *The Jewel of the Church*, and the edition and translation of the *Speculum duorum* by Lefèvre and Huygens (eds), Dawson (trans.), *Giraldus Cambrensis*, and the commentaries therein.

24 These works also did not appear to circulate widely in the medieval period, as they are extant in one or just a few medieval copies each; by comparison, the Welsh and Irish works circulated extensively; see Catherine Rooney, 'The Manuscripts of the Works of Gerald of Wales' (unpublished PhD thesis, University of Cambridge, 2005), 6–9, 101–13.

25 Rooney, 'The Manuscripts'; Shirin Khanmohamadi, *In Light of Another's Word: European Ethnography in the Middle Ages* (Philadelphia, 2014); Aisling Byrne, 'Family, Locality, and Nationality: Vernacular Adaptations of the *Expugnatio Hibernica* in Late Medieval Ireland', *Medium Aevum*, 82/1 (2013), 101–18.

# Appropriating the Past

# TWO

# Gerald of Wales
# and the Welsh Past

Huw Pryce
*Bangor University*

T HAT GERALD OF WALES engaged extensively with the past is evident from even a cursory survey of his writings. Thus he drew on sources such as Gildas, Bede, the *Lebor Gabála Érenn* ('The Book of the Takings of Ireland'), saints' Lives and Geoffrey of Monmouth's *Historia regum Britanniae* or *De gestis Britonum* to relate what he held to be the early history of the Irish and Welsh in the *Topographia Hibernica* and the two books on Wales, while he provided vivid depictions of the recent and contemporary history of the Angevin world in the *Expugnatio Hibernica*, the *De principis instructione* and the Life of Geoffrey, archbishop of York.[1] As the works mentioned reveal, Gerald, not surprisingly, was particularly interested in the histories and traditions of churches. This is exemplified by his rewriting of the Life of St David and the retrospective accounts of the St Davids struggle, which detailed both the historical precedents he claimed in support for the church's metropolitan status and the events of his own efforts to become, in effect, archbishop of Wales. However, he also wrote Lives of other saints as well as of eleventh- and twelfth-century churchmen, and his last work, the *Speculum ecclesiae*, has much on the history of religious orders as well as the churches of Rome. Gerald's writings prompt questions, then, about how this medieval author perceived and used the past.

What follows offers some observations on just one aspect of these questions: namely, the ways in which Gerald treated the Welsh past. His family background and ecclesiastical career gave him numerous opportunities to become acquainted with tales and tradition concerning the past of Wales, and it is clear that his engagement was shaped to a significant extent by his personal experience in and knowledge of Wales. At the same time, that engagement was subordinated to particular priorities, and did not extend to providing a sequential narrative of Welsh history. Rather, to generalise broadly, what we have are snapshots of, on the one hand, what purported to be early Welsh traditions (preserved both orally and in writing) and, on the other, recent and contemporary history, especially that in which either he or his extended kin were involved. And to generalise further, in common with many other medieval writers, he valued the past for its exemplary power — as a source of examples that could legitimise a particular viewpoint or teach moral lessons.

I will begin by examining two works that illustrate contrasting approaches to the Welsh past, namely the *Descriptio Kambriae* ('Description of Wales') and *Itinerarium Kambriae* ('Journey Through Wales'). This will lead on to a more detailed consideration of Gerald's treatment of the alleged history of the church of St Davids and its claims to metropolitan status.

## The *Descriptio Kambriae* and *Itinerarium Kambriae* on the Welsh Past

The Welsh work that Gerald comes closest to describing as a history is the *Descriptio Kambriae*, whose first redaction was completed *c.*1194. Of course, this may best be understood as an innovative exercise in ethnography, and it would be misleading to categorise it as principally a work of history, notwithstanding its strong historical dimension.[2] But in the First Preface, Gerald implicitly compared it with *historiae* of other peoples and declared his intention to rescue its *gesta* from neglect by devoting his energies to elucidating 'the poor histories of our lands' ('pauperes finium nostrorum historias').[3] And he ended by explicitly invoking Gildas as a model, whose lament for the fall of his people he had recounted in a true history.[4] As I have suggested elsewhere, the reference to Gildas is a vital clue to the work's purpose, as Gerald used the sixth-century writer's blaming the Britons' loss of Britain on their sins as a stick with which to beat the Welsh, whose confidence, Gerald insisted, was entirely misplaced because of the failings he had detailed in Book II of the work.[5] More generally, though, the dominant historical framework of the *Descriptio* was derived from the tradition of British history inaugurated by Gildas and most fully elaborated by Geoffrey of Monmouth, to whom Gerald was deeply indebted, while usually being reluctant to own up to this, as Julia Crick has emphasised.[6] This perspective was further sustained by reference to classical sources, especially Caesar and Lucan.[7] In other words, the Welsh of his own day were viewed through the lens of the Britons of the Roman and post-Roman periods, be it in the preference of their men for wearing moustaches, in the manner described by Caesar, or in devotional practices deriving from Germanus of Auxerre and Lupus of Troyes, such as sitting in threes to eat, in memory of the Trinity.[8]

By contrast, the *Descriptio's* coverage of the Welsh past from the seventh century to Gerald's own lifetime was limited, and consisted of two main elements. First, Gerald included material that redounded to the glory of, and probably ultimately derived from, the Welsh dynasty of Deheubarth, to whom he was related through his mother Angharad. In particular, he provided an account of the descendants of Rhodri Mawr (d. 878) which falsely asserted that his son Cadell, from whom the rulers of Deheubarth were descended, had 'obtained the monarchy of all Wales' ('totius Walliae . . . monarchiam obtinuit'), and that the position had been maintained by his successors until the time of Tewdwr.[9] Perhaps the notion drew on an idea already evidenced shortly after the death of Tewdwr's son, Rhys ap Tewdwr, at the hands of the Normans in 1093. According to John of Worcester, 'from that day kings ceased to rule in Wales' ('ab illo die regnare in Walonia reges desiere'), while *Brut y Tywysogyon* declared that with Rhys 'fell the kingdom of the Britons' ('y dygwydawd teyrnas y Brytanyeit') – verdicts that very probably reflect the debt of both sources to late eleventh-century Welsh Latin annals.[10] Even so, as J. E. Lloyd drily observed, Gerald's account 'was no doubt concocted to support certain South Welsh claims',[11] and its inclusion in the *Descriptio*, together with the precedence given to the genealogy of the Lord Rhys (d. 1197) of Deheubarth over that of the line of Gwynedd, surely reflects Gerald's family connections and alignment with the southern Welsh dynasty. The same may be true of the story in the *Itinerarium Kambriae* of how the birds of Llan-gors lake in Brycheiniog proclaimed through their singing that his great-uncle Gruffudd ap Rhys (d. 1137) was the true prince of south Wales, although that could have derived from local traditions preserved within Gerald's archdeaconry of Brecon.[12] Also significant in this context is Gerald's silence on the rape and abduction of his grandmother, Nest, related at length in the Welsh chronicles, which in turn very probably drew on a near contemporary account. Even if he believed Nest to have been an entirely innocent victim, Gerald had little incentive to report an episode that could have tarnished the highly favourable image he presented of her elsewhere.[13]

Secondly, Gerald explained that the first three Norman kings had been able to keep Wales in subjection partly because they had been content to focus their energies on the island of Britain, in the same manner as their Anglo-Saxon predecessors. Thus, Offa had built a dyke that had kept the Britons away from the English; Æthelfrith had destroyed Chester and massacred the monks of Bangor-on-Dee; and Harold had been especially successful, his victories being commemorated on stones bearing the inscription 'Here Harold was victorious' ('Hic fuit victor Haroldus').[14] While the reference to Æthelfrith of Bernicia evidently came from Bede,[15] the sources for Offa's dyke and Harold's victories are uncertain. Gerald may have derived his knowledge of the dyke directly from Asser's *Life of King Alfred*.[16] It is notable, though, that Harold's campaigns in Wales, recorded in several Anglo-Saxon and Anglo-Norman sources, were familiar to another curial cleric a generation before Gerald wrote, for they were praised by John of Salisbury in a passage of his *Policraticus* (1159) that also referred to Offa's dyke as the boundary separating the Welsh (termed, as in Gerald's account, *Britones*) from the English.[17] The account follows criticism of the failure to halt the expansion of 'the Britons of Snowdon' ('Niuicollini Britones'), evidently referring to campaigns by Owain Gwynedd (d. 1170).[18] Likewise, while not necessarily indebted to the *Policraticus*, Gerald may reflect a comparable awareness in Angevin court circles of earlier attempts to contain the Welsh as being particularly relevant in a period of Welsh recovery in the age of Owain Gwynedd and the Lord Rhys. Thus, Gerald cited these episodes, out of chronological order, as exempla to support his argument that the Welsh had recently enjoyed greater success because Henry II and his sons had been preoccupied with overseas commitments.[19]

The *Itinerarium Kambriae*, whose first redaction was completed *c.*1191, also throws valuable light on Gerald's perceptions of the Welsh past. In part, of course, this was an exercise in contemporary history, focused on some six weeks from early March to mid-April 1188, which offered the fullest account of the preaching of a medieval crusade that provided the ostensible occasion for the work's composition.[20] However, as is well known, the *Itinerarium* also contains numerous flashbacks to events and wonders in or near the places through which Archbishop Baldwin and Gerald travelled to preach the crusade. The material included seems to have varied according to the information available to Gerald, and is fullest for those parts of south Wales with which he was most closely connected, namely the archdeaconry of Brecon and Pembrokeshire, especially the church of St Davids.[21] Thus the second chapter of Book I, on Hay and Brecon, is the longest, followed by the chapters on the vale of Ewias and Llanthony Priory, Pembroke and St Davids.[22]

Here and elsewhere Gerald sometimes explicitly refers, or seems indebted, to written sources, and I shall return to his use of these below. However, it is very likely that he owed much of his material for the Welsh past from the late eleventh century onwards to oral transmission. In part, this seems to have consisted of minatory tales of the dangers of sacrilege committed against churches and especially the relics of their patron saints. Thus Gerald related how the hand of a boy who had tried to steal pigeon chicks from the church of St David at Llan-faes (Brycheiniog) became stuck to a stone on which he had leant,[23] and attributed the imprisonment of the Lord Rhys by his sons to the prince's seizure of St Cynog's torque belonging to the church of Merthyr Cynog. It should be added that the passage follows criticism of Rhys for having broken his oaths in previously capturing Nevern Castle from his son-in-law William fitz Martin and handing it over to his eldest legitimate son, Gruffudd: Gerald was not always kind to his Welsh kinsfolk.[24] Stories of the dire consequences of sacrilege were presumably preserved and transmitted by clergy of the churches concerned. However, Gerald also drew on texts for his accounts of Welsh saints, citing the authority of 'ancient and authentic writings' concerning St Illtud and the Life of St David.[25] As we shall see, the latter was one of several written sources he utilised for the history of the church of St Davids.

In addition, there are strong grounds for supposing that Gerald drew on family memory.[26] The numerous flashbacks in the *Itinerarium Kambriae* to events earlier in the twelfth century indicate that he viewed the relatively recent Welsh past from the perspective of the milieu in which he had been raised, namely the Marcher settlers who regarded themselves as subjects of the king of England. Accordingly, many of the events described consist of episodes in the (often violent) relations of the Welsh with the Marchers and/or the English Crown, with the chronology of events often indicated with reference to the reigns of kings of England, most often Henry I (1100–35) and his grandson Henry II (1154–89).[27] No source is given for most of the events related. However, a few stories involved Gerald's maternal uncle, David fitz Gerald, bishop of St Davids (1148–76),[28] and it may well be that some of the historical flashbacks derived from accounts related by David, and also perhaps by Gerald's mother Angharad.

## The History of St Davids

Let us move on to look at one of the major preoccupations of Gerald's life: the alleged metropolitan status of the church of St Davids. His interest in the question is evident while still employed as a royal clerk. The *Expugnatio Hibernica* (1189) refers to Diarmait Mac Murchada arriving at 'the ancient and genuine metropolitan see of St Davids' ('ad antiquam et authenticam metropolim Meneviam'), though other references to the see in the text make no comment on its status.[29] However, considerable attention is devoted to the church's history in two slightly later works, namely the first redaction of the *Itinerarium Kambriae* (c.1191), and in Gerald's new version of the Life of St David, probably composed in the early 1190s.[30] Gerald's writings on the subject thus antedate his unsuccessful attempt from 1198 to 1203 to gain confirmation of his election as bishop of St Davids and recognition of the church as a metropolitan see for Wales, and the works he subsequently wrote to vindicate his campaign. Rather, they reflect a readiness to give expression to traditions cherished by the church of St Davids. Gerald had been closely associated with the church since commencing his education with his uncle, Bishop David fitz Gerald (1148–76), a connection that led to his appointment as archdeacon of Brecon in the diocese of St Davids in 1175 and, he claimed, nomination as bishop in succession to his uncle on the latter's death in 1176.[31]

Gerald states that he was commissioned by his fellow canons of St Davids to write his version of the Life of St David.[32] This was based on the shorter Nero-Digby recension of Rhygyfarch's late eleventh-century Life composed during the pontificate of Bishop Bernard (1115–48).[33] As Robert Bartlett has shown, Gerald sought to update the Life to meet contemporary circumstances and expectations, both by adopting a 'scholarly style' and by 'demonasticizing' the content.[34] He also inserted an additional episode, not found in previous versions, concerning the 'imperfect Gospel' ('Evangelium imperfectum'), which St David had begun to copy but was completed in gold letters by an angel and enshrined in gold and silver as a relic, closed from view, revered for its miracles to the present day.[35] Here, we see Gerald's readiness to draw on St Davids traditions current in his lifetime, and more particularly to promote a secondary relic, presumably kept in the cathedral. The episode is thus of a piece with Gerald's accounts of other relics associated with native saints given in the Irish and Welsh works, and reflects his assumption that such objects conveyed the continuing power of the past in the present.[36]

In the present context, though, another change is particularly significant. According to the versions of Rhygyfarch's Life in both the Vespasian and Nero-Digby recensions, David was made archbishop twice: first by the patriarch of Jerusalem, then at the Synod of Brefi after successfully preaching against the Pelagian heresy.[37] The former reference, at least, looks like an interpolation to Rhygyfarch's original text, as the Life then goes on to refer to David as bishop until his elevation at Brefi.[38] Be that as it may, Gerald removed the inconsistency by stating that David had merely been made a bishop (*episcopus*) by the patriarch.[39] Furthermore, in his account of the saint's elevation as 'archbishop of all Wales' ('in Kambriae totius archiepiscopum'), he sought to accommodate a different explanation of David's elevation, namely that the saint had been ceded the dignity of archbishop by Dubricius.[40] This account derived, not from Rhygyfarch, but from Geoffrey of Monmouth, and Gerald included it in the *Itinerarium*.[41] Accordingly, in the Life, Gerald tries to reconcile the two traditions by stating that the saint had been made archbishop by the election of the synod of Brefi, while adding that he had already been ceded the honour by Dubricius.[42]

Turning next to the *Itinerarium*, Gerald emphasised the antiquity and former dignity of the see of St Davids by opening Book II of the work with the unequivocal statement that 'Menevia [St Davids] is the head of Wales, and formerly a metropolitan city' ('caput est Kambriae Menevia, et urbs olim metropolitana').[43] A lengthy chapter follows, headed 'Concerning the see of Menevia, with its notable things' ('De sede Menevensi, cum notabilibus suis').[44] Over half of this concerns the history of St Davids from the time of its patron saint,

David, to the pontificate of Bernard (1115–48), who had raised the metro-politan question earlier in the twelfth century.[45] Gerald cites two sources at the beginning of this account. The first is described as 'British histories' ('Bri-tannicae . . . historiae'), and evidently refers to the *De gestis Britonum*, whose author, Geoffrey of Monmouth, is not named, as was normal when it was in Gerald's interests to rely on him.[46] This was given as the authority for the claim that Archbishop Dubricius of Caerleon had ceded the metropolitan dignity to David, thereby ensuring its translation to Menevia. Secondly, David's sanctity is said to be witnessed by a book of the Life of St David, that is, some version of Rhygyfarch's late eleventh-century *Vita Sancti Dauid*. Gerald was anxious, then, to support key claims for the foundation of St Davids as a metropolitan see by reference to written texts.

There then follow two lists intended to demonstrate episcopal succession at St Davids from the time of its patron saint to that of King Henry I (1100–35; see Appendix below). The first list consists of alleged archbishops from St David to Samson, who is alleged to have taken the pallium to Dol in Brittany, thereby depriving St Davids of its metropolitan dignity. This is followed by an account of how Samson fled St Davids because of the 'yellow plague' ('flavam pestem') and took his pallium to Dol in Brittany, which consequently achieved metro-politan status while this was lost by Samson's successors at St Davids, though these continued to consecrate suffragan bishops in Wales and remained inde-pendent of any other church until the 'full conquest' of Wales ('ad plenam . . . Kambriae subactionem') by Henry I.[47] The names of those successors down to Bishop Wilfred (1085–1115) are then given in the second list.

Gerald gave two versions of the lists, one in the first and second redac-tions of the *Itinerarium* (*c.*1191 and *c.*1197 respectively), the other in the third redaction of *c.*1214. Both versions agree that there had been forty-four prelates from St David to Wilfred, and that the departure of Samson to Dol marked a significant turning point, after which the successors of St David were merely bishops, not archbishops, albeit allegedly still possessing some attributes com-mensurate with metropolitan status. In addition, the majority of the names in both versions are the same, differences in spelling being explicable as scribal variants. It is also possible that the repetition of Bleiddudd (*Blethuth*) in Version 1 and Sadyrnfai (*Sadernueu*) in Version 2 resulted from eye-skip, although either or both cases may equally well bear witness to deliberate editorial choice.

Nevertheless, there are also some substantive differences. Version 1 lists twenty-three archbishops and twenty-one bishops, as opposed to twenty-five and nineteen, respectively, in Version 2. Although it omits two of the names (one a repetition) from the list of bishops, Version 2 does not simply add two new names to the list of archbishops: rather, it omits three names given in Version 1, repeats one, and adds three of its own. These contrasts reflect the appearance in each version of three names that are unique to its lists. In Version 1 these consist of Cynog and Idwallon(?) (*Idwalauri/Idwalaun*) in the list of archbishops and Morfyw (*Morbiu*) in the list of bishops, while Version 2 adds Nobis (*Nouis*), Cadell(?) (*Catulus*) and Sulhaithfai (*Sulhaithuai*) to the list of archbishops.

The two versions of the list of archbishops differ in two main respects. First, Version 1 names David's successor, and thus the second archbishop of St Davids, as Cynog (*Kenauc*), who in turn is followed by Eliud, that is, St Teilo; whereas Version 2 omits Cynog and puts 'Eliud who is also called Teilo' ('Eliud qui et Theliau vocatur') second. The inclusion of Cynog may reflect the influence of the *Annales Cambriae*, two versions of which name him as the next bishop to have died after St David, although without identifying his see or claiming that he was David's successor.[48] Alternatively, or additionally, the list in the earlier redactions may have been indebted to Geoffrey of Monmouth, who claimed that, after David – termed archbishop of Caerleon – died in his abbey of Menevia, he was succeeded by Cynog (*Kinocus*), bishop of Llanbadarn.[49] The precedence given to the form Eliud, which is glossed as Teilo in the later list, may reflect a debt to the Life of St David, as this presented Eliud as one of the disciples of David in the latter's monastery, and also, together with Padarn, the saint's companion on the journey to the patriarch of Jerusalem.[50] The second difference is Version 2's expansion of the number of archbishops at the end of the sequence, with the repetition of the name Sadyrnfai (*Sadernueu*) and addition of three other names (*Nouis, Catulus* and *Sulhaithuai*) not found in the list given in the earlier redactions.[51]

The two versions' lists of bishops that succeeded Samson exhibit fewer differences than their lists of archbishops. Although their forms often differ, the names in the lists follow the same order in both versions, except that in Version 1 two additional names are inserted, Morfyw (*Morbiu*) and Bleiddudd (*Blethuth*), the latter being a repetition. The list in Version 2 also contains glosses on two of the names. Thus Morgenau is said to have been the first of the bishops of Menevia to have eaten meat, which led to his being killed by (presumably Hiberno-Scandinavian) pirates (*a piratis*); he then 'appeared to a certain bishop in Ireland, showing his wounds and saying, "Because I ate meat, I have become meat"' ('apparuit cuidam episcopo in Hibernia, ostendens vulnera sua et dicens, "Quia carnes comedi, caro factus sum"').[52] (Welsh chronicles record, in an annal for 999, that Menevia was ravaged by 'gentiles' ('gentiles'), a common term for Hiberno-Scandinavian raiders, and Bishop Morgenau killed.[53]) In addition, the list in Version 2 explains that Morgenau's successor but one, Ieuan, rendered *Iohannes* in Version 1, was bishop for only one night.[54]

Gerald gives no source for these lists. However, as argued below, it is likely that they originated independently of him, presumably at St Davids. Since the early modern period, scholars have considered the likely sources of the names listed,[55] and from the mid-nineteenth century have expressed strong reservations about the reliability of the lists, especially that naming archbishops, as evidence for early medieval episcopal succession at St Davids.[56] For W. Basil Jones and Edward Augustus Freeman, the lists were essentially fabricated by drawing on material in other texts: 'We are constrained to . . . observe that the compilers of lists and genealogies are frequently tempted to swell the numbers of them with names purloined from extraneous sources.'[57] Thus, following Edward Yardley in the mid-eighteenth century, they noted that some of the names, especially in the second list down to the eleventh century, correspond to bishops attested in the Welsh annals.[58] In these cases, which account for seventeen of the names taking both versions together, borrowing from one or more version of those annals is indeed likely. However, comparison of the name forms in the lists with those given in the three extant texts (A, B and C) of the Latin chronicles generically known as *Annales Cambriae* does not reveal a consistent pattern that could suggest that differences between the two versions reflected, at least in part, the use of different chronicle texts.[59] In addition, as John Reuben Davies has argued, several of these later bishops also appear in a list – extant in a fourteenth-century manuscript, but possibly deriving from an eleventh-century exemplar – of the bishops of Clas Cynidr (Glasbury, Radnorshire, near the Herefordshire border). This may point to translation from Glasbury to St Davids, to which it was somehow subordinate.[60] Nevertheless, Davies stresses that Gerald's lists are 'inherently untrustworthy', and they were clearly concocted in order to try and give historical substance to the claim that St Davids had possessed metropolitan status from the time of its patron saint until it was subjected to Norman power under Henry I.[61]

The inclusion of the lists of archbishops and bishops of St Davids in the *Itinerarium Kambriae* was clearly part of Gerald's wider aim of demonstrating the metropolitan status of that church. Given the opposition of King John and Archbishop Hubert Walter to Gerald's later prosecution of the metropolitan claim, this might seem surprising. After all, the first redaction of the *Itinerarium* was composed while its author was a clerk in the service of Richard I. It praised Archbishop Baldwin for undertaking his preaching tour in Wales,[62] and explicitly states that Baldwin asserted his metropolitan authority over the Church in Wales by celebrating mass in each of the Welsh cathedrals, 'as a sign of investiture of each one' ('singulis . . . investiturae cujusdam signum').[63] Gerald made this a cue to declare that 'before these last days and most recent times the church of St Davids did not use to regard Canterbury with any bond of obedience' ('ante finales hos dies et tempora novissima, Menevensis ecclesia Cantuariensem nullo subjectionis vinculo respiciebat'), citing as evidence Bede's account of the meeting between Augustine of Canterbury and the British bishops.[64] However, this merely served to emphasise that the metropolitan status of St Davids belonged to the past, and Gerald avoided making any explicit claim that that status should be restored in the present.[65] True, he explained that Bishop Bernard had been the only bishop since the Norman Conquest to advance the claim. However, he dampened any implications that this should inspire further such attempts by observing that circumstances had been particularly favourable at the time, and also by going on to expand on Bernard's excessive pomposity and ambition.[66] (His view of Bernard changed during his own attempt to secure recognition of the metropolitan status of St Davids from 1198 onwards, especially after finding evidence of papal bulls supportive of Bernard's metropolitan claim in the papal archives.[67]) Furthermore, Gerald contrasted the present state of St Davids very unfavourably with that of Canterbury, in terms of royal support, wealth and the number of suffragans and scholars, concluding that it would be difficult to restore the position of the former without major political and other changes.[68] By contrast, two additions to the second and third redactions of the *Itinerarium* sharpened the political significance of the metropolitan question. First, the loss of metropolitan status by Samson's successors at St Davids was now attributed, not only to laziness and poverty, but also 'to the coming of the English to the island and the enmity introduced by the Saxons' ('propter Anglorum adventum in insulam, et Saxonicam interpositam hostilitatem').[69] Secondly, Gerald introduced a paragraph describing how the canons of St Davids had sought in vain to persuade the Lord Rhys to prevent Baldwin from going to St Davids, as this would prejudice the recovery of its ancient metropolitan dignity.[70]

It may be, then, that the motivation for Gerald's account of the alleged early history of St Davids and its metropolitan status in the first redaction of the *Itinerarium* was primarily antiquarian. However, the same cannot be said of the works he subsequently wrote to record and vindicate his unsuccessful attempt to become bishop of St Davids and secure recognition of the church's metropolitan status. These were the autobiographical *De rebus a se gestis* ('On the Things He Has Achieved'), the collection of documents (both authentic and invented) entitled *De invectionibus* ('On Shameful Attacks'), and the *De iure et statu Menevensis ecclesiae* ('On the Rights and Status of the Church of St Davids'), a fictitious dialogue on the struggle; all were completed between about 1215 and 1218.[71] One interesting point here is that none of these works contain any version of the lists of the archbishops and bishops of the see, which appear only in the *Itinerarium*. True, Gerald states in both the *De invectionibus* and the *De iure* that there had been twenty-five archbishops from David to Samson, as well as a further nineteen bishops to his own day, thereby tacitly alluding to the lists in the third redaction of the *Itinerarium*.[72] However, the names themselves are not given. Since the *De iure* repeats the passage in the *Itinerarium* on how St Davids had lost the pallium under Samson, and adapts the earlier work's sections on Bishop Bernard, the omission of the lists, together with other differences, appears to have been deliberate. It may be that Gerald regarded material on the early history of the see as being of only tangential relevance to the *De iure*, whose main purpose was to relate the recent history of St Davids and especially to justify his struggle to be elected bishop and to gain recognition of the church's metropolitan status.[73]

As the repetition of the story of the loss of the pallium under Samson shows, however, the *De iure* did not ignore the purported early history of St Davids altogether. In particular, it quotes a memorandum on the early history of the Church in Britain and of St Davids that Gerald gave to the pope which is included in the *De invectionibus*.[74] The latter work was begun in Rome in 1200 and completed *c*.1216, and supports the metropolitan claim by two kinds of historical argument that expand upon, and in important respects augment, the history of St Davids presented in the *Itinerarium*. The first is the memorandum just mentioned, entitled 'A Chronicle of British Ecclesiastical History' ('Ecclesiastice hystorie Britannice cronographia').[75] This is an account of the early history of the British Church from the time of King Lucius, which is then linked to the history of St Davids down to Gerald's own day. The account is attributed to Bede and a volume by Pope Anacletus (that is, the *Notitia dignitatum*, an early fifth-century list of Roman offices and administrative divisions commonly ascribed to that first-century pope).[76] It is also indebted to material in Geoffrey of Monmouth that Gerald had already deployed in the *Itinerarium* and *Descriptio*, notably its quotation of Merlin's prophecy that 'St Davids will wear the pallium of Caerleon' ('Menevia pallio Urbis Legionum induetur'),[77] as well as its references to Brutus, Corineus and Kamber.[78] However, Gerald's reference to (otherwise unknown) 'historiae Dolenses' as establishing that Samson of Dol was originally from St Davids implicitly rejected Geoffrey, who stated that Samson had been archbishop of York, whence he was expelled and ended his days at Dol.[79] Secondly, a later chapter of the *De invectionibus* reproduces a letter from the chapter of St Davids to Pope Eugenius III (1145–53) which names bishops of Bangor, St Asaph and Llandaf who had allegedly been ordained by eleventh-century bishops of St Davids exercising their metropolitan functions despite the loss of the church's pallium under Samson.[80] The same work also contains a letter from the *conventus* of St Davids to Pope Honorius II (1124–30) outlining the historical basis of the claim to metropolitan status; this included the Lucius legend as well as the claims that St David was consecrated archbishop by Dubricius, that all his successors down to Wilfred had held the metropolitan dignity, and that Samson had taken the pallium to Dol after leaving St Davids because of the 'yellow plague' ('flavam pestem').[81]

If either or both of these letters are authentic, the claim that St Davids had lost its metropolitan status after Samson fled with the pallium to Brittany originated during or shortly after the pontificate of Bernard (1115–48). There is no earlier evidence for this claim than the letter to Honorius II, and the story was very probably invented in the second quarter of the twelfth century to provide a pseudo-historical explanation for St Davids having lost its alleged original status as an archbishopric.[82] This dating is consistent with other evidence. In the eleventh century the clergy of Dol had presented Samson as the first archbishop of their church as part of a renewed claim to metropolitan status, which had been briefly recognised by Pope Nicholas I (858–67), and the claim remained disputed until it was quashed by Pope Innocent III in 1199 in a definitive ruling subjecting Dol to the metropolitan authority of Tours.[83] That the clergy of St Davids under Bishop Bernard could have known of Dol's assertion of metropolitan status originating with Samson is suggested by the Book of Llandaf. This contains a version of Book I of the *Vita I S. Samsonis*, which, in contrast to its Breton source, refers to Samson as archbishop and asserts that Dol enjoyed 'pre-eminence' ('principatus') over all Brittany 'until today' ('usque hodie').[84] Perhaps reflecting an awareness of the Llandaf and/or St Davids claims, Geoffrey of Monmouth also presented Samson as archbishop of Dol.

The dependence of the distinction between the archbishops and bishops in the *Itinerarium*'s lists on Samson's alleged departure with the pallium could suggest, in turn, that at least one of those lists was compiled to support the metropolitan claims of St Davids from the time of Bishop Bernard onwards. The conclusion of the lists with Wilfred, Bernard's immediate predecessor, also supports this dating. True, neither the precise date of composition nor the authorship of the lists can be established with any certainty. It is also uncertain why the lists are attested in two versions. The similarities between them suggest that they are closely related, with one influencing the other or both deriving independently from a common lost exemplar. Although it increases the proportion of archbishops to bishops, neither this nor any other feature of Version 2 provides a significantly stronger basis for the metropolitan claim than Version 1. As regards dating, the possible influence of Geoffrey of Monmouth on Version 1 of the first list could indicate that this was composed after the publication of the *De gestis Britonum c.*1138. Be that as it may, moves to achieve metropolitan status by the St Davids clergy, first attested in the letter to Honorius II and subsequently promoted by Bishop Bernard, provide a plausible *terminus a quo* of 1124x1148 for both lists, whose purpose was clearly to furnish St Davids with an archiepiscopal and episcopal succession that would put flesh on the church's metropolitan claims.[85] A contemporaneous parallel is provided by a list of alleged archbishops of London, extant only in late sixteenth- and early seventeenth-century versions, that appears to derive from a twelfth-century text composed in the context of Gilbert Foliot's assertion of his see's metropolitan status.[86] Moreover, while the St Davids claims were dropped by Bishop Bernard's successors, David fitz Gerald (1148–76) and Peter de Leia (1176–98), members of the cathedral chapter continued to advance them.[87] It is entirely plausible, then, that the lists were drawn up by clergy at St Davids during the half-century or so before Baldwin's preaching tour, and quite possibly in the context of Bernard's campaign for metropolitan status.

Here it is worth adding that two other sources may indicate that at least one of the lists given by Gerald originated independently of him at St Davids. First, the letter from Owain Glyndŵr to Charles VI of France, dated at Pennal 31 March 1406, declaring the prince's readiness to transfer his allegiance to the Avignon Pope Benedict XIII, states that 'the chronicles and old books of the church of St Davids' ('cronicis et antiquis libris ecclesie Menevensis') contained the names of twenty-four archbishops of the see after St David, which are then cited in a list largely similar to, though not identical with, that of Version 2 in the third redaction of the *Itinerarium*.[88] Of course, the differences from the latter may have resulted from scribal error and emendation and thus do not conclusively preclude derivation, direct or indirect, from a manuscript at St Davids containing the third redaction of the *Itinerarium*.[89] Secondly, in the early seventeenth century Francis Godwin (1562–1633) published a list which he claimed to derive from the archives of St Davids, and which he distinguished from a list he ascribed to Gerald (and very probably taken from the conflated text of the *Itinerarium* published by David Powel in 1585 and reprinted by Camden).[90] However, as the list attributed to the archives is close to that of Version 2 in the third redaction of the *Itinerarium*, again we cannot rule out the possibility that it derived from Gerald rather than being Gerald's source.[91]

What does the inclusion of these lists in the *Itinerarium* reveal of Gerald's access to and use of sources for the Welsh past? Of particular interest here is the substitution of Version 2 of the lists in the third redaction of the *Itinerarium* c.1214. As he offers no comment on the change, and the differences between the two versions are fairly limited, it is unclear why Gerald came to consider the second version preferable. Possibly he was attracted by the naming of Teilo or Eliud, rather than Cynog, as David's successor, as, unlike the latter, Eliud appeared in his Life of St David, and the glosses on the fates of Morgenau and Ieuan may have appealed to his love of anecdote.[92] In any case, it seems likely that he only found Version 2 after completing the second redaction of the *Itinerarium* c.1197. This would be consistent with his greater knowledge of the St Davids archives subsequently, as evidenced by his discovery there of the original papal bulls to Bishop Bernard on returning from his first visit to press the metropolitan cause in Rome in 1200.[93]

One complication that arises here, however, is that Gerald seems not to have taken account of the later lists in the second redaction of the *Descriptio Kambriae*, dedicated to Stephen Langton, whose completion is usually dated to c.1214x1215,[94] and thus to about the same time as that of the third redaction of the *Itinerarium*. Indeed, Dimock argued that it was dedicated to Langton shortly *after* the dedication to him of the third redaction of the *Itinerarium*.[95] The second redaction of the *Descriptio* states that there had been twenty-three (not twenty-five) archbishops from David to Samson, and a further twenty-four thereafter 'to the present day' ('usque in hodiernum diem'), which would be consistent with the twenty-one down to Wilfred named in Version 1 in the earlier redactions of the *Itinerarium*, if we add Bernard, David fitz Gerald and Peter de Leia, bishop at the time the first redaction of the *Descriptio* was completed.[96] As Gerald explicitly refers in this passage of the *Descriptio* to the list of bishops' names in the *Itinerarium*, he clearly had a text of the first or second redactions of the latter text in mind. Since the *De invectionibus* and *De iure*, completed shortly afterwards, drew on the lists in the third redaction of the *Itinerarium*, this may indicate that the latter was completed after the second redaction of the *Descriptio*. If so, this could in turn suggest that Gerald only discovered the lists included in the third redaction of the *Itinerarium* shortly before completing that redaction, and thus over a decade after the conclusion of the St Davids struggle.[97] However, such are the complexities of the revisions Gerald made to his works, this can only be one possible explanation.[98]

What is clear, though, is that Gerald adapted the material he found on the purported early history of St Davids and integrated it into an interpretation that drew on his own understanding of Welsh history, notably in his emphasis on Henry I's accomplishing the 'full conquest' ('plenam . . . subactionem') of Wales. This is of a piece with his use of Henry I's reign elsewhere in his writings as a temporal marker, and reflects his understanding that the Norman conquests – from which he and his family had benefited – formed a crucial turning point, albeit one he wished to reverse when it came to the status of St Davids. In addition, Gerald tailored the material he presented on the history of St Davids to the purposes and intended readerships of the different works that dealt with this subject. Thus the first redaction of the *Itinerarium Kambriae*, while emphasising the metropolitan dignity of St Davids, is less concerned to draw out the implications of this for the church's status in the present than the later redactions, and especially the third, completed after the failure of his own struggle to secure metropolitan status for the see. In addition, that work contains more by way of local traditions on the alleged early history of the church than later works produced in the wake of his struggle. By contrast, the latter focus on arguments intended to persuade Pope Innocent III, and place greater emphasis on papal precedents in support of the independence of the Welsh church from Canterbury. This is especially clear in the 'Chronicle of British Ecclesiastical History' ('Ecclesiastice hystorie Britannice cronographia') included in the *De invectionibus*, and also quoted in the *De iure*, which explicitly refers to only two written sources, one of which is attributed to a pope, namely Anacletus, while the other, Bede's *Historia Ecclesiastica*, highlighted the role of Gregory the Great and his successors in the making of the Anglo-Saxon church, and provided evidence that the early archbishops of Canterbury, from Augustine to Theodore, lacked authority over the British bishops in Wales.[99]

## Conclusions

In his various accounts of the history of St Davids Gerald revealed his readiness to make the past serve his interests in the present. This instrumental view of the past as a key to understanding the present is likewise reflected in his accounts of the recent history of Anglo-Welsh conflict in which his family had played a prominent part. But it is also evident in his appeal to the more distant past: in the alleged influence of Trojan origins on the appearance and character of the Welsh, in parallels with the early Britons that had lessons for the Welsh of his own day, and in justifications of dynastic or ecclesiastical supremacy that looked back to the post-Roman and early medieval periods. Yet his treatment of the history of St Davids also shows that his use of the past was dynamic, and sometimes critical. Thus, with regard to the lists of archbishops and bishops, he rejected one source in favour of another, and he also sought to reconcile conflicting testimonies in the account of David's elevation as archbishop in his Life of the saint. Moreover, in the *Retractationes* he composed towards the end of his life Gerald acknowledged that, apart from what he had derived from Bede and the *Notitia dignitatum*, his account of the early British church and St Davids was 'based on common report and opinion rather than on any historical certainty' ('magis famam publicam et opinionem quam historiae cujuspiam certitudinem sunt secuta').[100]

It remains the case, though, that Gerald's knowledge and use of the Welsh past were selective. There is nothing to suggest that he sought to write a sequential narrative of Welsh history: indeed, to assess how far he succeeded in being a historian of Wales may be to miss his purpose.[101] Instead, he interpreted aspects of the past in the context of a broader engagement with the Wales of his own day. Small wonder, then, that Gerald does not seem to have utilised all the Latin historical sources in Wales potentially available to him. Particularly notable is his apparent neglect of the annals kept at St Davids and other ecclesiastical centres now extant in the Breviate and Cottonian Chronicles (otherwise known respectively as the B- and C-texts of *Annales Cambriae*), and which also underlie the lost Latin chronicle of the late thirteenth century that was translated in the Welsh chronicles generically known as *Brut y Tywysogyon* ('The Chronicle of the Princes').[102] Less remarkable is the only limited extent to which Gerald appears to have been acquainted with the literature and lore in Welsh embraced by the umbrella term of *cyfarwyddyd*, including the compendium of the bards' knowledge of early history and legend in *Trioedd Ynys Prydain* ('The Triads of the Island of Britain').[103] Yes, he shows some familiarity with Welsh words, quotes a couple of Welsh proverbs to illustrate the use of alliteration, and even feels qualified to comment on the quality of Welsh in different parts of Wales; he also describes the Welsh bards and states that they kept copies of genealogies written in Welsh.[104] Nevertheless, none of this suggests a deep immersion in the Welsh language and its literary culture, and there is therefore much to commend in Brynley Roberts's conclusion that 'Gerald is an observer of, never a participant in, native Welsh culture.'[105]

However, as that quotation indicates, Gerald was open to aspects of Welsh culture, and this certainly applies to his understanding of the Welsh past, which he seems to have viewed from two main perspectives. One was shaped by his own family background, and probably relied, in part, on memories transmitted by members of his family. Here, the focus was on the century or so following the first Norman conquests in Wales, and thus on struggles between kings of England, Marcher lords and Welsh rulers. This bears comparison with the earlier *Expugnatio Hibernica*, which highlighted conquests in which Gerald's kinsmen played a prominent – and, so Gerald maintained, undervalued – role.[106] However, he also took a longer view which shared affinities with key aspects of Welsh culture, and focused on origin legends concerning both the Welsh as a people and their saints and ecclesiastical traditions. In part, Gerald may have encountered such material orally, but he also relied heavily on Latin sources, especially Geoffrey of Monmouth. This no doubt partly reflected Geoffrey's popularity; but it probably also reflects Gerald's belief that the *De gestis Britonum* represented authentic Welsh tradition, already evident in the work of Gildas.[107] (The Irish parallel here, of course, is the use of a version of the *Lebor Gabála Érenn* in the *Topographia Hibernica*.[108]) Moreover, this tradition had potent implications for the present, being inextricably linked not only to a sense of territorial loss but also to concomitant hopes of political revival. After all, Gerald complained that all the Welsh of his own day believed – erroneously in his view – that the prophecies of Merlin would be fulfilled and that the Britons would recover their name and fate in the island of Britain.[109] And the translations of the *De gestis Britonum* into Welsh by the thirteenth century are eloquent testimony to how Geoffrey's vision of a glorious Brittonic past was appropriated, or, perhaps more accurately, reappropriated in Welsh historical writing.[110] For Gerald, then, the Welsh past was much more than a matter of history; rather, it was a powerful, and sometimes disturbing, presence in contemporary Wales that was central to his ecclesiastical career and literary ambitions.[111]

❖

# Appendix

## Lists of archbishops and bishops in the *Itinerarium Kambriae*, II.1

As explained above, two versions of these lists may be distinguished. The first version appears in the first and second redactions of the *Itinerarium Kambriae*, datable respectively to *c*.1191 and *c*.1197. It is printed here from Oxford, Bodleian Library, MS Rawlinson B. 188 (B), s. xii/xiii, a manuscript of the first redaction copied in London, British Library, Royal MS 13 B. viii (R), s. xii/xiii, which in turn was copied in Cambridge, University Library, MS Ff.1.27, part 2 (F), s. xiii.[112] Variant readings are noted from London, British Library, Additional MS 34762, s. xiii, a manuscript of the second redaction not used by Dimock, which gives better readings of at least two of the names that appear not to have been understood by B.[113] The second version appears in the third redaction of the *Itinerarium*, datable to *c*.1214. Its list is printed here from Aberystwyth, National Library of Wales, MS 3024C, s. xiv[2], whose original provenance is unknown but may have been copied at St Davids as it was given by Richard Davies, bishop of St Davids, to Sir William Cecil in 1564.[114] This has been chosen partly because it has not previously been published but also because it appears to contain more accurate renditions of some of the names than those in London, British Library, Cotton MS Domitian A. i (D), s. xiii[ex], printed by Dimock.[115] However, variant readings are also noted from the latter manuscript, as this was certainly written at St Davids, where it remained until Sir John Prise acquired it from John Lewis, treasurer of the cathedral 1523–41; thus its text of the *Itinerarium* may well derive from an earlier copy kept at that church, perhaps even one given to it by Gerald (the same may also be true of NLW 3024C).[116]

## A.   Archbishops of St Davids

| FIRST VERSION **B**, fol. 88r | SECOND VERSION **NLW 3024E**, fol. 43r–v |
|---|---|
| Dauid | Dauid |
| Kenauc | Eliud qui et Teliau[a] uocatur |
| Eliud | Keneu |
| Keneri | Morwal |
| Morwal | Haernueu |
| Haernueu[a] | Elwaid |
| Elwid[b] | Gurnueu |
| Gurneu | Leudiwit[b] |
| Lheudiuord | Gorwiust |
| Gorwiust[c] | Gogavn[c] |

Gugaun
Cledauc
Amuian
Eluoed
Ethelemun
Elauc
Maiscoit
Sadernueu
Nortwal[d]
Aser
Artwail[e]
Idwalauri[f]
Sampson

Cletauc[d]
Aman
Eludget[e]
Elduneu[f]
Elaue
Mailsvyd[g]
Sadernueu[h]
Catulus
Sulhaithuai
Nouis
Sadernueu[h]
Diothwal[i]
Asser
Arthuail[j]
Samson[k]

## B.  Bishops of St Davids

**B**, fol. 88v

**NLW 3024E**, fol. 44r

Ruelin
Retherch[g]
Elgiun[h]
Morbiu
Lunuerd
Nergu
Sulhidir
Eneuris

Riuelin[l]
Retherch[m]
Eluin
Lhunnerc[n]
Nergu
Sulidir
Eneuris
Morgeneu, qui primus inter episcopos Meneuie carnes comedit, et ibidem a piratis interfectus est . . . ('Morgeneu, who was the first among the bishops of St Davids to eat meat, and was killed by pirates in the same place')

Morgeneu
Nathan

Nathan
Ieu(an),[o] hic Ieuan[o] una sola nocte vixit episcopus ('Ieuan, this Ieuan was bishop for only one night')

Ioh(ann)es
August(us)[i]
Morgenueth
Blethuth

Arwistel
Morgennith[p]
Eruin
Tramerin

Eruin

Tramerin

Ioseph

Blethuth

Sulgen

Abraham

Wilfrid(us)

Ioseth

Bleidud[q]

Sulghein

Abraham

Wilfre

*First Version: Variants from London, British Library, Additional MS 34762, fols 145r, 146r*

[a] Harnueu  [b] Elwaid  [c] Gorwist  [d] Norwal  [e] Arthwail

[f] Idwalaun  [g] Retherc  [h] Elguin  [i] Arigustil

*Second Version: Variants from London, British Library, Cotton MS Domitian A. i (D), fol. 93r–v*

[a] Theliau  [b] Leudiwi  [c] Gogau  [d] Cledac  [e] Eludged  [f] Elduven

[g] Mailswid  [h] Sadurnueu  [i] Doithwal  [j] Archuail  [k] Sampson  [l] Kuielm

[m] Retherth  [n] Lunuerc  [o] Iewan  [p] Morgenennith  [q] Bleidhud

❖

## Notes

1    For assessments of Gerald as a historian, see Antonia Gransden, *Historical Writing in England c.550–c.1307* (London and Ithaca, 1974), pp. 221–2, 244–6; F. X. Martin, 'Giraldus as Historian', in A. B. Scott and F. X. Martin (eds and trans.), *Expugnatio Hibernica: The Conquest of Ireland, by Giraldus Cambrensis* (Dublin, 1978), pp. 267–84; Brynley F. Roberts, 'Gerald of Wales and Welsh Tradition', in Françoise H. M. Le Saux (ed.), *The Formation of Culture in Medieval Britain: Celtic, Latin and Norman Influences on English Music, Literature, History and Art* (Lampeter, 1995), pp. 129–47, at 134–8.

2    Robert Bartlett, *Gerald of Wales, 1146–1223* (Oxford, 1982), pp. 178–210. See also Michael A. Faletra, *Wales and the Medieval Colonial Imagination: The Matters of Britain in the Twelfth Century* (New York, 2014), pp. 155–6, 160.

3    *Descriptio*, 'Praefatio prima', p. 157.

4    *Descriptio*, 'Praefatio prima', p. 158.

5    Huw Pryce, 'Gerald of Wales, Gildas, and the *Descriptio Kambriae*', in Fiona Edmonds and Paul Russell (eds), *Tome: Studies in Medieval Celtic History and Law in Honour of Thomas Charles-Edwards* (Woodbridge, 2011), pp. 115–24.

6    Julia C. Crick, 'The British Past and the Welsh Future: Gerald of Wales, Geoffrey of Monmouth and Arthur of Britain', *Celtica*, 23 (1999), 60–75. For Gerald's debt to Geoffrey, see also Faletra, *Wales and the Medieval Colonial Imagination*, pp. 135, 138, 154–5, 157–9.

7    Bartlett, *Gerald of Wales*, p. 206.

8    *Descriptio*, i.11, 18, pp. 185, 202–3.

9    *Descriptio*, i.2, pp. 166–7.

10    P. McGurk (ed. and trans.), *The Chronicle of John of Worcester, Volume III: The Annals from 1067 to 1140 with the Gloucester Interpolations and the Continuation to 1141* (Oxford, 1998), pp. 64–5 (a passage argued to derive from Welsh Latin annals underlying *Brut y Tywysogyon* by McGurk, p. xxxii); Thomas Jones (trans.), *Brut y Tywysogyon, or, The Chronicle of the Princes, Peniarth MS. 20 Version* (Cardiff, 1952), p. 19. Cf. Thomas Jones (ed. and trans.), *Brut y Tywysogyon, or, The Chronicle of the Princes, Red Book of Hergest Version* (2nd edition, Cardiff, 1973), pp. 32–3: 'And then fell the kingdom of the Britons' ('ac yna y dygwydawd teyrnas y Brytanyeit').

11    J. E. Lloyd, *A History of Wales from the Earliest Times to the Edwardian Conquest*, 2/1 (3rd edition, London, 1939), p. 327, n. 27. See also David N. Dumville, 'The "Six" Sons of Rhodri Mawr: A Problem in Asser's *Life of King Alfred*', *Cambridge Medieval Celtic Studies*, 4 (1982), 5–18, at 11.

12    *Itinerarium*, i.2, pp. 34–5.

13    Huw Pryce, 'Giraldus and the Geraldines', in Peter Crooks and Seán Duffy (eds), *The Geraldines and Medieval Ireland: The Making of a Myth* (Dublin, 2016), pp. 53–68, at 60–3.

14    *Descriptio*, ii.7, p. 217.

15    Bertram Colgrave and R. A. B. Mynors (eds and trans.), *Bede's Ecclesiastical History of the English People* (Oxford, 1969), ii.2, pp. 140–1.

16  W. H. Stevenson (ed.), *Asser's Life of King Alfred* (Oxford, 1904), §14, p. 12; trans. in Simon Keynes and Michael Lapidge, *Alfred the Great: Asser's Life of King Alfred and Other Contemporary Sources* (Harmondsworth, 1983), p. 71. For Gerald's knowledge of Asser, see Caroline Brett, 'John Leland, Wales and Early British History', *Welsh History Review*, 15 (1990–1), 169–82, at 174–5.

17  Clement C. I. Webb (ed.), *Ioannis Saresberiensis episcopi Carnotensis Policratici sive De nugis curialium et vestigiis philosophorum libri VIII*, 2/2 (Oxford, 1909), vi.6, pp. 18–20; Cary J. Nederman (ed. and trans.), *John of Salisbury: Policraticus* (Cambridge, 1990), pp. 113–14. See also Kelly DeVries, 'Harold Godwinson in Wales: Military Legitimacy in Late Anglo-Saxon England', in Richard P. Abels and Bernard S. Bachrach (eds), *The Normans and their Adversaries at War: Essays in Memory of C. Warren Hollister* (Woodbridge, 2001), pp. 65–85, and sources cited there.

18  Webb (ed.), *Ioannis Saresberiensis*, 2/2, p. 18.

19  *Descriptio*, ii.7, p. 218.

20  Kathryn Hurlock, *Wales and the Crusades c. 1095–1291* (Cardiff, 2011), pp. 58–91.

21  J. F. Dimock (ed.), *Giraldi Cambrensis Opera*, 8/6 (London, 1868), pp. xliii–xlv; Thomas Jones, 'Gerald the Welshman's "Itinerary through Wales" and "Description of Wales": An Appreciation and Analysis', *National Library of Wales Journal*, 6 (1949–50), 117–48 and 197–22, at 126.

22  *Itinerarium*, i.2, 3, 12, ii.1, pp. 20–36, 37–47, 89–99, 101–10.

23  *Itinerarium*, i.2, pp. 23–4.

24  *Itinerarium*, ii.2, pp. 111–12.

25  *Itinerarium*, i.2, ii.1, pp. 28, 102. Cf. *Itinerarium*, ii.4, pp. 119–20, derived from *Vita Sancti Dauid*.

26  This section summarises the discussion in Pryce, 'Giraldus and the Geraldines', pp. 63–7.

27  For example, *Itinerarium*, i.4, ii.1, pp. 47–8, 103 (Henry I); i.1, 6, 13, pp. 19, 62, 100 (Henry II). For the only event dated with reference to a Welsh ruler (the death of Rhys ap Tewdwr in 1093), see *Itinerarium*, i.12, pp. 89–90.

28  *Itinerarium*, i.2, 8, pp. 24, 30–1, 73, 75–7.

29  *Expugnatio*, i.2, p. 30; cf. i.16, 28, 30, 38, pp. 64, 88, 92, 104–6.

30  Michael Richter, 'The Life of St. David by Giraldus Cambrensis', *Welsh History Review*, 4 (1968–9), 381–6, whose dating is followed by Robert Bartlett, 'Rewriting Saints' Lives: The Case of Gerald of Wales', *Speculum*, 58 (1983), 598–613, at 599–600, n. 6, and Richard Sharpe, 'Which Text is Rhygyfarch's *Life* of St David?', in J. Wyn Evans and Jonathan M. Wooding (eds), *St David of Wales: Cult, Church and Nation* (Woodbridge, 2007), pp. 90–106, at 97 and n. 31.

31  *De rebus*, i.2, 4, 9, pp. 22–3, 27, 41–2.

32  See *Vita Davidis*, 'Proemium', p. 377.

33  Sharpe, 'Which text is Rhygyfarch's *Life* of St David?', pp. 96–7.

34  Bartlett, 'Rewriting Saints' Lives', 604.

35  *Vita Davidis*, Lectio VI, p. 393; discussion in J. Wyn Evans, 'Transition and Survival: St David and St Davids Cathedral', in Evans and Wooding (eds), *St David of Wales*, pp. 20–40, at 29–30.

36   Bartlett, *Gerald*, pp. 118–22.

37   Richard Sharpe and John Reuben Davies (eds and trans.), 'Rhygyfarch's *Life* of St David', in Evans and Wooding (eds), *St David of Wales*, pp. 107–55, at §§46, 53, pp. 140, 146; J. W. James (ed. and trans.), *Life of St. David: The Basic Mid Twelfth-Century Latin Text* (Cardiff, 1967), §§46, 53, pp. 20, 24.

38   Sharpe and Davies (eds), 'Rhygyfarch's *Life* of St David', §§49–50, p. 142 (and cf. §§59–60, 68, pp. 148, 154); James (ed.), *Rhigyfarch's Life*, §§49–50, pp. 21–2.

39   *Vita Davidis*, Lectio VII, p. 398.

40   *Vita Davidis*, Lectio VIII, p. 401.

41   Michael D. Reeve (ed.) and Neil Wright (trans.), *Geoffrey of Monmouth: The History of the Kings of Britain. An Edition and Translation of De gestis Britonum [Historia Regum Britanniae]* (Woodbridge, 2007), IX.158.404–5, p. 214; *Itinerarium*, i.5, ii.1, pp. 56, 101.

42   *Vita Davidis*, Lectio VIII, p. 401.

43   *Itinerarium*, ii, p. 101.

44   *Itinerarium*, ii.1, p. 101.

45   *Itinerarium*, ii.1, pp. 101–10.

46   *Itinerarium*, ii.1, p. 101; Crick, 'The British Past', p. 68.

47   *Itinerarium*, ii.1, p. 103.

48   *Annales Cambriae*, s.a. 606, Edmond Faral (ed.), *La légende arthurienne: études et documents*, 3/3 (Paris, 1929), p. 46 (*Cinauc*); Henry W. Gough-Cooper (ed.), 'Annales Cambriae: The B Text from London, National Archives, MS E164/1', *Welsh Chronicles Research Group* (2015), pp. 2–26, 27 (*Kenauc*), http://croniclau.bangor.ac.uk/documents/AC%20B%20first%20edition.pdf (accessed 27 July 2016). Cf. William Basil Jones and Edward Augustus Freeman, *The History and Antiquities of Saint David's* (London, 1856), p. 254.

49   Reeve (ed.) and Wright (trans.), *Geoffrey of Monmouth*, XI.179.90–6, pp. 254–5. Geoffrey's *Kinocus* is identified with Gerald's *Cenauc* in James Ussher, 'Britannicarum Ecclesiarum Antiquitates, quibus inserta est pestiferae adversus Dei gratiam a Pelagio Britanno in ecclesiam inductae haereseos Historia' [Dublin, 1639], in Charles Richard Elrington (ed.), *The Whole Works of the Most Rev. James Ussher, D.D.*, 16/5 (Dublin, 1864), p. 106.

50   Sharpe and Davies (eds), 'Rhygyfarch's *Life* of St David', §§15, 44–5, pp. 120–1, 138–41.

51   The repetition could, perhaps, have resulted from eye-skip; however, this cannot explain the additional names, as these are not found earlier in the list.

52   *Itinerarium*, i.2, p. 104.

53   For example, Jones (trans.), *Brut y Tywysogyon, Peniarth MS. 20 Version*, p. 10; Henry W. Gough-Cooper (ed.), 'Annales Cambriae: The C text from London, British Library Cotton MS Domitian A.i, ff. 138r–155r', *Welsh Chronicles Research Group* (2015), p. 24, http://croniclau.bangor.ac.uk/documents/AC%20C%20first%20edition.pdf.

54   *Itinerarium*, i.2, p. 104.

55   For example, Ussher, 'Britannicarum Ecclesiarum Antiquitates', in Elrington (ed.), *Whole Works*, 16/5, pp. 105–9.

56 Jones and Freeman, *History and Antiquities*, pp. 248–67. See also A. W. Haddan and William Stubbs (eds), *Councils and Ecclesiastical Documents relating to Great Britain and Ireland*, 3/1 (Oxford, 1869–78), p. 145 ('manifestly late compilations, and untrustworthy').

57 Jones and Freeman, *History and Antiquities*, p. 258.

58 Jones and Freeman, *History and Antiquities*, pp. 254, 257–8, 261–3, 266–7; Francis Green (ed.), *Menevia Sacra by Edward Yardley, S. T.B.* (London, 1927), pp. 22–31.

59 How far differences resulted from the use of Latin chronicles no longer extant can, of course, only be guessed.

60 John Reuben Davies, 'The Archbishopric of St Davids and the Bishops of *Clas Cynidr*', in Evans and Wooding (eds), *St David of Wales*, pp. 296–304, at 301.

61 *Itinerarium*, ii.1, p. 103.

62 Huw Pryce, 'Gerald's Journey through Wales', *Journal of Welsh Ecclesiastical History*, 6 (1989), 17–34, at 20, 27–8, 33–4.

63 *Itinerarium*, ii.1, pp. 104–5. However, this clause was omitted in the second redaction of *c.*1197, completed shortly before his election as bishop of St Davids, and dedicated to Bishop Hugh of Lincoln: *Itinerarium*, ii, p. 105, n. 1.

64 *Itinerarium*, i.2, p. 105.

65 Likewise, while Gerald observed in the *Itinerarium* that Dol had recently lost its metropolitan status owing to pressure from Tours, it was only in the *De invectionibus*, completed in 1216, that he used Innocent III's definitive ruling on the matter in 1199 to argue that St Davids should also be restored to its original, i.e. metropolitan, status; for edition see W. S. Davies (ed. and trans.), 'The Book of Invectives of Giraldus Cambrensis', *Y Cymmrodor*, 30 (1920), 1–248, hereafter cited as *De invectionibus*, at ii.5, p. 139.

66 *Itinerarium*, i.2, pp. 105–6.

67 James Conway Davies (ed.), *Episcopal Acts and Cognate Documents relating to Welsh Dioceses, 1066–1272*, 2/1 (Cardiff, 1946–8), pp. 215–19; Michael Richter, *Giraldus Cambrensis: The Growth of the Welsh Nation* (2nd edition, Aberystwyth, 1976), p. 112.

68 *Itinerarium*, i.2, p. 107.

69 *Itinerarium*, ii.1, p. 103 and n. 2.

70 *Itinerarium*, i.1, pp. 15–16 and 15 n. 2.

71 Bartlett, *Gerald*, p. 219.

72 *De invectionibus*, ii.1, pp. 131–2; *De iure*, ii, p. 151. The latter work states that twenty-four bishops had succeeded Samson to 'these times of ours' ('haec nostra tempora'), which, if this referred to the pontificate of Geoffrey de Henlawe (1203–14), would be consistent with the nineteen down to Wilfrid given in the third redaction of the *Itinerarium*.

73 As noted by Dimock (ed.), *Giraldi Cambrensis Opera*, 8/6, pp. 103, n. 1 and 105, n. 7, with reference to *De iure*, ii, pp. 151–2, 152–3.

74 *De iure*, ii, pp. 169–75.

75 In *De invectionibus*, ii.1, pp. 130–5. Comment in Richter, *Giraldus Cambrensis*, pp. 112–14.

76   Christopher N. L. Brooke, *The Church and the Welsh Border in the Central Middle Ages* (Woodbridge, 1986), p. 25.

77   Reeve (ed.) and Wright (trans.), *Geoffrey of Monmouth*, VII.112.48–9, p. 145; *Itinerarium*, i.5, p. 56.

78   Cf. *Descriptio*, i.1, 7, pp. 165, 178.

79   *De invectionibus*, ii.1, pp. 47, 130–5; Reeve (ed.) and Wright (trans.), *Geoffrey of Monmouth*, VIII.130.292, IX.151.192–6, IX.158.406–7, pp. 175, 203, 215. Geoffrey's claim is rejected in favour of Gerald's evidence, followed by Roger of Howden, in Ussher, 'Britannicarum Ecclesiarum Antiquitates', in Elrington (ed.), *Whole Works*, 16/5, pp. 94–7. The 'historiae Dolenses' are dismissed as invention by Gerald in F. Duine, *Le métropole de Bretagne. Chronique de Dol composée au XI^e siècle et Catalogues des Dignitaires jusqu'à le révolution* (Paris, 1916), p. 54, n. 2.

80   *De invectionibus*, ii.6, pp. 139–41.

81   *De invectionibus*, ii.10, pp. 143–6. On the letter and its authenticity, see Richter, *Giraldus Cambrensis*, pp. 40–2; Julia Barrow (ed.), *St Davids Episcopal Acta 1085–1280* (Cardiff, 1998), p. 4; John Reuben Davies, *The Book of Llandaf and the Norman Church in Wales* (Woodbridge, 2003), p. 110.

82   For the implausibility of the claim, see Jones and Freeman, *History and Antiquities*, pp. 263–4.

83   Duine, *Le métropole de Bretagne*, p. 41. For the background, see Paula De Fougerolles, 'Pope Gregory VII, the Archbishopric of Dol and the Normans', *Anglo-Norman Studies*, 21 (1999), 47–66; George Conklin, 'Les Capétiens et l'affaire de Dol de Bretagne, 1179–1199', *Revue d'histoire de l'Église de France*, 78/201 (1992), 241–63. Gerald claimed that Dol had already lost to Tours by *c*.1191, stating that Samson's successors at Dol had received the pallium 'almost until these times of ours, during which the accidental dignity passed away owing to the power of the archbishop of Tours' ('usque ad nostra haec fere tempora, quibus praevalente Turonorum archipraesule adventita dignitas evanuit'): *Itinerarium*, ii.1, p. 103 (a passage found in all three redactions).

84   J. Gwenogvryn Evans and John Rhys (eds), *The Text of the Book of Llan Dâv* (Oxford, 1893, repr. Aberystwyth, 1979), pp. 22, 24. Samson is also described as archbishop of Dol in the *Vita S. Teliaui*, in Evans and Rhys, *The Text of the Book of Llan Dâv*, p. 109. The *Vita I* describes Samson's consecration as bishop (in Wales) and Dol as a *monasterium*: Pierre Flobert (ed. and trans.), *La Vie ancienne de Saint Samson de Dol* (Paris, 1997), i.44, 52, 61, pp. 206–8, 222, 234. See also Davies, *The Book of Llandaf*, pp. 116, 128–9, 130.

85   R. R. Davies, *The Revolt of Owain Glyn Dŵr* (Oxford, 1995), p. 172, suggests that the lists 'may well have been initially compiled' as part of Bishop Bernard's campaign to secure metropolitan status for St Davids. Although Gerald appears to have gained knowledge of Version 2 of the lists after he found Version 1, it does not necessarily follow, of course, that Version 2 was originally compiled after Version 1.

86   Helen Birkett, 'Plausible Fictions: John Stow, Jocelin of Furness and the Book of British Bishops', in Clare Downham (ed.), *Jocelin of Furness: Proceedings of the 2011*

*Conference* (Donington, 2013), pp. 91–120. I am grateful to Dr Birkett for drawing this parallel to my attention and providing me with a copy of her paper.

87 Michael Richter (ed.), 'A New Edition of the So-called *Vita Dauidis Secundi*', *Bulletin of the Board of Celtic Studies*, 22/3 (1967), 245–9, at 247–8; *De invectionibus*, ii.1, pp. 134–5; *De rebus*, ii.3, pp. 48–9.

88 T. Matthews (ed.), *Welsh Records in Paris* (Carmarthen, 1910), p. 53; also in Michael Livingston and John K. Bollard (eds), *Owain Glyndŵr: A Casebook* (Liverpool, 2013), p. 124, with commentary at pp. 348–9.

89 Apart from giving different spellings of names in Version 2, the list in the 1406 letter omits two of the alleged early archbishops (*Eludget* and *Elduneu*), adds *Menevie* (apparently mistaken as a separate name) after *Morwal*, and inserts *David secundus* before Samson.

90 David Powel (ed.), *Pontici Virunnii viri doctissimi Britannicae historiae libri sex magna et fide et diligentia conscripti . . .* (London, 1585), pp. 161–2.

91 Francis Godwin, *A Catalogue of the Bishops of England, since the first planting of Christian religion in this island, together with a briefe history of their lives and memorable actions, so neere as can be gathered out of antiquity* (London, 1601; revised, London, 1615), pp. 505–9 (p. 506: 'A certaine Antiquity belonging vnto the Church of S. Dauid, reporteth a Catalogue somewhat different from this of Giraldus, to witte, this that followeth'); Francis Godwin, *De praesulibus Anglicae commentarius* (London, 1616), pp. 601–3 (p. 602: 'We have taken this list from Gerald; but have not thought fit to hide from the reader that the contrary is to be had in the archives of the church of St Davids' ('Catalogum istum ex Giraldo desumpsimus; a quo diversum haberi in archivis Ecclesiae Menevensis lectorem celandum non duximus').

92 See above, and, on anecdotes, Gransden, *Historical Writing*, p. 222.

93 Cf. Richter, *Giraldus Cambrensis*, p. 112.

94 Dimock (ed.), *Giraldi Cambrensis Opera*, 8/6, pp. xli–xlii (end 1213 x June 1215; probably end 1214 or early 1215; later than *Itinerarium*); Bartlett, *Gerald*, p. 216 (*c.*1215). I follow Dimock and Bartlett in identifying two redactions, though Lewis Thorpe (trans.), *Gerald of Wales, The Journey through Wales and The Description of Wales* (Harmondsworth, 1978), pp. 49–50, identifies three. See further Catherine Rooney, 'The Manuscripts of the Works of Gerald of Wales' (unpublished PhD thesis, University of Cambridge, 2005), 92–6.

95 Dimock (ed.), *Giraldi Cambrensis Opera*, 8/6, p. xli.

96 *Descriptio*, i.4, pp. 169–70 and 170, n. 1.

97 Alternatively, though, he may have known of those lists when revising the *Descriptio*, but found it simpler to refer to the earlier redactions of the *Itinerarium*, as the third redaction had not yet been completed.

98 Cf. Rooney, 'The Manuscripts', 29; Georgia Henley, 'Quotation, Revision, and Narrative Structure in Giraldus Cambrensis's *Itinerarium Kambriae*', *Journal of Medieval Latin*, 24 (2014), 1–52, at 40–6.

99 *De invectionibus*, ii.1, pp. 130, 132–3.

100 J. S. Brewer (ed.), *Giraldi Cambrensis Opera*, 8/1 (London, 1861), p. 426; Davies, *De invectionibus*, p. 17. Compare how Gerald was more cautious in the third redaction

of the *Itinerarium* with respect to his discovery of Merlin Silvester's prophecies at Nefyn than in the first two redactions: the latter state that he 'found' ('invenit') the prophecies, whereas the third redaction states that he 'is said to have found' ('dicitur invenisse') them: *Itinerarium*, ii.6, p. 124 and n. 5.

101   For a different perspective, see Faletra, *Wales and the Medieval Colonial Imagination*, pp. 138, 159.

102   For an overview of these chronicles with references to editions and secondary scholarship, see the 'Welsh Chronicles' website, *http://croniclau.bangor.ac.uk/index. php.en* (accessed 27 July 2016). For Gerald's relationship to, and possible influence on, Welsh Latin chronicles, see David Stephenson, 'Gerald of Wales and *Annales Cambriae*', *Cambrian Medieval Celtic Studies*, 60 (2010), 23–37.

103   By contrast, the St Davids metropolitan cause in the time of Bishop Bernard is apparently echoed in the first triad in the Early Version of *Trioedd Ynys Prydain*: Rachel Bromwich (ed.), *Trioedd Ynys Prydain: The Triads of the Island of Britain* (2nd edition, Cardiff, 1978), pp. cxi, 3.

104   *Descriptio*, i.3, 6, 12, 15, 17, pp. 167–8, 177, 187–8, 194, 200. See also Bartlett, *Gerald*, pp. 209–10, and Ben Guy's contribution in this volume.

105   Roberts, 'Gerald of Wales', pp. 139–42, at 139.

106   Pryce, 'Giraldus and the Geraldines'.

107   For a different interpretation, which presents the absence of a sequential history of Wales in Gerald's writings as a failure to provide a Welsh counter-narrative to Geoffrey, see Faletra, *Wales and the Medieval Colonial Imagination*, pp. 138, 159.

108   Jeanne-Marie Boivin, *L'Irlande au moyen âge. Giraud de Barri et la Topographia Hibernica (1188)* (Paris, 1993), pp. 91–100.

109   *Descriptio*, ii.7, pp. 215–16; see also Pryce, 'Gerald of Wales, Gildas', pp. 121–3.

110   For a recent reappraisal of the various versions of these translations (known generically as *Brut y Brenhinedd*), extant in manuscripts from the thirteenth century onwards, see Patrick Sims-Williams, *Rhai Addasiadau Cymraeg Canol o Sieffre o Fynwy* (Aberystwyth, 2011).

111   I would like to thank those who commented on the version of this paper given at the conference in Harvard.

112   Rooney, 'The Manuscripts', 47, 151. Dimock, whose edition was based on London, British Library, Cotton MS Domitian A. i (D), a manuscript of the third redaction, gives as variant readings a conflated text of the first version of both lists based on R, B and Hc (a manuscript of the second redaction), stating that these witnesses had 'no variants worth noticing' and 'scarcely any variation in the spelling of the names': *Itinerarium*, ii.1, pp. 102, n. 4; 103, n. 6.

113   See Version 1, textual notes f and i, where, in contrast to B, London, British Library, Additional MS 34762, gives plausible Welsh forms, the latter also found in the B-text of *Annales Cambriae*. London, British Library, Harley MS 3859 (Hc), s. xvi[ex], used by Dimock, was copied from either BL Add. 34762 or an exemplar common to both: Rooney, 'The Manuscripts', 77–8.

114   Robin Flower, 'Richard Davies, William Cecil, and Giraldus Cambrensis', *National Library of Wales Journal*, 3/1–2 (1943), 11–14, at 11. I follow the dating in Daniel

Huws, *Repertory of Welsh Manuscripts and Scribes* (forthcoming), entry for NLW 3024C (Mostyn 83), which states that the manuscript was 'probably written in south-west Wales, very likely at St Davids'. (I am grateful to Ann Parry Owen for supplying me with a copy of this description.) By contrast, Rooney, 'The Manuscripts', 80, dates NLW 3024C to s. xiii[ex].

115 See textual notes c, d, 1. Flower, 'Richard Davies', 13, states that NLW 3024C was used by David Powel for his edition of the *Itinerarium* (1585). If so, however, it is clear, as Dimock pointed out in *Giraldi Cambrensis Opera*, 8/6, pp. liii–liv, that he also drew on a copy of the second redaction; and his text was 'very inaccurate'. In the case of the two lists, Powel both rendered the names inaccurately and conflated Version 2 with a text of Version 1 by inserting *Cenauc* after David and omitting the second *Sadernueu*: Powel (ed.), *Pontici Virunnii viri doctissimi Britannicae historiae libri sex*, pp. 161–2.

116 For Cotton Domitian A. i, see Rooney, 'The Manuscripts', 80, 158; John Prise, *Historiae Britannicae Defensio*, in Ceri Davies (ed. and trans.), *Historiae Britannicae Defensio: A Defence of the British History* (Toronto, 2015), pp. xxvii, 55, 67, 280, n. 26.

# THREE

# Gerald and Welsh Genealogical Learning

Ben Guy
*University of Cambridge*

T HE QUESTION OF GERALD'S READING and deployment of written sources has prompted much fruitful enquiry from scholars in the past century and a half or so since the publication of the first volume of *Giraldi Cambrensis Opera* in 1861.[1] It is widely recognised that Gerald drew upon a variety of biblical, classical and patristic texts, and recent work has demonstrated the ways in which quotations from these texts were skilfully deployed by Gerald in order to construct rigorous rhetorical arguments.[2] Among historical texts, the works of Gildas, Bede and Geoffrey of Monmouth are named specifically by Gerald as texts known to him, and each of them clearly influenced the ways in which he chose to present the historical process, particularly in his works on Wales and on St Davids' metropolitan claims.[3]

Much less work has been done on the texts known to Gerald that had been written in Wales. In part, this is due to the lack of such surviving written material from twelfth-century Wales, but it is also testimony to the approach taken by scholars. The only direct attempt to answer the question was made by Brynley Roberts in 1995.[4] The question posed by Roberts in this article is 'how much traditional learning might one expect to find in the *Itinerary through Wales* and the *Description of Wales*?'[5] By 'traditional learning', Roberts meant the body of inherited knowledge concerning the history and lore of Wales that is believed to have been well known to those immersed in Welsh vernacular culture, such as the Welsh *beirdd* ('poets').[6] In this chapter, I take a different approach, which I hope will lead to slightly firmer results. I ask instead: what is the evidence that Gerald had read texts produced in Wales, and what were these texts? Whatever one might think about 'traditional learning' in medieval Wales, that subject can only be approached from the point of view of the written texts that have survived, and consequently the latter must initially form the object of enquiry.

I focus here on two texts with which Gerald explicitly claims familiarity, one written in Latin and the other in Welsh.[7] Both of these texts have been loosely classified as 'early Welsh genealogical tracts' by modern scholars, although, as will be seen, the two texts are very different in format, purview and origin.[8] The first text is called *De situ Brecheniauc* ('Concerning the Establishment of Brycheiniog'), and is a Latin account of Brychan, founder of Brycheiniog (Brecknockshire), and his saintly progeny. The second is an agnatic pedigree belonging to what I call the 'Rhodri Mawr recension' of Welsh genealogies, an important version of an earlier collection of genealogies that was developed during the course of the twelfth century. Gerald encountered these two texts in different circumstances, as is explained for each text below, and it is clear that his reactions to the texts were shaped by incidental conditions such as language, genre and codicological context.

In Book I.2 of the *Itinerarium Kambriae*, Gerald offers his readers a number of particulars about the region of Brycheiniog in south-central Wales, with which he was particularly well acquainted thanks to his tenure of the archdeaconry of Brecon.[9] In the course of his discussion comes the following passage:

Erat autem antiquitus regionis illius, quae Brecheniauc dicitur, dominator vir potens et nobilis, cui nomen Brechanus; a quo et terra Brecheniauc denominata. De quo mihi notabile videtur, quod ipsum viginti quatuor habuisse filias historiae Britannicae testantur, omnes a pueritia divinis deditas obsequiis, et in sanctitatis assumptae proposito vitam feliciter terminasse. Extant autem basilicae adhuc per Kambriam multae, earum nominibus illustratae: quarum una in provincia de Brecheniauc, non procul a castro principali de Aberhotheni, in collis cujusdam vertice sita, quae Sanctae Aelivedhae ecclesia dicitur: hoc etenim virginis sanctae nomen extiterat, quae et ibidem terreni regis nuptias respuens, aeterno nubens regi, felici martyrio triumphavit.

. . .

And in ancient times there was a ruler of this region, which is called Brycheiniog, a powerful and noble man, whose name was Brychan, and from whom the land of Brycheiniog was also named. Concerning him, it seems noteworthy to me that *historiae Britannicae* testify to him having had twenty-four daughters, all dedicated from youth to religious lives, and to him having ended his life happily, by adopting a resolution of sanctity. And there are still many churches throughout Wales made famous by their names, one of which is in the province of Brycheiniog, not far from the principal castle of Aberhonddu, situated on the top of a certain hill, which is called the church of Saint *Aelivedha*; for this is the name of a holy virgin, who, in that very place, by rejecting marriage with an earthly king and marrying the eternal king instead, triumphed in happy martyrdom.[10]

The question of import in the present context is the meaning of *historiae Britannicae*. Which particular 'Britannic histories' did Gerald have in mind? They do not seem to have included Geoffrey of Monmouth's *Historia*, to which he refers as a *historia Britannica* elsewhere.[11] The *historiae* in question seem to have provided details about Brychan and the sanctity of his twenty-four daughters, including, most probably, the daughter whose church Gerald knew to stand near Aberhonddu castle. A text of exactly this kind is indeed known to have existed in Gerald's time. This text survives in four versions, two written in Latin and two in Welsh, and is generally known as *De situ Brecheniauc*, after the title of the earliest Latin version. Each of these four versions derives from the same lost archetype. I have argued elsewhere that the original text was composed in the first few decades of the twelfth century in the newly founded Brecon Priory, as a response to the predatory claims of Llandaf and St Peter's Abbey in Gloucester with regard to the ownership of certain churches in Brycheiniog.[12] The earliest extant copy of the text, contained in London, British Library, Cotton MS Vespasian A. xiv, was written during Gerald's lifetime, most probably at St Mary's Priory in Monmouth.[13] In the sixteenth century, another copy was discovered by Henry VIII's agent Sir John Price, most probably in Brecon Priory itself, which Price began to lease in 1537 and which he subsequently bought outright in 1542.[14] Price copied this text into London, British Library, Cotton MS Domitian A. i, originally a thirteenth-century manuscript from St Davids. The text was also translated into Welsh on at least two occasions: it is found as sections 1–3 of the genealogical collection in Oxford, Jesus College MS 20 (*c*.1400), and as the tract known as *Plant Brychan*, surviving in many manuscripts of the fifteenth to eighteenth centuries.[15] It is probable that Gerald would have been able to access a copy of *De situ Brecheniauc* in the very place where it was composed, only a stone's throw from his archidiaconal residence in Llanddew.[16]

*De situ Brecheniauc* would certainly have provided Gerald with the information relayed in the *Itinerarium*. The best surviving version of the text, preserved in Vespasian A. xiv, begins by stating that 'Brycheiniog took its first name from Brychan' ('Brecheniauc primum a Brachano nomen accepit'), using the same Old Welsh spelling for Brycheiniog employed by Gerald himself.[17] Then comes a hagiographical narrative about the birth and upbringing of Brychan and the conception of his son, St Cynog. Following the narrative are lists of

Brychan's sons and daughters of the type mentioned by Gerald. Thanks to the vagaries of textual transmission, each of the four versions of *De situ Brecheniauc* attributes to Brychan slightly differing numbers of daughters: twenty-five in Vespasian A. xiv, twenty-four in Domitian A. i, twenty-three in Jesus College 20, and twenty-two in *Plant Brychan*. If Gerald had seen a version of the Brychan text, it could quite plausibly have listed twenty-four daughters. Moreover, St *Aelivedha* herself is one of the daughters of Brychan mentioned in three of the four versions of the text, as shown below:

> Vespasian A. xiv: 'Eiliwedd daughter of Brychan in Crug Gorsafael' ('Eiliueth filia Brachan yGrugc Gors Auail')[18]
> Domitian A. i: 'Eiliwedd on the hill of Gorsafael, who was martyred for the love of chastity' ('Elyuet in Monte Gorsauael, que pro amore castitatis martirizata est')[19]
> *Plant Brychan*: 'Elined daughter of Brychan in Crug Gorsafael' ('Elinet[20] ferç Vryçan yGrug Gorsabaụl')[21]

The entry preserved in Domitian A. i is particularly reminiscent of Gerald's story. The latter may well have been inspired by an entry of this kind, perhaps supported by a piece of local folklore.

It seems more than likely that Gerald had seen a version of *De situ Brecheniauc*, most probably one located in Brecon Priory. Perhaps he had seen more than one version, accounting for his use of the plural *historiae*. What is interesting is that Gerald shows no kind of suspicion towards this particular *historia Britannica*. His faith was probably supported by a number of factors. One was that the text was written in Latin. This contrasts with the other genealogical source mentioned by Gerald, as shall be seen, and probably helps to account for Gerald's designation of the text as a '*historia*'. Another factor is that the text was of a familiar kind. The narrative preceding the lists of Brychan's sons and daughters is essentially a hagiographical narrative, whose style and topoi are of a piece with contemporary saints' Lives. Gerald himself wrote no less than five saints' Lives.[22] Interestingly, one of these, the Life of St David, was a reworking of an earlier Life of St David whose original text is best preserved in Vespasian A. xiv, the same manuscript as *De situ Brecheniauc*. However, it has been demonstrated that Gerald's version derives not directly from the original eleventh-century Life, as preserved in Vespasian A. xiv, but from the twelfth-century 'Nero-Digby' recension of the Life preserved elsewhere.[23]

Gerald's faith in the *historiae Britannicae*, including the Brychan text, may be compared with what he says of another genealogical text. In Book I.3 of the *Descriptio Kambriae*, Gerald quotes two genealogies, one of the Welsh princes of south Wales, and the other of the Welsh princes of north Wales. The genealogies are followed by Gerald's observations on the Welsh practice of writing these genealogies down in books.[24] Note that Gerald's comments on these matters are repeated, almost verbatim, in *Epitome Historiae Britanniae*, a Latin chronicle associated with Glamorgan found in three fifteenth-century manuscripts.[25]

> Haec itaque est generatio principum Sudwalliae: Resus filius Griphini, Griphinus filius Resi, Resus filius Theodori, Theodorus filius Cadelh, Cadelh filius Eneae, Eneas filius Oenei, Oeneus filius Hoeli da, id est Hoeli boni, Hoelus filius Cadelh, Cadelh filius Roderici magni.

> De Cadelo igitur, filio Rotherici magni, descenderunt principes Sudwalliae. De Mervino principes Nortwalliae, in hunc modum: David filius Oenei, Oeneus filius Griphini, Griphinus filius Canani, Cananus filius Iago, Iago filius Ythewal, Ythewal filius Meuric, Meuric filius Anaudrech, Anaudrech filius Mervini, Mervinus filius Rotherici magni.

> De Anaraut autem generatio non provenit. Unde et principes Powisiae suam habent per se generationem.

> Hoc etiam mihi notandum videtur, quod bardi Kambrenses, et cantores, seu recitatores, genealogiam habent praedictorum principum in libris eorum antiquis et authenticis, sed tamen Kambrice scriptam; eandemque memoriter tenent, a Rotherico magno usque ad beatam Virginem, et inde usque ad Silvium, Ascanium, et Eneam; et ab Enea usque ad Adam generationem linealiter producunt. Sed quoniam tam longinqua, tam remotissima generis enarratio, multis trutanica potius quam historica esse videretur, eam huic nostro compendio inserere ex industria supersedimus.

> . . .

> And this is the descent of the princes of South Wales: Rhys son of Gruffudd, Gruffudd son of Rhys, Rhys son of Tewdwr, Tewdwr son of Cadell, Cadell son of Einion, Einion son of Owain, Owain son of Hywel Dda, i.e. Hywel the Good, Hywel son of Cadell, Cadell son of Rhodri Mawr.

> Thus the princes of South Wales descended from Cadell, son of Rhodri Mawr. The princes of North Wales are from Merfyn, in this manner: Dafydd son of Owain, Owain son of Gruffudd, Gruffudd son of Cynan, Cynan son of Iago, Iago son of Idwal, Idwal son of Meurig, Meurig son of *Anaudrech*, *Anaudrech* son of Merfyn, Merfyn son of Rhodri Mawr.

> However, no descent stemmed from Anarawd. And as a result the princes of Powys have their own descent.

Yet it seems to me that it should be noted that Welsh bards, singers or reciters have a genealogy of the aforementioned princes in their old and authentic books, written, however, in Welsh; and they retain this in memory, from Rhodri Mawr to the blessed Virgin, and thence back to Silvius, Ascanius and Æneas; and from Æneas back to Adam they trace the descent linearly. But because an exposition of descent so distant and remote might seem to many to be more fictitious than historical, we have with due diligence omitted to include it here in our treatise.

It would appear that the tale of Brychan of Brycheiniog's twenty-four saintly daughters did not necessitate the same caveat as the genealogy of the princes of Wales, traced back to the blessed Virgin, Æneas and Adam. Yet Gerald's apparent incredulity should not necessarily be mistaken for modern historical sensibility; after all, elsewhere he subscribed wholeheartedly to the story of the Trojan origin of the Britons and the foundation of Wales by Kamber son of Brutus.[26] One might wonder instead whether his observation that the books of the bards were 'old and authentic, but written, however, in Welsh' ('antiquis et authenticis, sed tamen Kambrice scriptam') indicates his scepticism about the reliability of texts written in the vernacular, especially those that contained recognisably Galfridian elements. Gerald seems not to have followed Geoffrey in ascribing latent authority to texts written in the Welsh vernacular, as a handful of other writers influenced by Geoffrey did in the twelfth and thirteenth centuries.[27] Gerald seems rather to have viewed Latin as the only proper vehicle for historical truth, and vernacular texts as inherently suspicious. The same view caused an outraged William of Newburgh to remark that Geoffrey 'has dressed up stories about Arthur, taken from the old fictions of the Britons and augmented by himself, in the honest name of history, by drawing the style of the Latin language over it' ('fabulas de Arturo ex priscis Britonum figmentis sumptas et ex proprio auctas per superductum Latini sermonis colorem honesto historiae nomine palliavit').[28] One may compare the situation in England more generally, where, by c.1200, Latin was overwhelmingly the dominant medium for scholarly and historical exposition.[29]

Since genealogies of the kind described by Gerald are indeed found in extant vernacular manuscripts, Brynley Roberts posited that it was here, in Gerald's chapter on genealogies, that 'he comes closer to the native tradition'.[30] But just how 'traditional' was this type of genealogy? The earliest surviving versions of Rhodri Mawr's genealogy know nothing of Silvius, Ascanius or Æneas, let alone Adam. An example is provided by the Harleian genealogies, so-called because they are preserved in London, British Library, Harley MS 3859 (s. xi/xii), which represent a tenth-century redaction of a ninth-century collection of genealogies assembled at the court of Rhodri Mawr of Gwynedd himself.[31] In this text, Rhodri Mawr's genealogy ends with '*Amalech*, who was son of Beli

Mawr, and Anna, his mother, whom they say was cousin of the Virgin Mary, the mother of our lord Jesus Christ' ('Amalech, qui fuit Beli magni filius, et Anna, mater eius, quam dicunt esse consobrina Mariae uirginis, matris Domini nostri Iesu Christi').[32] Other early, textually related versions of the same genealogy end with much the same words, as is seen in the Lives of saints Cadog and Carannog, the Life of the Breton saint Gurthiern, and the Welsh genealogies in Jesus College 20.[33] For this reason, I see no need to subscribe to the view, first expressed by David Powel in 1585 and subsequently followed by later scholars, that Gerald's reference to the genealogy of Rhodri Mawr being traced back to the blessed Virgin is a mistake for Beli Mawr, through a misunderstanding of the abbreviation 'B. M.' as 'beatus Marius' ('blessed Mary').[34] It seems to me far more likely that Gerald had before him a genealogy that included a statement of the type found in the Harleian genealogies.[35]

However, if the genealogy was traced back to Mary, why the references to Æneas, Adam and the like, who are absent from all of the genealogical sources quoted so far? The Harleian genealogies and the saints' Lives are witnesses to a genealogical compilation that was current in Wales from the ninth to the eleventh century. During the twelfth century, this compilation continued to be copied, but was developed in two significant respects. First, the role of the ninth-century king Rhodri Mawr as a crux within the overall genealogical scheme was emphasised through a series of forged links between Rhodri and the genealogies of various older, now defunct dynasties.[36] This is most clearly visible in the Jesus 20 genealogies, which, although occurring in a manuscript of c.1400, contain what is textually the earliest extant redaction of the developments that led to the creation of a distinct 'Rhodri Mawr' recension of the genealogical collection.[37] Rhodri was granted this new degree of prominence because, by the middle decades of the twelfth century, he had become the common ancestor of the two most important native dynasties in Wales, those of Owain Gwynedd and the Lord Rhys of Deheubarth. Gerald himself was cognisant of the new pre-eminence attributed to Rhodri Mawr. In the chapter of the *Descriptio* immediately preceding the genealogies already quoted, Gerald relates a story about Rhodri dividing Wales between his three sons, the successors of one of whom, Cadell, continued to rule Wales until the time of Tewdwr, great-grandfather of the Lord Rhys. Gerald's emphasis on the lineage of Tewdwr is no doubt designed to magnify his own position, since he was descended from the same line of princes, but nevertheless the fiction of Rhodri dividing power in Wales between his sons is redolent of a wider historiographic trend that transformed the historical rule of Rhodri Mawr into a teleological origin legend for the dynasties of Owain Gwynedd and the Lord Rhys.[38] It is possible that the story about Rhodri in Book I.2 of the *Descriptio Kambriae* was either taken from the same 'ancient and authentic books' ('libris antiquis et authenticis') of the bards in which Gerald found the genealogies, or else was related to him by the books' bardic owners.[39] The story and the genealogy were certainly connected in Gerald's mind, because both display the same idiosyncrasy in presenting Rhodri's son Merfyn, rather than his brother Anarawd, as the progenitor of the dynasty of Gwynedd.[40]

The second aspect of the development of the 'Rhodri Mawr recension' was the creation of a fictitious patrilineal genealogy for Rhodri, and the subsequent extension of this genealogy back in time.[41] The earliest dateable version of this genealogy is found in the *Vita Griffini filii Conani*, the twelfth-century Life of Gruffudd ap Cynan, king of Gwynedd, written between 1137 and 1170.[42] In the first instance, Rhodri's male-line ancestry was extended back to Llywarch Hen and the heroes of the Brittonic Old North.[43] A genealogy extended in exactly this way is found in the Jesus 20 genealogies, which, as already noted, contains the textually earliest version of the 'Rhodri Mawr recension'. At a stage later than the redaction of the version in Jesus 20, the patriline was extended back much further in time, through a combination of at least two sources. One was a pedigree of obscure British heroes traced back to an eponymous Prydain son of Aedd Mawr, which Peter Bartrum has argued might be linked with the earlier genealogical scheme of the *Historia Brittonum*.[44] The supposed father of this Aedd Mawr, a certain Antonius, was then connected to a line of kings in the second source, the *Historia regum Britanniae* of Geoffrey of Monmouth.[45] This line includes Silvius, Ascanius and Æneas, just as in the genealogy known to Gerald. Finally, Æneas's ancestry was traced back through a line that incorporated the heroes of Greek mythology and the biblical genealogy of Noah, reaching back to Adam, another figure in the genealogy known to Gerald.[46]

It was clearly a genealogy of exactly this type that was seen by Gerald in the books of the bards. No other genealogy produced in medieval Wales ever contained the same combination of figures. And, interestingly, this genealogy was not very old by the time it was seen by Gerald, sometime in the last quarter of the twelfth century. A genealogy in this form can only have been constructed after the publication of Geoffrey's *Historia*, probably around 1138, and before the composition of the Life of Gruffudd ap Cynan, no later than 1170.[47] Although textual evidence demonstrates that the Life of Gruffudd ap Cynan cannot have contained the original version of the genealogy, the genealogical source used by the author of the Life evidently cannot have been much older than the Life itself. It is not likely that the Life of Gruffudd ap Cynan was Gerald's direct source, since it was written in Latin rather than Welsh, and also because its genealogy of the more recent line of Gwynedd erroneously includes the name 'Elisse', which Gerald's version does not.[48] However, the genealogical source used by the author of the Life of Gruffudd ap Cynan may have been particularly closely related to the text seen by Gerald: of all the surviving versions of the genealogy of the dynasty of Gwynedd, of which there are many, only the versions in Gerald's

*Descriptio Kambriae* and in the Latin and Welsh Lives of Gruffudd ap Cynan omit the name of Idwal Foel, son of Anarawd ap Rhodri Mawr.

It may thus be seen that there was nothing particularly 'traditional' about the genealogy that Gerald had seen, nor can the books to which he refers have been particularly *antiquus* by the late twelfth century.[49] Presumably the books in question were relatively recent productions designed to grant the bards access to an up-to-date version of the genealogy of their patrons.[50] This phenomenon in itself may have been a relatively new state of affairs. It is not at all clear that secular professionals such as poets would have owned manuscripts of this kind prior to the twelfth century. They almost certainly did in the thirteenth and fourteenth centuries. For example, it has been argued by Thomas Charles-Edwards that the *loci* of the kind of textual variation seen in the fluid textual traditions of medieval Welsh prose tales were the books of the professional literary class.[51] Similarly, there is evidence that manuscripts of medieval Welsh law were actively used by professional lawyers. A good example of this is London, British Library, Harley MS 1796, a mid-thirteenth-century Latin law manuscript that was glossed by three different hands, writing in both Welsh and Latin.[52] Law manuscripts in particular might form an instructive parallel to the now lost bardic books seen by Gerald. It has been argued by Huw Pryce that at least the prologue of the earliest of the three extant recensions of the Laws of Hywel Dda, the Cyfnerth recension, took shape during the reign of the Lord Rhys, sometime between 1170 and 1197.[53] Perhaps this is indicative of a wider trend wherein the composition of Welsh legal tracts coincided with the growth in accessibility of manuscripts, and most particularly vernacular manuscripts, to the professional classes. Malcolm Parkes has noted that the twelfth century was exactly the period in England for which substantial evidence for the lay ownership of manuscripts can be marshalled.[54] On Gerald's evidence, such manuscripts in Wales must have contained, among other things, written genealogies.

The evidence thus suggests that Gerald had seen at least two genealogical texts that had been produced in Wales. One, a version of the Latin *De situ Brecheniauc*, he probably found in an ecclesiastical manuscript, most probably in Brecon Priory, and he warmed to its contents because it presented a text comprehensible within the parameters of the familiar hagiographical genre. The other, a version of the patrilineal genealogy of Rhodri Mawr, he saw in a vernacular manuscript owned by a bard, the contents of which, much like the contents of Geoffrey's *Historia*, he mistrusted but nonetheless employed to a certain extent in his work. Neither of the texts used by Gerald was particularly old, or composed or transmitted primarily through an oral medium; it is thus questionable whether their analysis through the paradigm of 'Welsh tradition' is either helpful or necessary.

❖

## Notes

1   J. S. Brewer, J. F. Dimock and G. F. Warner (eds), *Giraldi Cambrensis Opera*, 8 vols (London, 1861–91).

2   Georgia Henley, 'Quotation, Revision, and Narrative Structure in Giraldus Cambrensis's *Itinerarium Kambriae*', *Journal of Medieval Latin*, 24 (2014), 1–52; Georgia Henley, 'Through the Ethnographers Eyes: Rhetoric, Ethnicity and Quotation in the Welsh and Irish Works of Gerald of Wales', in Georgia Henley and Paul Russell (eds), *Rhetoric and Reality in Medieval Celtic Literature: Studies in Honor of Daniel F. Melia*, CSANA Yearbook, 11–12 (Hamilton, 2014), pp. 63–74. Cf. J. F. Dimock (ed.), *Giraldi Cambrensis Opera*, 8/6 (London, 1868), pp. lxv–lxviii.

3   Michael Richter, *Giraldus Cambrensis: The Growth of the Welsh Nation* (Aberystwyth, 1972), p. 67; Robert Bartlett, *Gerald of Wales, 1146–1223* (Oxford, 1982), pp. 67 (n. 44); 183; 190 (n. 65); and 206–7 on Gildas; pp. 140–1 and 180 on Bede; Brynley F. Roberts, 'Gerald of Wales and Welsh Tradition', in Françoise H. M. Le Saux (ed.), *The Formation of Culture in Medieval Britain: Celtic, Latin and Norman Influences on English Music, Literature, History and Art* (Lampeter, 1995), pp. 129–47, at 135; Huw Pryce, 'Gerald of Wales, Gildas, and the *Descriptio Kambriae*', in Fiona Edmonds and Paul Russell (eds), *Tome: Studies in Medieval Celtic History and Law in Honour of Thomas Charles-Edwards* (Woodbridge, 2011), pp. 115–24; Julia C. Crick, 'The British Past and the Welsh Future: Gerald of Wales, Geoffrey of Monmouth and Arthur of Britain', *Celtica*, 23 (1999), 60–75. For specific references by Gerald, see the following: for Gildas: *Descriptio*, 'Praefatio prima' and ii.2, pp. 158 and 207–9; Lewis Thorpe (trans.), *Gerald of Wales, The Journey through Wales and The Description of Wales* (Harmondsworth, 1978), pp. 214 and 257–9. For Geoffrey: *Itinerarium*, i.5, p. 58; Thorpe (trans.), *Gerald*, pp. 117–18. For Bede: *Itinerarium*, ii.1, p. 105; Thorpe (trans.), *Gerald*, p. 164.

4   Roberts, 'Gerald'.

5   Roberts, 'Gerald', p. 133.

6   For classic statements of this concept, see Rachel Bromwich, 'The Character of Early Welsh Tradition', in Nora K. Chadwick (ed.), *Studies in Early British History* (Cambridge, 1954), pp. 83–136; Rachel Bromwich, *Trioedd Ynys Prydein: The Triads of the Island of Britain* (4th edition, Cardiff, 2014), pp. lviii–lxix; Brynley F. Roberts, 'Oral Tradition and Welsh Literature: A Description and Survey', *Oral Tradition*, 3 (1988), 61–87; Brynley F. Roberts, 'Geoffrey of Monmouth and Welsh Historical Tradition', *Nottingham Medieval Studies*, 20 (1976), 29–40; the latter two articles are reprinted as chapters one and two in Brynley F. Roberts, *Studies in Middle Welsh Literature* (Lampeter, 1992).

7   Other texts written in Wales that Gerald had seen include the Nero-Digby recension of the *Vita Sancti Dauid* and the source for his list of the archbishops and bishops of St Davids. On the former, see below, and on the latter, see John Reuben Davies, 'The Archbishopric of St Davids and the Bishops of *Clas Cynidr*', in J. Wyn Evans and Jonathan M. Wooding (eds), *St David of Wales: Cult, Church and Nation* (Woodbridge, 2007), pp. 296–304, and Huw Pryce's contribution to this volume.

8   Cf. P. C. Bartrum (ed.), *Early Welsh Genealogical Tracts* (Cardiff, 1966), pp. 14–19 and 35–7.

9   Gerald was archdeacon of Brecon from *c.*1175 until he resigned in favour of his nephew in 1203: Richter, *Giraldus*, pp. 4 and 11, n. 27; Bartlett, *Gerald*, pp. 28–9.

10   *Itinerarium*, i.2, pp. 31–2. Translation is my own.

11   The *Itinerarium* refers to Geoffrey's *Historia* as 'The History of the Britons redacted by Geoffrey Arthur' ('Historia Britonum a Galfrido Arthuro tractata'): *Itinerarium*, i.5, p. 58; Thorpe (trans.), *Gerald*, p. 117. The beginning of Book II of the *Itinerarium* refers to Geoffrey's work in similar terms, saying 'just as the British histories report' ('sicut Britannicae referunt historiae': *Itinerarium*, ii.1, p. 101; translation my own). Another similar reference appears in the *Topographia Hibernica*, which says 'just as the British history reports' ('sicut Britannica refert historia': *Topographia*, iii.8, p. 148; translation my own). Note that the original title of Geoffrey's work was probably *De gestis Britonum*: Michael D. Reeve (ed.) and Neil Wright (trans.), *Geoffrey of Monmouth: The History of the Kings of Britain. An Edition and Translation of De gestis Britonum [Historia Regum Britanniae]* (Woodbridge, 2007), p. lix.

12   Ben Guy, '*De situ Brecheniauc* and Related Texts: Their Origin and Purpose', in David Parsons et al. (eds), *The Cult of Saints in Wales* (forthcoming).

13   Silas M. Harris, 'The Kalendar of the *Vitae Sanctorum Wallensium*', *Journal of the Historical Society of the Church in Wales*, 3 (1953), 3–53, at 10–12; Kathleen Hughes, 'British Library MS. Cotton Vespasian A. XIV ("Vitae Sanctorum Wallensium"): Its Purpose and Provenance', in Nora K. Chadwick (ed.), *Studies in the Early British Church* (Cambridge, 1958), pp. 183–200, at 197; rev. in D. N. Dumville (ed.), *Celtic Britain in the Early Middle Ages: Studies in Scottish and Welsh Sources* (Woodbridge, 1980), pp. 53–66, at 64. Diplomatic editions of the Latin texts, accompanied by translations, are available in A. W. Wade-Evans (ed. and trans.), 'The Brychan Documents', *Y Cymmrodor*, 19 (1906), 18–48. Texts and translations may also be found in A. W. Wade-Evans (ed. and trans.), 'Brychan Brycheiniog', *The Transactions of the Brecknock Society*, 1 (1930), 7–24, and the texts are reprinted in A. W. Wade-Evans (ed.), *Vitae sanctorum Britanniae et genealogiae: The Lives and Genealogies of the Welsh Saints* (Cardiff, 1944; new edition, 2013, with introduction and updated bibliography by Scott Lloyd), pp. 313–18.

14   Neil R. Ker, 'Sir John Prise', *The Library*, 5th Series, 10 (1955), 1–24, at 4; repr. in Neil R. Ker, *Books, Collectors and Libraries: Studies in the Medieval Heritage* (London, 1985), pp. 471–96, at 474; Glanmor Williams, 'Sir John Pryse of Brecon', *Brycheiniog*, 31 (1998/9), 49–63, at 55.

15   For editions of the Welsh texts, see Bartrum (ed.), *Tracts*, pp. 42–4 and 81–4. Bartrum's edition of *Plant Brychan* is highly unsatisfactory, since it has conflated a number of distinct recensions of the text. The best witness to the thirteenth-century original may be found in Cardiff, Central Library MS 3.77, pp. 40–4, the text of which was copied from a non-extant medieval witness by John Jones of Gellilyfdy in 1640.

16   Cf. *Itinerarium*, i.3, p. 47; Thorpe (trans.), *Gerald*, p. 107.

17 *De situ Brecheniauc*, §1; Wade-Evans (ed. and trans.), 'The Brychan Documents', pp. 24 and 31. In particular, both use *e* for / ə/ and then *e* for /ei/.

18 *De situ Brecheniauc*, §12.20; Wade-Evans (ed. and trans.), 'The Brychan Documents', pp. 26–7 and 34.

19 *Cognacio Brychan,* §15.18; Wade-Evans (ed. and trans.), 'The Brychan Documents', pp. 30 and 37.

20 Note that here a *u* for /w/ has been misread as an *n*.

21 Since this item is, by the chance of textual error, missing from the best copy of *Plant Brychan* in Cardiff, Central Library MS 3.77, pp. 40–4, the text here has been taken from another copy of the text at p. 10 of the same manuscript. The text at p. 10 was copied into the Cardiff manuscript from the lost medieval manuscript Hengwrt 33. For the importance of Cardiff, Central Library MS 3.77 as a witness to Hengwrt 33, see Bartrum (ed.), *Tracts,* pp. 75–7; P. C. Bartrum, 'Bonedd yr Arwyr', *Bulletin of the Board of Celtic Studies*, 18 (1959), 229–52, at 230–1; P. C. Bartrum, 'Achau Brenhinoedd a Thywysogion Cymru', *Bulletin of the Board of Celtic Studies*, 19 (1961), 201–25, at 201–5.

22 Bartlett, *Gerald,* pp. 217–18.

23 J. W. James (ed. and trans.), *Life of St. David: The Basic Mid Twelfth-Century Latin Text* (Cardiff, 1967), p. xxxii. James's conclusion about this particular point is accepted explicitly by Richter and implicitly by Sharpe: Michael Richter, 'The *Life* of St. David by Giraldus Cambrensis', *Welsh History Review,* 4 (1968–9), 381–6, at 366; Richard Sharpe, 'Which Text is Rhygyfarch's Life of St David?', in Evans and Wooding, *St David,* pp. 90–106, at 96–8.

24 *Descriptio*, i.3, pp. 167–8; translation below is my own. In the first recension of the *Descriptio Kambriae,* the genealogy of the princes of south Wales is traced back from the Lord Rhys, while that of the princes of north Wales is traced back from Dafydd, son of Owain Gwynedd. In London, British Library, Royal MS 13 B. xii, a manuscript of the second recension as defined by Dimock, the northern line appears differently, being traced instead from Llywelyn ab Iorwerth, Dafydd's nephew, who was pre-eminent in Gwynedd by the time of the redaction of the second recension in *c.*1215 (Dimock (ed.), *Giraldi Cambrensis Opera,* 8/6, pp. xxvi–xxvii and 167, n. 2). This manuscript was later designated by Lewis Thorpe as a witness to a putative third recension, on account of this and other changes apparent in the manuscript that might stem from Gerald himself (Thorpe (trans.), *Gerald,* p. 50). When Thorpe made this suggestion, Royal 13 MS B. xii, a late sixteenth-century manuscript, was the only known witness to this hypothetical third recension. Subsequently, Catherine Rooney discovered other witnesses, including one from the second half of the fourteenth century (Aberystwyth, National Library of Wales MS 3024C), suggesting that Thorpe may have been correct to designate this version as a third recension produced by Gerald: Catherine Rooney, 'The Manuscripts of the Works of Gerald of Wales' (unpublished PhD thesis, University of Cambridge, 2005), 92–6. See also Catherine Rooney's contribution to this volume. For the date of the second recension of the *Descriptio,* see Dimock (ed.), *Giraldi Cambrensis Opera,* 8/6, pp. xli–xlii;

Bartlett, *Gerald*, p. 216. The text printed here is that of the first recension, as edited by Dimock.

25 The full text of this chronicle is found in two manuscripts of the fifteenth century, whilst an abbreviated version, omitting the genealogical comments, is found in the early fifteenth-century manuscript Aberystwyth, National Library of Wales, Peniarth MS 32, *Y Llyfr Teg*. For general comment, see Diana Luft, 'The NLW Peniarth 32 Latin Chronicle', *Studia Celtica*, 44 (2010), 47–70 (especially p. 51). For text and translation, see W. J. Rees, *Lives of the Cambro-British Saints* (Llandovery, 1853), pp. 278–86 and 612–22 (the paraphrase of the *Descriptio Kambriae* is at pp. 283–4).

26 For example, *Descriptio*, i.7, p. 178; Thorpe (trans.), *Gerald*, pp. 231–2.

27 Sara Harris, 'Twelfth-Century Perceptions of the History of Britain's Vernacular Languages' (unpublished PhD thesis, University of Cambridge, 2013), 64 and 68–71.

28 William of Newburgh, *Historia rerum Anglicarum* I.3, in P. G. Walsh and M. J. Kennedy (eds and trans.), *The History of English Affairs, Book I* (Warminster, 1988), pp. 28–9; translation is my own. Cf. Harris, 'Twelfth-Century Perceptions', 81.

29 For the relative statuses of Latin, English and French in England during this period, see M. T. Clanchy, *From Memory to Written Record: England 1066–1307* (2nd edition, Oxford, 1993), pp. 197–223.

30 Roberts, 'Gerald', p. 137. Elsewhere, Roberts implies that the books known to Gerald would have contained lists of British kings, in addition to genealogies, but there is no evidence that this was the case (Roberts, 'Geoffrey', 38). Wales is notable in an Insular context for wholly lacking a tradition of creating king-lists, as David Dumville has pointed out: D. N. Dumville, 'Kingship, Genealogies, and Regnal Lists', in P. H. Sawyer and I. N. Wood (eds), *Early Medieval Kingship* (Leeds, 1979), pp. 72–104, at 96–7. The only king-lists appearing in Welsh manuscripts derive ultimately from Geoffrey of Monmouth, such as those in Oxford, Jesus College MS 20 (*c*.1400) and the lost medieval manuscript known as Hengwrt 33. See Bartrum (ed.), *Tracts*, pp. 49–50 and 109–10.

31 Ben Guy, 'The Origins of the Compilation of Welsh Historical Texts in Harley 3859', *Studia Celtica*, 49 (2015), 21–56; Ben Guy, 'The Textual History of the Harleian Genealogies', *Welsh History Review*, 28 (2016), 1–25.

32 Harleian genealogies, §1; Egerton Phillimore (ed.), 'The *Annales Cambriae* and the Old-Welsh Genealogies from *Harleian MS. 3859*', *Y Cymmrodor*, 9 (1888), 141–83, at 170; Bartrum (ed.), *Tracts*, p. 9; translation is my own.

33 For the Lives of Cadog and Carannog, see Wade-Evans (ed.), *Vitae*, pp. 118–19 and 148–9 and Bartrum (ed.), *Tracts*, pp. 25–6. For the Life of St Gurthiern, see Léon Maître and Paul de Berthou (eds), *Cartulaire de l'Abbaye de Sainte-Croix de Quimperlé* (2nd edition, Rennes, 1904), p. 42 and Léon Fleuriot, 'Old Breton Genealogies and Early British Tradition', *Bulletin of the Board of Celtic Studies*, 26 (1974–6), 1–6, at 2. For Jesus College 20, see Bartrum (ed.), *Tracts*, p. 44.

34 '*Cambriae descriptio, auctore sil. Giraldo Cambrense. cum annotationibus Davidis Poveli sacrae theologiae professoris*', in William Camden (ed.), *Anglica, Normannica, Hibernica, Cambrica, a veteribus scripta* (Frankfurt, 1602), pp. 879–92, at 883; Dimock (ed.),

*Giraldi Cambrensis Opera*, 8/6, p. 168, n. 1; Roberts, 'Gerald', p. 137. The edition of David Powel used by Camden had been originally published by Powel himself in 1585: see Dimock (ed.), *Giraldi Cambrensis Opera*, 8/6, pp. liii–lviii (especially p. liv, n. 3) and Thorpe (trans.), *Gerald*, p. 44. Bartrum attributed the suggestion to George Owen Harry, who, however, was writing later than both Powel and Camden: George Owen Harry, *The Genealogy of the High and Mighty Monarch James* (London, 1604), p. 17; Bartrum (ed.), *Tracts*, p. 126, n. 1.

35    This was also Dimock's view: see Dimock (ed.), *Giraldi Cambrensis Opera*, 8/6, p. 168, n. 1.

36    Patrick Sims-Williams, 'Historical Need and Literary Narrative: A Caveat from Ninth-Century Wales', *Welsh History Review*, 17 (1994), 1–40, at 25–6; David E. Thornton, *Kings, Chronologies and Genealogies: Studies in the Political History of Early Medieval Ireland and Wales* (Woodbridge, 2003), pp. 111–15.

37    For the dating of Jesus 20, see Daniel Huws, *Medieval Welsh Manuscripts* (Cardiff and Aberystwyth, 2000), p. 60.

38    For the development of this legend, see David N. Dumville, 'The "Six" Sons of Rhodri Mawr: A Problem in Asser's *Life of King Alfred*', *Cambridge Medieval Celtic Studies*, 4 (1982), 5–18, at 11–12.

39    At two points in his works, Gerald describes an encounter with one of Llywelyn ab Iorwerth's bards at the prince's court: *De invectionibus*, v.3, pp. 127–8; *De iure*, iii, pp. 209–10. The passage is translated in H. E. Butler (ed. and trans.), *The Autobiography of Giraldus Cambrensis* (London, 1937), pp. 233–4. My thanks to Huw Pryce for this point.

40    As noted by J. E. Lloyd, *A History of Wales from the Earliest Times to the Edwardian Conquest*, 2/1 (3rd edition, London, 1939), p. 326, n. 27.

41    Egerton Phillimore was the first to suggest that Rhodri Mawr's patriline was fabricated: see Phillimore, '[The Dynasty of Rhodri Mawr]', in Henry Owen (ed.), *The Description of Penbrokshire [sic] by George Owen of Henllys, Lord of Kemes*, 4/3 (London, 1892–1936), pp. 207–10, at 209.

42    *Vita Griffini filii Conani*, §3; Paul Russell (ed. and trans.), *Vita Griffini filii Conani: The Medieval Latin Life of Gruffudd ap Cynan* (Cardiff, 2005), pp. 52–5.

43    For this section of the genealogy, see Sims-Williams, 'Historical Need', 26–30. For one view of the role of Llywarch Hen as an ancestral figure, see Patrick Ford, 'Llywarch, Ancestor of Welsh Princes', *Speculum*, 45 (1970), 442–50.

44    P. C. Bartrum, 'Was There a British "Book of Conquests"?', *Bulletin of the Board of Celtic Studies*, 23 (1968–70), 1–6.

45    For the view that the *Historia regum Britanniae* and the genealogy in the Life of Gruffudd ap Cynan are independent witnesses to a pre-existing king-list, see Bromwich, 'Character', p. 98, n. 3.

46    For the origins of the classical and biblical ancestry of Æneas, see David E. Thornton, 'Power, Politics and Status: Aspects of Genealogy in Medieval Ireland and Wales' (unpublished PhD thesis, University of Cambridge, 1991), 30–49.

47    Cf. Sims-Williams, 'Historical Need', 28. For the dating of the *Historia regum Britanniae*, see Jaakko Tahkokallio, 'Monks, Clerks, and King Arthur: Reading

Geoffrey of Monmouth in the Twelfth and Thirteenth Centuries' (unpublished PhD dissertation, University of Helsinki, 2013), 19–22; John Gillingham, 'The Context and Purposes of Geoffrey of Monmouth's *History of the Kings of Britain'*, *Anglo-Norman Studies*, 13 (1991), 99–118, repr. in John Gillingham, *The English in the Twelfth Century: Imperialism, National Identity and Political Values* (Woodbridge, 2000), pp. 19–39, at 20, especially n. 5. For the dating of the *Vita Griffini filii Conani*, see D. Simon Evans (ed.), *Historia Gruffud vab Kenan* (Cardiff, 1977), pp. ccxliii–ccxlix; Russell (ed. and trans.), *Vita Griffini*, pp. 46–7.

48    The *Vita Griffini filii Conani* was probably not translated into Welsh until the early thirteenth century: see Evans, *Historia*, p. ccxci.

49    Patrick Sims-Williams has made the same point about the books seen by Gerald: 'Historical Need', 29.

50    Cf. Bromwich, 'Character', p. 98.

51    T. M. Charles-Edwards, 'The Textual Tradition of Medieval Welsh Prose Tales and the Problem of Dating', in Bernhard Maier and Stefan Zimmer (eds), *150 Jahre "Mabinogion"–Deutsche-walisische Kulturbeziehungen* (Tübingen, 2001), pp. 23–40; cf. Paul Russell, 'Texts in Contexts: Recent Work on the Medieval Welsh Prose Tales', *Cambrian Medieval Celtic Studies*, 45 (2003), 59–72.

52    Paul Russell (ed.), *Welsh Law in Medieval Anglesey: British Library Harleian MS 1796 (Latin C)* (Cambridge, 2011), pp. xxvii–xxviii.

53    Huw Pryce, 'The Prologues to the Welsh Law Books', *Bulletin of the Board of Celtic Studies*, 33 (1986), 151–87, at 153–4; Huw Pryce, 'The Context and Purpose of the Earliest Welsh Lawbooks', *Cambrian Medieval Celtic Studies*, 39 (2000), 39–63, at 52–7.

54    Malcolm Parkes, 'The Literacy of the Laity', in David Daiches and Anthony K. Thorlby (eds), *Literature and Western Civilisation: The Mediaeval World*, 5/2 (London, 1973), pp. 555–76; repr. in Malcolm Parkes, *Scribes, Scripts and Readers: Studies in the Communication, Presentation and Dissemination of Medieval Texts* (London, 1991), pp. 275–97, at 277–8. Parkes also pointed out that the mid-thirteenth century marks a watershed for the survival of books owned and used by lawyers, just as in Wales (pp. 282–3). Michael Clanchy lists a number of prominent book-owning laymen living in the thirteenth century: Clanchy, *From Memory*, p. 105.

❖

# FOUR

# Gerald of Wales, Walter Map and the Anglo-Saxon History of Lydbury North

Joshua Byron Smith
*University of Arkansas*

OR A MEDIEVAL BISHOP, bragging rights were always welcome. The bishop of Hereford, although he oversaw a rather poor diocese, had something that very few of his contemporaries did. He could boast that he was one of the small number of ecclesiastics to hold a Marcher lordship.[1] The fifty-three-hide estate of Lydbury North was a significant source of pride, and income, for the bishop of Hereford.[2] It became a sort of *secunda sedes* in the diocese, with the manor of Lydbury North being closely associated with the archdeacon of Shropshire, a position presumably created to help uphold the bishop's authority in the northern reaches of the diocese.[3] But enforcing the bishop's will was not the only challenge that the diocese faced in this remote area: border warfare was a very real threat, and by 1087 the bishop had built a castle there to safeguard his holdings. As a result, this lordship came to be known as the Bishop's Castle. How the bishop of Hereford first came to possess this important estate, located far to the north-west of the cathedral, is poorly understood by modern scholars.[4] Medieval minds, too, were occupied with this same issue. In the late twelfth century, two canons of Hereford, Gerald of Wales and Walter Map, provided answers to what must have been an important question for the bishop – by what right did the diocese hold Lydbury North?

Gerald and Walter, though colleagues at Hereford Cathedral, wrote strikingly different accounts of the gift of Lydbury North. Neither account has won much trust from modern historians. Walter's story, which includes a particularly fanciful tale concerning the offspring of a fairy-bride, is at odds with the established chronology, regardless of one's opinions on the existence of fairies.[5] Gerald's account, on the other hand, is the sole source for a late legend about King Offa and is widely suspected to be Gerald's own invention. This chapter argues that these disparate narratives have more in common than it may otherwise seem. In particular, both accounts show that these Hereford canons were part of an intellectual climate in which the Anglo-Saxon past was invoked, and also invented, to lend weight to important claims. Gerald and Walter, both of whom took significant interest in the Anglo-Saxon past, gave Lydbury North an Anglo-Saxon seal of approval.

Hereford Cathedral was not alone in having to explain a gap in its history. Vikings, fires, the Norman invasion and even changes in script meant that many twelfth-century English ecclesiastical establishments had embarrassingly little information regarding their past, a regrettable situation that could leave them vulnerable to legal challenges.[6] Not every historical gap was caused by a single traumatic event: poor record keeping and a break in oral tradition are just two mundane reasons a church could find itself without any documentation of its properties. Hereford Cathedral, however, could point to one particularly disastrous moment to explain why it had no early records. In 1055 the ascendant Welsh prince Gruffudd ap Llywelyn (d. 1063) laid waste to Hereford and destroyed its cathedral.[7] Almost everything was lost, including the relics of St Æthelbert. The low point, however, occurred the next year when Gruffudd defeated the entire party sent against him in retaliation from Hereford. Leofgar, the newly consecrated bishop of Hereford, several of the cathedral's canons and Ælfnoth, the sheriff of Hereford, all fell. Gruffudd's devastating attack explains why very few documents from the cathedral survive from before 1055. It also clarifies why no convincing explanation for the church's possession of Lydbury North came down to us, or to Walter Map and Gerald of Wales in the late twelfth century.

The bishops of Hereford had good reason to worry about their hold on Lydbury North. Bishop Gilbert Foliot (1148–63) had seen Lydbury North forcefully occupied by Hugh de Mortimer during his rebellion of 1155. Although Gilbert successfully regained Lydbury North after pleading to the king, the unlawful occupation of the manor seems to have touched a nerve: during Hugh's occupation, the canons of nearby Wigmore sent two men to guard the church at Lydbury. When Gilbert returned, he memorably had them thrown out and a brief struggle over the church at Lydbury ensued.[8] Cleary, he did not like others occupying property that rightfully belonged to his church.

Furthermore, anyone associated with Hereford Cathedral would have remembered that Henry II, at the height of his battle with the Church, had taken control of Bishop's Castle from 1167 until 1174, during which time the see of Hereford remained vacant. Even if no immediate threat appeared in the late twelfth century, the bishop of Hereford would have been aware of these recent injustices, and would have felt a strong need to produce some narrative that could explain why the church held the manor of Lydbury North. Walter and Gerald both sought to remedy this situation.

Walter Map enjoyed a long association with Hereford Cathedral.[9] He almost certainly received his prebendary at the cathedral from the patronage of the Foliots, his life-long supporters. Gilbert Foliot, Walter's greatest patron, was bishop of Hereford from 1148–63, and Robert Foliot – a relative of Gilbert's – was bishop from 1174–86.[10] The exact date that Walter obtained his position at Hereford is impossible to discern, and it may have been as early as 1158, but at any rate he was witnessing charters in the 1170s and 1180s.[11] The cathedral chapter supported him in 1199, trying, and failing, to elect him bishop.[12] Walter, in turn, supported the cathedral by creating a story for its possession of Lydbury North. His explanation, however, is anything but a simple historical tale of ecclesiastical endowment.

In Walter's account, the Anglo-Saxon folk hero Eadric the Wild is made responsible for the donation of the manor.[13] Eadric, a nobleman in western Shropshire during the reign of William the Conqueror, abducts a fairy woman and takes her as his wife. The story catches King William's ear, and he summons the odd couple to London so that he may look on them. The court holds a trial of sorts, and 'the weightiest argument in favour of an otherworldly nature was the woman's novel appearance, which nobody had seen before' ('maximum erat fatalitatis argumentum inuisa prius et inaudita species mulieris').[14] The king's curiosity having been satisfied, the two return home and live happily until Eadric insults his wife, breaking her commandment never to reproach her, and she disappears. She does, however, leave behind a son, Alnoth, a man 'of great holiness and wisdom' ('magne sanctitatis et sapiencie').[15] In his old age, Alnoth becomes afflicted with palsy. Scorning the advice of physicians to travel to Rome for a cure, he has himself brought to Hereford first, because of his devotion to St Æthelbert. Upon being restored to his former health, 'in an act of thanks he gave his manor of Lydbury, which is in Welsh country, to God and the Blessed Virgin and to the Holy King Æthelbert, with all its appurtenances' ('et cum graciarum accione donauit in perpetuam elemosinam Deo et beate Virgini et sancto regi Edelberto Ledebiriam suam, que in terris Wallie sita est, cum omnibus pertinenciis suis').[16] That is, he gave the manor to Hereford Cathedral, whose patron saints were the Virgin and Æthelbert, King and Martyr. Walter brings the tale of Eadric and Alnoth to an end by cataloguing the worth of Lydbury North, writing that 'it is still in the lordship of the bishop of Hereford, and it is reported to yield its lords thirty pounds a year' ('que adhuc nunc in dominio episcopi Herefordensis est, diciturque triginta libras annuas facere dominis suis').[17] Thus, as far as I am aware, Walter has written the only fairy story that draws to a close with the formulaic language of charters, for which he deserves, perhaps, some praise.

Interestingly, Walter Map's *De nugis curialium* ('Courtiers' Trifles') preserves another, shorter version of this foundation story in Distinctio IV.[18] Although greatly reduced, the narrative is largely the same: a man, who is distinguished, but unnamed, captures a fairy-bride, and the couple is subsequently admired by King William. Their son Alnoth, cured of palsy, donates the manor of Lydbury North to the bishop of Hereford. In this account, the only detail not present in the version in Distinctio II is the explanation that the bishop who currently holds it is the 'sixth from the one who received it from Alnoth's hand' ('sextus ut dicitur ab eo qui eam de manu Alnodi suscepit').[19] These two stories are not the only doublets present in the *De nugis curialium*. There are several.[20] An analysis of these doublets reveals that in every instance the stories found in Distinctiones I and II are revised, later versions of those found in Distinctiones IV and V.[21] The story of the donation of Lydbury North is no exception. The fuller version of the story in Distinctio II is an expansion of the earlier version in Distinctio IV. Walter has altered the tale so radically that only a few phrases are left intact from the earlier version (e.g. 'se iussit Herefordiam deferri' ('he ordered that he be carried to Hereford') remains as 'se deferri fecit Herefordiam' ('he had himself carried to Hereford')).[22] Walter was a tireless reviser.

What is important for our present purposes is that, in rewriting this tale, Walter has attached the story of Alnoth's donation of Lydbury North to Eadric the Wild (also known as Eadric Cild), an Anglo-Saxon thegn who held lands in Herefordshire and Shropshire near the Welsh border.[23] After the Conquest, Eadric participated in several campaigns against William, and for Walter's contemporaries he was probably a well-known legendary outlaw. At first glance, Eadric seems an odd match for this fairy-bride story. In addition to the fairy-bride element, which was a favourite motif of Walter's, the historical Eadric joined forces with the Welsh and even harried Herefordshire in 1067.[24] The rewritten tale does, however, fit comfortably in its new context in Distinctio II, which concerns the offspring of mortals and their fairy lovers. Furthermore, Eadric's heir Alnoth is described as a 'man of great holiness and wisdom' ('uirum magne sanctitatis et sapiencie'), making him good company for the other holy men in Distinctio II.[25] Still, one of Walter's aims in revising the tale is to explain the possession of Lydbury North, but the earlier version already does a decent job of that. So why Eadric the Wild? His persona does not seem necessary for the fairy-bride story. Yet the new, charter-like ending of the story and the care that Walter shows in revising the tale make it clear that he wanted this Anglo-Saxon figure to be part of the history of Lydbury North. Eadric's insertion into the manor's history makes better sense when considered alongside Gerald's version, even though the two versions differ in almost every way.

Like Walter, Gerald was a canon of Hereford Cathedral, but he seems to have obtained his prebendary later than Walter, under the episcopacy of Bishop William de Vere (1186–98).[26] During his tenure as bishop, William made a concerted effort to patronise several writers, Gerald included.[27] Around 1195 Simon de Freine, a canon of the cathedral, wrote a flattering poem to Gerald, urging him to move to the city 'where a multitude of liberal arts shine brightly' ('ubi tot radiant artes').[28] Simon's poem seems to have worked, and Gerald took up residence in the glow of Hereford's scholarly chapter, though probably for only a brief period. While there, Gerald turned his pen towards one of the cathedral's patron saints, Æthelbert. According to legend, Æthelbert, king of the East Anglians, had travelled to Mercia to obtain a suitable bride, but he was betrayed and murdered by Offa in 794. His body was subsequently discovered and interred at Hereford, although his head found its way to Westminster, where it was enshrined. Unfortunately for Hereford Cathedral, which became a popular destination for pilgrims, the relics of St Æthelbert were destroyed during the Welsh attack of 1055, along with any *vitae* that the cathedral had possessed of their patron saint. Losing Æthelbert's acephalous body was insult enough. The cathedral ought to at least have a *vita*.

Unsurprisingly, an anonymous author provided one at the beginning of the twelfth century.[29] Osbert of Clare, in turn, revised this earlier Life in the middle of the twelfth century.[30] It was Osbert's Life that Gerald adapted and revised during his time at Hereford.[31] According to Gerald, his fellow canons (concanonicorum) had urged him to improve the earlier Life, which was 'crammed with tedious digressions and crude language' ('longis autem ambagibus rudique sermone congestam').[32] In rewriting Osbert's Life, Gerald gave the legend of Æthelbert a more modern, scholastic feel, and he substantially altered the style of the earlier Life, but the substance of the legend remained largely the same.[33] Nonetheless, one of the few additions that Gerald did make was a short account of the donation of Lydbury North.[34]

Like Walter, Gerald associates Lydbury North with the miraculous healing of an Englishman stricken by palsy. Gerald describes how King Offa sent out two bishops to investigate the posthumous miracles of Æthelbert at Hereford. They return with the tale of Edwin Shaky-Head (*Edwinus quatiens caput*): as Edwin holds a devout vigil over the tomb of St Æthelbert, he falls asleep and an unknown man graciously holds his head in his lap. When Edwin awakens, he asks for the man who held him as he slept, but his retainers say that they have seen no one. Edwin, noticing that his palsy has ceased, recognises this strange dream for what it was – the miraculous intervention of St Æthelbert. To show his thanks, 'in a laudable act of generosity, he granted Lydbury North, in full with all its appurtenances, to Æthelbert the Martyr' ('martiri Æthelberto Lede-buriam borialem cum omnibus integre pertinenciis suis laudabili munificencia largitus est').[35] Not to be outdone by Edwin, Offa himself decides to donate some of his own land to the cathedral, property that the cathedral 'also holds until this very day' ('eciam usque hodiernum diem tenet').[36] This story has been bequeathed to posterity, Gerald assures his readers, by 'the trustworthy ancients' ('fidelis antiquitas').[37] Creative exaggeration never bothered Gerald too much, and it seems that this pronouncement is nothing more than a red herring. Yet if Gerald himself is responsible for the majority of this legend, it is even more pertinent to ask why Walter and Gerald, fellow canons at Hereford, do not agree in their accounts of Lydbury North.

First, however, we must confront the spectre of plagiarism, which arises whenever Gerald and Walter are discussed in tandem. Gerald did, to be sure, take from others without attribution, Peter the Chanter being the most igno-minious instance.[38] Walter Map is often said to be another victim of Gerald's intellectual larceny, and so it is worth asking whether Gerald took the germ of his story – an Englishman being cured by palsy – from Walter. I think that is unlikely, primarily because the claim that Gerald plagiarised Walter, widespread in secondary scholarship, originates from an article by Alan Keith Bate, which, to my mind, is not particularly convincing.[39] On the basis of chronology and shared language, Bate concludes that Gerald 'had *De Nugis* in front of him when writing *De principis instructione*' and that 'in all these cases of similar lan-guage it is obvious that Gerald is plagiarising Map'.[40] Gerald looks guilty again.

However, it helps to understand that the real aim of Bate's article is not to pillory Gerald, but to show that Walter Map's *De nugis curialium* actually circulated in his lifetime. If, as Bate claims, Gerald and Walter were not friends, then the only explanation for the shared passages is that Gerald had gotten hold of Walter's text. Nonetheless, I think this claim deserves a second look. Their shared language is better explained as stories from the same cultural milieu rather than plagiarism. One similarity is clearly due to liturgical influ-ence, another to a shared knowledge of Horace.[41] Their anti-Cistercian anec-dotes, while very similar in some respects, differ quite radically in others, and the verbal correspondences are never more than slight.[42] Perplexingly, Bate also includes similar derogatory comments about the Welsh as evidence that Gerald has been using Walter's work.[43] Such a claim is puzzling because I find it unbe-lievable that Gerald would need to rely on *anybody* when it came to describing the faults of the Welsh. At any rate, their similar comments regarding the Welsh are no more than common medieval stereotypes. The last piece of evidence for plagiarism is that the two share a jocular anecdote about the French.[44] Yet the verbal correspondence appears only in the story's short punchline, which, given the mnemonic nature of punchlines, is poor evidence for written dependence.[45] Most of us can recall a joke with little effort.

The fact that Gerald plagiarised Peter the Chanter does not serve as more evidence to condemn him of the same when it comes to Walter. Instead, it helps exonerate him. Nothing in the passages suspected to be taken from Walter shows the direct, continuous lifting of prose that occurs when Gerald passes off Peter's writing as his own. The best explanation for the similarities is that the two clerics were part of the same intellectual circles.[46] They clearly knew one another. Although Walter does not mention Gerald in any of his surviving work – and this is unsurprising given what little survives – Gerald mentions Walter a total of twelve times.[47] From these references, we can see that they seem to have been on friendly terms. Gerald sent Walter a walking stick. The two traded poems. On multiple occasions Gerald praised Walter's wit. And Gerald, after realising that he would never have his cherished bishopric, even proposed Walter as an alternative for bishop of St Davids. Although Gerald and Walter, like a quarter of their fellow canons, were not in continuous residence at Hereford Cathedral, they did make frequent visits to the diocese.[48] The two men knew each other, shared many of the same interests, and almost certainly spent time together at Hereford Cathedral. They also probably wrote their stories around the same time.

Although neither story can be dated precisely, it seems that Walter and Gerald both wrote their accounts within two decades of one another. It is tempting to date Walter's story of Eadric the Wild to the episcopacy of Robert Foliot (1174–86). Robert and Walter were roughly the same age and part of the same social circle. Both men were archdeacons of Oxford and canons of Lincoln. Furthermore, they both were part of the English delegation to the Third Lateran Council in 1179, and some material in the *De nugis curialium* was clearly written during the early 1180s, including stories in Distinctio II, where the story of Eadric the Wild appears.[49] Furthermore, in the earlier story Walter provides a vague date for Alnoth's donation: he writes that the current bishop is now the sixth to hold it. If Walter wrote this passage under the tenure of Robert Foliot or William de Vere, then it is imagined to take place during the time of Bishop Reinhelm (1107–15) or Geoffrey de Clive (1115–29). This would make sense to Walter's audience: plausible dates for the generation after William the Conqueror and Eadric the Wild. However, given the fact that Walter was a thorough reviser, and that sections of the *De nugis curialium* shows clear signs of unfinished revisions, it remains difficult to date sections of the *De nugis curialium* with any certainty. Gerald, as far as we can tell, seems to have written his version in the *Vita Ethelberti* in or shortly after 1195, when he arrived in Hereford.

Even though they both date to the last twenty years of the twelfth century, the two accounts of Lydbury North show a clear lack of coordination among the canons of Hereford. Perhaps the differences arose because they were written under different bishops (if, in fact, Walter's was written before 1186). For various reasons, Robert Foliot might have preferred a connection with Eadric the Wild and Alnoth, while William de Vere thought Offa and Edwin a better fit with diocesan propaganda. But the two different accounts certainly owe as much to their authors as to diocesan leadership. Walter's story, in particular, combines one of his favourite motifs – the fairy-bride – with the donation of Lydbury North.[50] Gerald's, on the other hand, shows his typical willingness to invent historical fact when needed. Audience, too, played a role. Gerald was writing for his fellow canons, many of whom may not have shared the same appreciation for secular wonders as their colleague Walter. Gerald's version is standard hagiographical fare, and when read aloud on Æthelbert's feast day, it would not draw any sidelong glances from those at the service. Walter's audience is more difficult to envision, however. While parts of the *De nugis curialium* clearly circulated on their own, Distinctio II, which contains the Lydbury North story, seems to have not. Its incomplete ending suggests that Walter never finished it. Nonetheless, the imagined audience would not have found the story of Eadric and Alnoth to be an outlier, since Distinctio II concerns the deeds of extraordinary men, religious as well as secular. With other supernatural oddities and saintly men, Eadric and Alnoth have happy company in Distinctio II. Couching the history of Lydbury North in a fairy story might strike modern readers as a farce, but many twelfth-century readers would have had little problem with this odd mixture.

I believe that these shared stories are notable not for their lack of coordination, but for their similar use of the Anglo-Saxon past. Both men have created authorising strategies that create links to the Anglo-Saxon past, giving Lydbury North a history that stretches back before the anarchy of King Stephen's reign and even before the Norman Conquest. In both Gerald and Walter, the Anglo-Saxon past acts as a kind of vouchsafe for the antiquity of Lydbury North. For their source, Walter and Gerald were working with the same germ of a legend, which was probably all Hereford retained after their documents had been destroyed a century earlier: local tradition must have held that Lydbury North was granted to Hereford Cathedral from a rich Englishman who had been cured of palsy through the miraculous intervention of St Æthelbert. The textual histories of the *De nugis curialium* and the *Vita Ethelberti* show how both authors took this local legend and grounded it in the Anglo-Saxon past. Gerald has framed the story around King Offa. Who better to confirm and praise Edwin's gift of Lydbury North than Offa, the region's most famous Anglo-Saxon king? Walter, however, has attached the legend to Eadric

Streona, a great landowner in Herefordshire and Shropshire, who was, rather famously, an Anglo-Saxon holdout against William the Conqueror, and one who had Welsh allies. Thus, Walter's addition of Eadric is not as farfetched as it has been made out to be: his status as a well-known Marcher lord in Herefordshire and Shropshire makes him an ideal candidate for a supporter of Hereford trying to craft an explanation for who could have possibly granted such a large and important manor to the diocese.

Invoking the Anglo-Saxon past was a familiar and useful strategy for both Gerald and Walter. Walter even records another Anglo-Saxon donation to Hereford Cathedral. He is the only source that records Edmund Ironside's death at Ross-on-Wye.[51] According to Walter, as Edmund lay dying, he granted the church of Ross to Hereford Cathedral – another convenient claim for the diocese. Elsewhere, Walter shows a general interest in previous English kings, telling stories about Offa and Edward the Confessor.[52] He even wrote a short history of later Anglo-Saxon England from Edgar to the Conquest.[53] Gerald, too, knew how to manipulate the Anglo-Saxon past. In the *Vita Ethelberti*, Gerald inserts a passage from Asser, whom Gerald calls 'the trustworthy reporter of the deeds of King Alfred' ('veraxque relator gestorum Regis Alfridi'), directly before his story of Lydbury North.[54] It is striking that Gerald knew this work, as it makes him one of only a few early readers of Asser, and possibly the only witness to Asser's circulation in Wales, although Gerald certainly could have encountered a copy in England.[55] Nonetheless, Gerald's reading of Asser's *Life of Alfred* reflects his interest in the Anglo-Saxons. Of course, simply being willing to rewrite the *Vita Ethelberti* shows that Gerald enjoyed exploring the English past. Moreover, Gerald, always a keen observer of language, knew that the dialect of Old English spoken in Wessex was prestigious. In the *Descriptio Kambriae*, after remarking how the Welsh spoken in north Wales is typically seen as the purest, Gerald observes that the English spoken in the south, especially around Devon, seems the less affected, since the Danes and Norwegians had overrun the north. He continues with this remarkable comment: 'That [i.e. the intrusion of foreigners] is not even the only evidence for this fact: you are also able to have proof of it, since you will find all the English books of Bede, Hrabanus and King Alfred, or anyone else, written in this characteristic dialect' ('Cujus etiam rei non solum argumentum, set et certitudinem inde habere potes, quod omnes libros Anglicos Bedae, Rabani, regis Aeluredi, vel aliorum quorumlibet, sub hujus idiomatis proprietate scriptos invenies').[56] This is a puzzling claim: the reference to Alfred's programme of translation is the only one that we would consider correct.

While Bede's *Historia ecclesiastica* was translated into Old English, it has Mercian – not West-Saxon – dialectal characteristics.[57] Nonetheless, this passage reflects the tradition that King Alfred had Bede translated into Old English, which would explain Gerald's association of the Old English translation with West Saxon English.[58] However, claiming that Hrabanus Maurus wrote in Old English is less explicable. Hrabanus was certainly known in Anglo-Saxon England, and it might be that Gerald is drawing upon an erroneous tradition that has confused the Carolingian monk for an Old English author.[59] Excerpts of Hrabanus's writing did end up being translated into Old English, and Gerald's odd reference here might ultimately point to this translation.[60] Gerald, though, was not an exacting historian; I merely wish to draw attention to his interest in the Anglo-Saxon past.

Gerald and Walter were not alone in finding convenient 'facts' in the Anglo-Saxon past. Writers throughout the twelfth century showed great industriousness in examining pre-Conquest England, producing not only genuine historical research, but also imaginative invention.[61] While many of the specifics remain unknowable, when Walter and Gerald gave Lydbury North an Anglo-Saxon heritage, they were both participating in a widespread cultural process of reimaging and rethinking earlier English history. Nonetheless, their two accounts have only been mentioned in passing, typically only for their glaring discrepancies. And although Gerald and Walter are often studied together, the story of Lydbury North has never been seen as a story that the two share. Yet for this reason it has never been seen as one of Gerald's plagiarised stories, either.

As the principal aim of this volume is to offer new perspectives on Gerald of Wales, I would like to end by proposing that the story of Lydbury North presents a better model for thinking about the literary relationship between Gerald and Walter. While the claim that Gerald occasionally plagiarised from Walter has been repeated, a review of the evidence shows that in fact such a claim has little in its support. Gerald's and Walter's versions of the granting of Lydbury North elaborate on the same basic theme – an Englishman cured of palsy donated the manor – and they display the same widespread cultural impulse to invoke the Anglo-Saxon past to explain contemporary rights and privileges. These similarities are unremarkable for two contemporary canons of Hereford when faced with the same gap in the historical record. Similarly, their other shared passages result from the fact that the two men were working in the same courtly and ecclesiastical environments, that they had similar interests and that they were, in all likelihood, friends. Gerald of Wales may have never been completely intellectually honest, but he did not plagiarise Walter Map.

❖

# Notes

1    R. R. Davies, *Lordship and Society in the March of Wales, 1282–1400* (Oxford, 1978), pp. 39–40.

2    Cited in Julia Barrow, 'A Lotharingian in Hereford: Bishop Robert's Reorganisation of the Church of Hereford 1079–1095', in David Whitehead (ed.), *Medieval Art, Architecture, and Archaeology at Hereford* (London, 1995), pp. 29–49, at 30.

3    Barrow, 'A Lotharingian in Hereford', p. 33; 'Introduction', in J. S. Barrow (ed.), *Fasti Ecclesiae Anglicanae 1066–1300: Volume 8, Hereford* (London, 2002), pp. xxi–xxxiv, at n. 18, *www.british-history.ac.uk/fasti-ecclesiae/1066-1300/vol8/xxi-xxxiv* (accessed 10 June 2016).

4    Barrow, 'Introduction'; Patrick Sims-Williams, *Religion and Literature in Western England, 600–800* (Cambridge, 1990), pp. 90–1.

5    Hereford held the manor at the time of Domesday, but Walter's version dates the donation to the early twelfth century. See Barrow, 'Introduction', n. 9.

6    Robert Bartlett, 'The Viking Hiatus in the Cult of Saints as Seen in the Twelfth Century', in Martin Brett and David A. Woodman (eds), *The Long Twelfth-Century View of the Anglo-Saxon Past* (Farnham, 2015), pp. 13–25. For the creation of twelfth-century narratives about the destruction of Anglo-Saxon monasteries at the hands of Vikings, see Julia Barrow, 'Danish Ferocity and Abandoned Monasteries: The Twelfth-Century View', in Brett and Woodman (eds), *The Long Twelfth-Century View*, pp. 77–93.

7    Michael Swanton (ed. and trans.), *The Anglo-Saxon Chronicle* (New York, 1998), pp. 184–7 (C). See also Simon Keynes, 'Diocese and Cathedral before 1056', in Gerald Aylmer and John Tiller (eds), *Hereford Cathedral: A History* (London, 2000), pp. 4–20, at 18–20; Barrow, 'Athelstan to Aigueblanche, 1056–1268', in Aylmer and Tiller (eds), *Hereford Cathedral*, pp. 21–47, at 22–3; Michael Davies and Sean Davies, *The Last King of Wales: Gruffudd ap Llywelyn c. 1013–1063* (Stroud, 2012), pp. 65–8.

8    R. W. Eyton, *Antiquities of Shropshire*, 12/11 (London, 1854–60), pp. 196–7.

9    M. R. James (ed. and trans.), *Walter Map: De nugis curialium. Courtiers' Trifles*, rev. C. N. L. Brooke and R. A. B. Mynors (Oxford, 1983), pp. xii–xv, hereafter cited as *DNC*. Translations are my own.

10    Walter clearly considered Gilbert a friend. See *DNC*, i.13, p. 36; i.24, p. 80; iv.5, p. 313.

11    *DNC*, p. xv, n. 2.

12    Decima L. Douie and David Hugh Farmer (eds), *Magna Vita Sancti Hugonis: The Life of St Hugh of Lincoln*, 2/2 (Oxford, 1961–2), pp. 131–2; Barrow, 'Athelstan to Aigueblanche', p. 30.

13    *DNC*, ii.12, pp. 155–9. See also Ralph Hanna, 'The Matter of Fulk: Romance and History in the Marches', *Journal of English and Germanic Philology*, 110 (2011), 337–58, at 347–8.

14    *DNC*, ii.12, pp. 156–9.

15    *DNC*, ii.12, pp. 158–9.

16  *DNC*, ii.12, pp. 158–9.

17  *DNC*, ii.12, pp. 158–9.

18  *DNC*, iv.10, pp. 348–51.

19  *DNC*, iv.10, pp. 350–1.

20  A. G. Rigg, review of M. R. James (ed. and trans.), rev. C. N. L. Brooke and R. A. B. Mynors, *Walter Map: De nugis curialium. Courtiers' Trifles*, *Speculum*, 60 (1985), 177–82, at 182.

21  See my book *Walter Map and the Matter of Britain* (Philadelphia, 2017). I also argue that the *De nugis curialium* was never meant to be a single book and that what has come down to us is very likely five separate works in various stages of completion, all of which have been unified by scribal interpolation. See also Rigg, review of James, 182.

22  *DNC*, iv.10, p. 350; ii.12, p. 158.

23  For the historical Eadric, see S. Reynolds, 'Eadric Silvaticus and the English Resistance', *Bulletin of the Institute of Historical Research*, 54 (1981), 102–5.

24  For Eadric's Welsh allies, see Lindy Brady, *Writing the Welsh Borderlands in Anglo-Saxon England* (Manchester, 2017). I would like to thank Lindy for allowing me to read her book before publication.

25  *DNC*, ii.12, p. 158.

26  For Gerald in Hereford, see Daniel Birkholz, 'Hereford Maps, Hereford Lives: Biography and Cartography in an English Cathedral City', in Keith Lilley (ed.), *Mapping Medieval Geographies: Geographical Encounters in the Latin West and Beyond, 300–1600* (Cambridge, 2013), pp. 225–49, especially 228–36.

27  Julia Barrow, 'A Twelfth-Century Bishop and Literary Patron: William De Vere', *Viator*, 18 (1987), 175–90.

28  *Symbolum electorum*, Juvenalia 42, pp. 382–4, at 383.

29  This early Life, found in Cambridge, Corpus Christi College MS 308, is edited in M. R. James, 'Two Lives of Ethelbert, King and Martyr', *The English Historical Review*, 32 (1917), 214–44, at 236–44. A later redaction of this Life exists in London, British Library, Harley MS 2253, edited in Susanna Fein, with David Raybin and Jan Ziolkowski (ed. and trans.), *The Complete Harley 2253 Manuscript*, 3/2 (Kalamazoo, 2014), no. 18, *http://d.lib.rochester.edu/teams/text/fein-harley2253-volume-2-article-18-introduction* (accessed 10 June 2016).

30  Gotha, Forschungsbibliothek MS Memb. I 81, fols 30r–39r. Richard of Cirencester used a large portion of Osbert's text in John E. B. Mayor (ed.), *Speculum historiale de gestis regum Angliae*, 2/1 (London, 1863–9), pp. 262–94. An abridged version of Osbert's Life is found in Carl Horstman (ed.), *Nova legenda Anglie*, 2/1 (Oxford, 1901), pp. 412–18.

31  Edited in James, 'Two Lives of Ethelbert', 222–36, hereafter cited as *Vita Ethelberti*.

32  *Vita Ethelberti*, p. 236.

33  Robert Bartlett, 'Rewriting Saints' Lives: The Case of Gerald of Wales', *Speculum*, 58 (1983), 598–613.

34  *Vita Ethelberti*, pp. 232–3; Bartlett, 'Rewriting Saints' Lives', 610, n. 59.

35  *Vita Ethelberti*, p. 233.

36    *Vita Ethelberti*, p. 233.

37    *Vita Ethelberti*, p. 232.

38    André Boutemy, 'Giraud de Barri et Pierre le Chantre: une source de la *Gemma ecclesiastica*', *Revue du moyen âge latin*, 2 (1946), 45–62; E. M. Sanford, 'Giraldus Cambrensis' Debt to Petrus Cantor', *Medievalia et humanistica*, 3 (1945), 16–32.

39    Alan Keith Bate, 'Walter Map and Giraldus Cambrensis', *Latomus*, 31 (1972), 860–75, at 873–5. See also Hugh M. Thomas, *The Secular Clergy in England, 1066-1216* (Oxford, 2014), p. 202, n. 68. Robert Bartlett has brought to my attention another shared passage that Bate missed, in which both Gerald and Walter seem to be drawing on the same source for information on ancient Rome: see *DNC*, iv.3, pp. 298–9 and London, British Library, Cotton MS Julius B. xiii, fol. 68v (*De principis instructione*). I am grateful to Prof. Bartlett for sharing his transcription of this passage with me.

40    Bate, 'Walter Map and Giraldus Cambrensis', 875.

41    Bate himself suspects that the phrase 'by robbing the Egyptians and enriching the Hebrews' ('spoliando Aegypios et ditando Hebraeos') is a medieval commonplace, inspired by Exodus 12:35–6. But for its use in English liturgies for Easter Vigil, see Marbury B. Ogle, 'Bible Text of Liturgy?', *The Harvard Theological Review*, 33 (1940), 191–224, at 217–18. The misquotation of Horace, which Bate finds significant, is not exact, and, moreover, appears in other twelfth-century authors, e.g. Nigel Whiteacre, *Tractatus contra curiales*, in André Boutemy (ed.), *Nigellus de Longchamp dit Wireker* (Paris, 1959), p. 181.

42    Bate, 'Walter Map and Giraldus Cambrensis', 873–4. In both works, the Cistercians are said to have removed boundary markers to confiscate desired land; ploughed up and manured a field overnight, only to claim in the morning that they have always possessed it; sold thick bacon to villagers, only to squeeze out the fat before they cart it away; salted a field so that its owner, believing it to be barren, sold it cheaply; and fraudulently altered charters to gain more land at Neath. However, the stories actually differ in many respects. In the bacon story alone, alongside a host of minor discrepancies, there are two major ones: Walter's story is set in Pontigny, near Auxerre in France, while Gerald's takes place near Lincoln. In Walter's version the monks' scam is uncovered by a shepherd, while in Gerald's an expelled, and apparently disgruntled, monk reveals how the other monks had deceived the buyer. We find the same situation in each of these shared episodes. While the mechanism of the deceit is largely the same, the details do not line up. The Cistercians in Walter's account use goats and salt to destroy a field's productivity. In Gerald's, they only use salt. Walter provides specifics in his story of the moved boundaries: it takes place at Coxwold in North Yorkshire, and Roger, archbishop of York, orders the boundary moved back to its original place. Gerald merely states that the story takes place in the northern borders of England, and it is the village elders and their lord who discover and put right the monks' deceit. More discrepancies between the two can easily be deduced.

43    Bate, 'Walter Map and Giraldus Cambrensis', 874.

44    Bate, 'Walter Map and Giraldus Cambrensis', 873–4.

45 Compare Walter's version, '"In France, we don't have anything except bread, wine and good time." I took note of this phrase, since it was was wittily and truly said' ('"Nos in Francia nihil habemus nisi panem et uinum et gaudium." Hoc uerbum notaui, quia comiter et uere dictum': *DNC*, v.5, p. 451), with Gerald's '"While many other kingdoms are mentioned, nothing similar is said about France" and without skipping a beat he said, "At any rate, we have bread, wine and a good time." Behold how remarkable and mild the reply of such a prince was' ('"Inter caetera uero regna de Francia quoque nil dicitur!" Statimque subjungens, "Et nos certe panem," inquit, "habemus et uinum et gaudium." Sed ecce, quam mirum fuit hoc et quam mansuetum tanti principis uerbum': *De principis instructione*, iii.30, p. 318). Again, however, some of the details are different: Gerald mentions Spain, Walter does not. Walter talks of Charlemagne, Gerald does not. And Gerald spends much more time describing the wealth of England than Walter does. Moreover, unlike Walter, Gerald does not claim to have heard the joke from Louis VII himself. Rather, he simply states that he has thought the king's quip (*dictum*) worthy of mentioning (*memoratu dignum*).

46 Another example, which Bate does not discuss, is Gerald's tale of Reginald de Giens, which has the same plot as Walter's story of Rollo and Rhys. See Tony Davenport, 'Sex, Ghosts, and Dreams: Walter Map (1135? –1210?) and Gerald of Wales (1146–1223)', in Ruth Kennedy and Simon Meecham-Jones (eds), *Writers of the Reign of Henry II: Twelve Essays* (New York, 2006), pp. 133–50, at 144–6.

47 For Gerald and Walter, see Lewis Thorpe, 'Walter Map and Gerald of Wales', *Medium Aevum*, 47 (1978), 6–17. Cf. Davenport, 'Sex, Ghosts, and Dreams', p. 136.

48 Barrow, 'Athelstan to Aigueblanche', p. 34.

49 *DNC*, pp. lii–liv. See also J. Hinton, 'Walter Map's *De Nugis Curialium*: Its Plan and Composition', *Proceedings of the Modern Language Academy*, 32 (1917), 81–132.

50 For Walter's mixing of 'low' and 'high' culture, see Alberto Várvaro, *Apparizioni fantastiche: Tradizioni folcoriche e letteratura nel medioevo: Walter Map* (Bologna, 1994).

51 *DNC*, v.4, pp. 430–1.

52 *DNC*, ii.17, pp. 166–75; ii.23, pp. 192–3.

53 *DNC*, v.3–4, pp. 412–37.

54 *Vita Ethelberti*, pp. 231–2, which corresponds to W. H. Stevenson (ed.), *Asser's Life of King Alfred* (Oxford, 1904), §14–15, pp. 12–14; trans. in Simon Keynes and Michael Lapidge, *Alfred the Great: Asser's Life of King Alfred and Other Contemporary Sources* (Harmondsworth, 1983), pp. 71–2.

55 For the short list of early uses of Asser, see Keynes and Lapidge, *Alfred the Great*, pp. 56–8. The discussion of Gerald here, however, is slightly mistaken and was later corrected in Simon Keynes, 'The Power of the Written Word: Alfredian England 871–899', in Timothy Reuter (ed.), *Alfred the Great: Papers from the Eleventh-Century Conferences* (Aldershot, 2003), pp. 175–97, at 181, n. 31.

56 *Descriptio*, i.6, pp. 177–8.

57 Dorothy Whitelock, 'The Old English Bede', *Proceedings of the British Academy*, 48 (1962), 57–90; repr. in Eric Stanley (ed.), *British Academy Papers on Anglo-Saxon*

*England* (Oxford, 1990), pp. 227–50; Janet Bately, 'Old English Prose Before and During the Reign of Alfred', *Anglo-Saxon England*, 17 (1988), 93–138.

58   Ælfric of Eynsham, writing in the late tenth century, claims that King Alfred had Bede's '*Historia Anglorum*' translated into Old English in B. Thorpe (ed.), *The Homilies of the Anglo-Saxon Church: The First Part, containing the Sermones Catholici, or Homilies of Ælfric,* 2/2 (London, 1844–6), pp. 116–19. William of Malmesbury later claimed the same. See R. A. B. Mynors, completed by R. M. Thomson and M. Winterbottom (ed. and trans.), *William of Malmesbury: Gesta regum Anglorum: The History of the English Kings,* 2/1 (Oxford, 1998), §II.123.1, pp. 192–3. See also Dorothy Whitelock, 'William of Malmesbury on the Works of King Alfred', in D. A. Pearsall and R. A. Waldron (eds), *Medieval Literature and Civilization: Studies in Memory of G. N. Garmonsway* (London, 1969), pp. 78–93.

59   For Hrabanus in Anglo-Saxon England, see Frederick Biggs, Thomas Hill and Paul Szarmach (eds), *Sources of Anglo-Saxon Literary Culture: A Trial Version* (Binghamton, 1990), pp. 130–3. For Anglo-Saxon copies of Hrabanus, see Helmut Gneuss and Michael Lapidge, *Anglo-Saxon Manuscripts: A Bibliographic Handlist of Manuscripts and Manuscript Fragments Written or Owned in England up to 1100* (Toronto, 2014), nos. 12, 59, 65.5, 73, 131, 140, 178, 243, 258, 398, 498.4, 644, 779, 814, and 919.3.

60   Hrabanus's interpretation of the canonical hours from the second book of his *De clericorum institutione* was translated into Old English. For an edition and discussion of the translation, see James M. Ure (ed.), *The Benedictine Office: An Old English Text* (Edinburgh, 1957), especially pp. 15–16. For the manuscripts, see Gneuss and Lapidge, *Anglo-Saxon Manuscripts*, nos. 65.5 and 644.

61   For some key studies of the uses of the Anglo-Saxon past in the twelfth century, see James Campbell, 'Some Twelfth-Century Views of the Anglo-Saxon Past', *Peritia*, 3 (1984), 131–50; the essays in Brett and Woodman (eds), *The Long Twelfth-Century View*; Elaine Treharne, *Living Through Conquest: The Politics of Early English, 1020–1220* (Oxford, 2012); and Mary Swan and Elaine Treharne (eds), *Rewriting Old English in the Twelfth-Century* (Cambridge, 2000).

❖

# TWO

# Gerald the Writer: Manuscripts and Authorship

# FIVE

# Gerald of Wales and the History of Llanthony Priory

Robert Bartlett
*University of St Andrews*

T HE *HISTORY OF LLANTHONY PRIORY* survives in one late thirteenth-century manuscript, London, British Library, Cotton MS Julius D. x, fols 31–53v. This book also contains two other works, a Life of Robert, bishop of Hereford (1131–48), who had been a canon and prior of Llanthony, written by William of Wycombe, a later prior of Llanthony, and an Anglo-Norman genealogy of the lords of Brecon, so it has a clear local focus.[1] The text of the *History* is about 10,700 words long, although it is incomplete, breaking off abruptly in the middle of a chapter. Much of the *History* has appeared in print. Approximately 60 per cent of the surviving text appeared in Dugdale's *Monasticon* in 1661.[2] In 1977 Michael Richter published another 20 per cent of the text, including the preface, table of contents and the two final chapters of the text as it stands.[3] This leaves another 20 per cent as yet unprinted. Because of fire damage, suffered in the Cottonian fire of 1731, these unprinted passages are not always completely legible, but their main sense is not in doubt. They consist of two complete chapters, *De prelatis* and *De subditis*, on the duties of superiors and subjects; and two shorter sections, a brief rhetorical lament for the fate of Llanthony when Robert of Bethune departed to take up his position as bishop of Hereford, and a passage on the relics of Llanthony, which includes a story of a miracle involving a piece of the Virgin Mary's hair.

The *History* tells how, around the year 1100, William, a household knight of the Norman baron Hugh de Lacy, came into the remote vale of Llanthony while out hunting, and resolved to take up a hermit life there. Eventually his fame came to the ears of Ernisius, a former chaplain of Queen Matilda, wife of Henry I, who had himself become a hermit in the English Midlands, and, in 1103, Ernisius joined William in the valley. There they built a simple church dedicated to John the Baptist, which was consecrated in 1108, and enjoyed the secular patronage of Hugh de Lacy, lord of the region. The next step, undertaken with the approval and advice of Archbishop Anselm, was to transform 'this fellowship of two into a monastery of many' ('contubernium duorum transiret in cenobium multorum').[4] So the two hermits adopted the Augustinian rule, recruited canons from the Augustinian houses of England and founded a priory with Ernisius as its first prior.[5]

The *History* goes on to recount the sequence of priors and the changing fortunes of the priory down to the late twelfth century. The most dramatic event in this story is the partial abandonment of the original site of the priory during the troubled times that followed the death of Henry I in 1135: 'instantly those who had previously been checked by fear of royal punishment rather than by love of justice, erupt in ferocious feuds and violent hostilities' ('Grassantur illico feralibus inimicitiis, sediciosisque simultatibus quos prius regalis districtionis timor non amor iusticie cohercuit').[6] Llanthony Priory was particularly vulnerable, since it was located, according to the author of the *History*, 'in the midst of a crooked and perverse nation' ('in medio nationis prave et perverse').[7] A neighbouring Welshman, seeking refuge from his enemies, took up residence in the priory along with his household and followers. The canons' dining hall was filled with Welsh women dancing. Finding the situation intolerable, most of the canons accepted the invitation of the bishop of Hereford, their former prior, to take up residence in his cathedral city.

The canons did not stay long in Hereford. Miles of Gloucester, one of the dominant barons of the region, whose father had ended his days as a canon of Llanthony, offered them a site just outside the walls of Gloucester and provided them with a rich endowment. In 1136 their new church was consecrated, not in honour of John the Baptist but in honour of the Virgin Mary. This community is usually termed Llanthony (or Lanthony) Secunda, the original site in Wales, Llanthony Prima. The relationship between the two was to be a vexed and troubled one. The author of the *History* is undoubtedly a champion of Llanthony Prima. For him, the move to Gloucester was not a permanent relocation, but an expedient measure in troubled times. Eventually, he explained, the canons intended to re-establish full religious life at their site in Wales, leaving only the minimum number of brethren in the daughter house at Gloucester. But he acknowledged that there was a question. Recognising that Miles of Gloucester had not donated the site at Gloucester to the canons of the church of John the Baptist in Wales, he nevertheless asserted 'he could not deny that he had donated it to those who had professed their vows in that church and in no other' ('illius ecclesie et non alterius professis illum se contulisse negare non poterit').[8] In fact, the question would be answered in various ways: until

1205 there was one prior for both houses; in that year or thereabouts the two houses were separated; at the end of the Middle Ages, in 1481, Llanthony Prima became a dependency of Llanthony Secunda.[9]

The *History* naturally takes us nowhere near so far. It tells of Prior William of Wycombe, author of the Life of Bishop Robert of Hereford; recounts the failure of the canons to restore Llanthony Prima, indeed, their ransacking of the books, the vestments and even the bells of the mother house to adorn the house at Gloucester; praises the theological writings of Clement, William of Wycombe's successor as prior (these writings survive in numerous manuscripts),[10] but criticises the nepotism he displayed in later life. After the end of the chapter on Clement, at the bottom of folio 50, there is a conspicuous change in the handwriting of the manuscript (Dugdale ended his excerpts at this point). The last section, folios 50v–53v, concerns the time of Prior Roger of Norwich, that is, the 1170s and 1180s. It contains a long anecdote about a squabble between the canons of Llanthony and the monks of Canterbury, and an assessment of Roger, whose health and temper degenerated with age. On Roger's death, the canon Geoffrey of Henlawe, who had been Roger's doctor, became prior. The last words of the *History* as it survives are as follows: 'But before we say anything about the election or appointment of Geoffrey, the seventh prior, let us follow up certain things that are not to be kept silent, which happened shortly before the death of Prior Roger, of whom we have written, or in the lifetime of this Geoffrey, namely the conflict between the fathers' ('Prius autem quam uel de electione uel de substitutione Galfridi prioris septimi aliquod dicamus, quedam que paulo ante mortem Rogeri prioris de quo scripsimus uel in uita istius Galfridi acciderant, de conflictu paternorum scilicet, non reticenda prosequamur').[11] Here the text, tantalisingly, breaks off.

Gerald of Wales was familiar with both Llanthony Prima and Llanthony Secunda. He was educated as a boy at Gloucester Abbey, about a quarter hour's walk from Llanthony Secunda outside the city walls. He also knew Llanthony Prima well. It was within his archdeaconry of Brecon and he gave an appreciative description of it in his *Itinerarium Kambriae*.[12] A friendly exchange of letters with Prior Roger survives.[13] In a letter of *c*.1213 written to a later prior of Llanthony, Gerald refers to Llanthony as 'a beautiful, worthy and adequately endowed monastery' (monasterio pulcro et honesto et sufficienter opimo gregi').[14] Less amicably, the Llanthony prior Geoffrey of Henlawe was his successful rival as a candidate for the see of St Davids. And, beyond this general familiarity and these personal relations, there is no doubt that there is some textual relationship between the *History* and parts of Gerald's works.

Michael Richter pointed out in the 1970s that some parts of the *History* are identical to passages in Gerald's works.[15] The most striking example is a long passage that begins with the anecdote about Prior Roger, who, while visiting Canterbury, sent one of his canons to prepare for him to celebrate mass at an altar in the cathedral. The canon was, however, accosted by a Canterbury monk who barred him, as a cleric, from celebrating mass there, and told him his proper place was in one of the town churches, among the clerics. Sometime later a Canterbury monk was a guest at Llanthony Secunda, and, as he prepared to celebrate mass, was told that, as a monk, he should go into Gloucester town and celebrate there with the monks of St Peter's Abbey. This tit-for-tat exchange is followed by a long disquisition on the differences between monks and clerics, very much to the advantage of the latter. The whole passage is about 750 words in length and forms a substantial part of the last surviving chapter of the *History* and recurs in almost exactly the same wording in one of Gerald's last works (after 1219), *Speculum ecclesiae*.[16] There is no question that there is a relationship, which must, logically, be either the *History* copying Gerald, or Gerald copying the *History*, or both following a common source. And there are other instances of such verbal overlap.

Richter developed a quite elaborate theory about the relationship between Gerald and the *History*. He suggested that:

1.  Some of Gerald's passages on Llanthony in the *Itinerarium Kambriae* are 'copied . . . directly' from the *History*.[17]
2.  There is also a 'direct dependence' the other way, of the *History* on Gerald's *Speculum duorum*, in the case of some citations from canon law, with framing comment.[18]
3.  The occurrence in identical wording of the passage about Prior Roger and the altercation with the Canterbury monk, which is in the *History* and in Gerald's late *Speculum ecclesiae*, is explained in a particularly intricate way: 'there can be no doubt that Giraldus had written down this particular story at an earlier stage . . . the whole chapter is borrowed into the *History* of Llanthony from Giraldus's notes which later formed the *Speculum Ecclesiae*'.[19]

Might there not, however, be a simpler theory, that Gerald was himself the author of the *History*?

The case for Gerald's authorship can begin with the well-established fact of the existence of exactly similar passages and phrases in the *History* and in Gerald's works. The anecdote about Prior Roger has already been mentioned. As found in the *History* and in the *Speculum ecclesiae*, the passage breaks down into 250 words of narrative, followed by 500 words of reflection and citation of authorities. While the narrative cannot be discovered other than in these two places, the same is not true of the reflections and citations. In fact, the *Topographia Hibernica*, Gerald's earliest work, has more than half of these reflections, spurred by Gerald's observation that most Irish bishops were drawn from the monks rather than from clerics, which, he thought, explained their neglect of their flocks: 'A monk is so called from being the guardian of one alone and has care only for himself. But a cleric is obliged to exercise care of many' ('Monachus enim tanquam unius custos, vel singularis dictus, sui solius curam agit. Clericus vero circa multorum curam solicitari tenetur').[20] Gerald is notorious for his outspoken championing of clerks against monks, and this passage in the *Topographia*, published around 1187, fits very well with his views elsewhere. In fact he recycled it entirely in his autobiographical account, *De rebus a se gestis* ('On the Things He Has Achieved'), of 1208–16, and there presented it as being part of a sermon he had given at Dublin in March 1186.[21] This discrete and distinctive block of text thus appears in three of Gerald's works over a period of more than thirty years.

The last part of these reflections and quotations that follow the anecdote about Prior Roger is taken up mainly by a long quotation from a letter of St Augustine as enshrined in Gratian's *Decretum*.[22] Its subject is the ambitions of monks for clerical office, which Augustine distrusts. Its first appearance in Gerald's works is in a letter to Peter de Leia, bishop of St Davids (1176–98), in the context of an attack on one of his enemies, an *ex-monachus*.[23] It is repeated in his polemical *De invectionibus*, where he discusses episcopal elections in Wales.[24] Thus its appearance in the *Speculum ecclesiae* is its third recycling. The long section about Prior Roger and the Canterbury monk, and its extensive train of reflections and quotations, as found in the *Speculum ecclesiae*, thus contain much material that Gerald had been using and reusing since 1186 or 1187. It is not impossible that another author, writer of the *History*, had then copied it all from the *Speculum* text, and, since it may be the case that the unique manuscript of the *Speculum* is actually from Llanthony,[25] this would make its use by an anonymous writer there a possibility. But the only writer we know for sure who had access to the *Speculum* is Gerald himself.

Another reasonably extensive verbal overlap between Gerald's works and the *History* is curious, not to say bizarre. The *History* describes the sad decline of Prior Roger, who drifted into gluttony and drunkenness before being smitten with a stroke. But his physical ailments did not check his greed and avarice. The author cites a line based on Cicero: 'What greater madness is there, than to seek greater supplies as the journey draws to its end?' ('Que maior amentia, quam cum minus uie restat, plus uiatici quterere?').[26] This entire passage, of paragraph length, also occurs, in exactly the same words, in Gerald's polemical work, *De iure et statu Menevensis ecclesiae* ('On the Rights and Status of the Church of St Davids').[27] But there it refers not to Prior Roger, but to Geoffrey of Henlawe, Roger's physician and successor as prior, and Gerald's successful rival for the see of St Davids. An anonymous writer may have borrowed Gerald's account from the *De iure* and reapplied it to his long dead prior (Geoffrey of Henlawe died in 1215, Prior Roger in or shortly before 1189[28]), or Gerald may have come across the passage in the *History* and lifted it, but an easier solution might be to see the same pen at work in both passages. We know that Gerald was a great recycler of his own words.

Shorter cases of overlap are, in some sense, even more illustrative, because they do not have the narrative attraction of a good anecdote or pen portrait, and are thus less likely to be cases of borrowing by one author from another. For instance, the closing words of the *History*, quoted above, can be set beside a passage from Gerald's *De rebus*:

> *Prius autem quam uel de electione uel de substitutione Galfridi prioris septimi aliquod dicamus, quedam que paulo ante mortem Rogeri prioris de quo scripsimus uel in uita istius Galfridi acciderant, de conflictu paternorum scilicet, non reticenda prosequamur.*
>
> . . .
>
> *But before we say anything about the election or appointment of Geoffrey, the seventh prior, let us follow up certain things that are not to be kept silent, which happened shortly before the death of Prior Roger, of whom we have written, or in the lifetime of this Geoffrey, namely the conflict between the fathers.*[29]

In his *De rebus*, Gerald writes:

> *Prius autem quam uel de obitu Meneuensis episcopi Dauid, uel electione aut alterius substitutione dicamus, quedam que paulo ante acciderant non reticenda prosequemur.*
>
> . . .
>
> *But before we say anything about the death of David the bishop of St Davids, or about the election or appointment of another, let us follow up certain things that are not to be kept silent, which happened shortly before.*[30]

The overlap, indicated by italics, is indisputable. These are not short stock phrases. Either the author of one text had seen the other text and borrowed a fairly complex construction, but not one carrying a great burden of meaning, or the author of the two texts was the same man.

Moving on from similarities of wording to more general resemblances of outlook and theme, one of the parallels that Michael Richter pointed out concerns the description of Llanthony in the *History* and in Gerald's *Itinerarium Kambriae*.[31] Gerald begins with a depiction of the situation of the valley, mentions the decrepit chapel of St Davids there, 'adorned only with woodland moss and ivy' ('musco silvestri solum et hederae nexibus adornata'; compare the *History*'s 'musco et hedera silvestri circumdata'), and then gives an etymological explanation of the place-name.[32] This is exactly how the *History* opens. But the similarities between what Gerald says about Llanthony in the *Itinerarium* and what is said in the *History* go well beyond this. Gerald moves on from the description of the site to lament the fate of the mother house, supplanted by the daughter house at Gloucester on account of 'the opulence of English luxury' ('ob Anglicani luxus opulentiam'), and he recounts the fates of those priors who had oppressed the Welsh house: William, deposed by the brethren and not buried among the priors; Clement, neglectful of discipline and struck by paralysis; Roger, who carried off the books, ornaments and charters from the mother house, likewise paralysed for a long time before his death.[33] Gerald relates the history of the house, from the time of William and Ernisius, under the patronage of Hugh de Lacy, and the foundation of the daughter house by Miles of Gloucester, and then writes a carefully balanced rhetorical contrast of the mother and daughter houses ('Ibi . . . hic; ibi . . . hic'), painting the difference between the bustle and worldliness of the Gloucester house and the devout spirituality of the poor Welsh house. All this fits the tone of the *History* extremely well. One chapter of that work begins by lamenting 'the devastation and despoliation of the mother house' ('de desolatione et spoliatione matricis ecclesie') for the benefit of the daughter house, asking rhetorically, 'who can write about all that comes to mind without sobs and sighs?' ('Sed [Si MS] quis omnia etiam que memorie occurrent sine singultu et suspiriis stilo prosequetur?'),[34] and continuing with a sustained comparison of the two sites: 'the city of Gloucester and the Hatterall Hill, the river Severn and the water of Honddu, the very wealthy English and the very poor Welsh; there fertile fields, here barren woodlands' ('urbem Gloucestrie et montem Hatyre, et fluvium Sabrine et aquam Hodanie, Anglos ditissimos et Walenses pauperrimos; illic agros fertiles, hic saltus steriles').[35] The author describes with outrage how the canons of Llanthony Secunda belittle the mother house, even expressing the wish for it to be swallowed up into the depths, and using it as a kind of retreat home for the older and weaker canons. And, as has been pointed out above, the author is not sparing in his criticisms of the failings of priors William, Clement and Roger. Gerald and the author of the *History* have common ground as champions of Llanthony Prima against Llanthony Secunda.

But, even if they clearly felt that the mother house had been treated very badly by the daughter house, both Gerald and the author of the *History* thought that the Augustinian canons, taken as a whole, were the best of the religious orders. This point comes out strongly early on in the *History*. When the two first hermits in Llanthony are pondering which order to adopt, they decide against the black monks because of their excesses, against the Cistercians because of their aloofness and avarice, and conclude that the Augustinians are the best, because of their charity and their moderate ways. Since they supposedly undertook this selection process after 1108, but in the time of Archbishop Anselm, who died in 1109, it can be given a clear and narrow date in the narrative. The date makes the story impossible, however, since at that time the Cistercians had not yet founded a single daughter house, let alone one in England or Wales. The author clearly wanted to use the story to praise the Augustinian canons for their ideal moderate way, neither self-indulgent like the Benedictines nor grasping like the Cistercians, and he did not let a minor issue like anachronism inhibit him. Likewise, in his account of Llanthony in the *Itinerarium*, Gerald of Wales singles out the Augustinians for their 'moderation and temperance' ('mediocritate ... atque modestia'),[36] contrasting them with the gluttony of the Benedictines and the avarice of the Cistercians, and elsewhere he tells a story about Ranulf de Glanville, chief justiciar of Henry II, in which that great noble makes exactly the same judgements about the religious orders as the two hermits had reportedly done. Wanting to found a monastic house, Glanville rejected the black monks as 'too devoted to their bellies' ('ventri ... nimis addictos'), the Cistercians as 'too grasping and self-seeking' ('nimis cupidos et ambitiosos'), and eventually chose the Augustinians, 'more moderate than the rest' ('caeteris ... modestiorem').[37] Both Gerald and the author of the *History* are thus clear about the virtues and the failings of these three orders, and employ narratives that show protagonists choosing between them, on identical grounds.

The preface to the *History* also throws light on its author. Although Michael Richter thought that at least the last chapters of the *History* were written 'by a member of the Llanthony community',[38] the author of the preface says he is writing 'at the request of certain (of the) brethren' ('rogatu quorundam fratrum'),[39] a phrase that distances him from the canons of Llanthony, rather than identifying him with them. When Gerald wrote saints' Lives for St Davids and for Hereford, communities of which he was a member, he identified those who had requested his works as 'fellow canons' ('concanonici').[40] The author of the *History* gives no such grounds for seeing him as a member of the community for which he is writing.

The classical allusions in the preface are also revealing. Almost the first words of the preface are a quotation from Horace, lamenting the passage of time:

> multa ferunt anni venientes commoda se cum,
> multa recedentes adimunt.
>
> . . .
>
> many blessings do the advancing years bring with them;
> many, as they retire, they take away.[41]

Exactly these words are cited by Gerald in the *Itinerarium Kambriae*.[42] They are by no means a standard citation of the period.[43] A few lines later, the author says it is proper and useful to produce writing in praise of our holy predecessors, so that 'through common exercise each may read it again and again and thumb it over' ('lectitet teratque uiritim puplicus usus').[44] This is again a quotation from Horace,[45] which is also found in several of Gerald's works, namely, the third edition of the *Topographia Hibernica*, the later editions of the *Expugnatio Hibernica* (and incorporated from these two works into his anthology, the *Symbolum electorum*), the *Gemma ecclesiastica*, and the Letter to the Chapter of Hereford.[46] All these can be dated to the 1190s, except the last, but in this case Gerald explicitly says he is quoting from the *Gemma*. As in the previous case, this is not a common quotation.[47]

The overall structure of the preface of the *History* is as follows. The author has contemplated the wonderful devotion of the fathers of old. The moderns (*moderni*) can scarcely be compared with the men of old (*antiqui*), but it is proper to record the praises of those past heroes as an example and from gratitude.[48] However, nowadays the illiterate despise literature and envy is everywhere. Nevertheless, the author is going to write the history of Llanthony 'in scholastic speech' ('scolastico sermone'), as Gerald of Wales rewrote the Life of St David 'in scholastic style' ('scholastico . . . stilo').[49] He will tell the story from the first settlement down to his own times, as he has learned it from the mouths of the elders or certain writings. He is 'a most diligent investigator' ('diligentissimus inuestigator').[50] If anyone should ask how he dares to narrate things he has not seen, then there is the example of Mark and Luke, who recorded in the Gospels what they had heard rather than what they had seen. It is much more profitable that the author should tell the truth, even if in a rough style, than that someone else should compose arbitrary falsehoods. Since he is writing this at the request of some of the brethren, he earnestly entreats that his little work 'may be strengthened by the authority of all of them against the poisonous cunning of those who suppress and falsify' ('auctoritate circa uirulentam suppressorum et falsariorum astuciam efflagito roborari').[51] It may be a matter of subjective judgement, but this distinctive mixture of boasting, defensiveness and paranoia seems absolutely characteristic of Gerald's mind.

The unprinted chapters, *De prelatis* and *De subditis*, on the duties of superiors and subjects, also have a strongly personal and opinionated tone.[52] In a fine example of apophasis or *praeteritio*, the author says that he will not mention the vices of the secular clergy, their simony, illiteracy, disorder, greed and lust, but concentrate on those living in religious houses. As might be expected, these two chapters contain several references to passages of scripture, but they are also sprinkled with citations from the Roman poets Horace, Ovid, Persius and

Statius (one of the quotations from Horace in these chapters appears in exactly the same form in the *Itinerarium Kambriae*).[53] The author is well informed about the dynamics of religious communities, especially their failings, but does not write as if he were himself a member of one. He pictures those coming to the monastic life who have earlier held important secular office or been renowned in the schools, and their envy when they see others being asked for advice and counsel, since they seem to themselves to be wiser than all the rest. If they do eventually attain the headship of the community, they disdain the food, repose and clothing of the other brethren, demand better food, longer sleep and more delicate clothes, and spend their time in their private chamber and bedroom rather than in the common refectory and dormitory. The great monastic founders like St Benedict, writes our author, were satisfied with hair-shirts and sheepskins, unlike modern superiors, with their vanities and their concern for external things.

The subjects (*subditi*) do not come out much better. They may enter the religious life with good intentions, but become resentful and recalcitrant when they are issued with commands or prohibitions, and mutter against their superiors and can only be brought very unwillingly to obedience. Some are interested only in food, sending the servants out in pursuit of delicacies; some are too concerned with warm clothing; some gossip about others, reproaching the virtuous for pride and deriding the humble. Many are ambitious for external office, undervaluing the benefits of life within the cloister and willingly becoming entangled with the litigation and troubles of the outside world. 'But', the author concludes this chapter,

> if I were to discuss one by one both the things I have briefly touched upon here and the things that I have refrained from treating, the brief space of this little book would extend into great prolixity and perhaps indignation might be stirred up against me rather than charity.
>
> ...
>
> Verum si tam ea que hic breviter tetigi, tam ea que breviter tangere dissimulavi, singillatim digererem, libelli huius brevitas in amplam extenderetur prolixitatem et fortassis cicius michi indignacio quam karitas oriretur.[54]

Gerald of Wales is well known as a critic of monks.[55] The *Speculum ecclesiae*, a work of his last years already mentioned, surviving in one, fire-damaged manuscript, is dedicated to a prolonged critique of the Benedictines and Cistercians, with short passages on some of the other orders (Gilbertines, Carthusians and Grandmontines) whose austerity serves to highlight the failings of the two major monastic orders. The work exhibits a special concern with the infringement of the command not to eat meat.[56] The Augustinians are praised for their moderation in this respect: 'St Augustine allowed his canons, and those in the Order that he instituted for clerics so honourably and so moderately, to eat meat three times a week in the common refectory' ('Augustinus canonicis suis et in ordine tam honesto tamque modesto clericaliter ab ipso institutis, ter in hebdomada . . . in refectoriis etiam publicis, discrete quidem uti carnibus indulsit').[57] This moderation is, in Gerald's view, preferable to a more extreme austerity that is actually continually being infringed and subverted. The eating of meat was a subject also given concentrated treatment in the *History of Llanthony Priory*, since one of the chapter headings (the chapter itself is missing) is 'Concerning the eating of meat' ('De esu carnium'). Unfortunately we do not know what the author had to say on the topic.

All these points mean that the hypothesis of Gerald's authorship of the *History* is not improbable. There are, however, two objections that could be raised against Gerald's authorship. The first concerns the list of chapter headings that precedes the work. This contains not only headings for the extant material but also headings for chapters that presumably once existed in the exemplar of the text. These include chapters dealing with the ninth to fourteenth priors of Llanthony Prima. They can be roughly dated as follows:

> De Rogero de Godest' priore nono [occurs 1209, 1211x1213].
> De Waltero priore decimo [occurs 1224].
> De Stephano priore undecimo.
> De Phillippo priore duodecimo.
> De Dauid priore decimo tercio.
> De Thome priore quartodecimo [1242x1253].
>
> . . .
>
> On Roger of Godest', the ninth prior
> On Walter, the tenth prior
> On Stephen, the eleventh prior
> On Phillip, the twelfth prior
> On David, the thirteenth prior
> On Thomas, the fourteenth prior.[58]

The conclusion of the work with Prior Thomas in the mid-thirteenth century fits well with the dating of the script of the manuscript to the later part of that century.[59] The existence of a version of the *History* that extended to the middle of the thirteenth century, when Gerald was long dead, does not, however, constitute a definitive objection to the idea of his authorship. This is for two reasons. First, it is well known that monastic histories were very frequently compiled over long periods of time by different authors. The 'Deeds of the Abbots of St Albans' ('Gesta abbatum monasterii sancti Albani'), for example, which goes under the name of Thomas Walsingham and was produced in the 1390s, is actually a layer cake, in which Walsingham used earlier historians, Matthew Paris down to 1255 and then an anonymous continuator down to 1308, before launching into his own composition to cover the years 1308–93.[60] The text appears continuous, with each abbot numbered, from Willegod, first abbot, to Thomas de la Mare, the thirtieth abbot, but it is a compilation. The fact that Matthew Paris drew on earlier sources, and that Walsingham's work was subsequently continued down to 1411, simply underlines the point about multiple authorship and the common practice of continuing earlier works of monastic history. A text composed by Gerald could certainly have been continued at Llanthony by a writer or writers of a subsequent generation.

But a more telling point than this generality is that there is some evidence, in the text of the *History* as we have it, of a date of composition in Gerald's lifetime. The author refers to oral sources (*seniorum relatione*) in his preface, and says that the spiritual qualities of Prior Clement, who died between 1167 and 1174, are attested by 'the elders who are yet alive' ('seniores qui adhuc supersunt'),[61] thus implying a date of composition at the very end of the twelfth century or during the first quarter of the thirteenth, and certainly ruling out the mid-thirteenth century. Moreover, the incident involving Prior Roger and the Canterbury monk, which must date to the 1170s or 1180s, is described as happening 'in these our days' ('hiis nostris diebus').[62]

The second objection to Gerald's authorship will also involve some consideration of the date of the text. Gerald is famous for not hiding his light under a bushel, yet nowhere does he mention authorship of the *History*, either when talking of Llanthony in his other works, or in the list of his writings that he sent to the Chapter of Hereford.[63] Since it includes the *Speculum ecclesiae*, this list must date from the last few years of Gerald's life, as the *Speculum* was finished after 1219 and Gerald was dead by 1223. Clearly, one implication of claiming that Gerald wrote the *History* is that it dates from this period. This would harmonise with the fact that two of the most striking parallels between Gerald's texts and the *History*, the anecdote about Prior Roger and the story of Ranulf de Glanville choosing the Augustinians, concern the *Speculum ecclesiae*, a work of these years. If that is the case, the *History* was Gerald's last work. We know that he died in, or in close proximity to, the diocese of Hereford, since it was the dean of Hereford who undertook the task of informing relevant authorities of his death.[64] Llanthony is fifteen miles or so from Hereford. Perhaps that is where Gerald spent his last days.

In summary, we can say that the author of the *History* was an educated, if somewhat cantankerous, cleric of the late twelfth or early thirteenth century, who had ties of affection with Llanthony Prima, and compared Llanthony Secunda unfavourably with it. This description fits Gerald perfectly. The author was able to cite freely from several works of Gerald of Wales and used many of the same classical and legal quotations in exactly the same phrasing. He had precisely the same views about the different religious orders as Gerald, and illustrated them with similar stories. It is, of course, possible that all this was true of an anonymous author, but a strong case can be made that the *History of Llanthony Priory* is a late work by Gerald of Wales.

## Notes

1   The former text is edited by Henry Wharton, *Anglia sacra*, 2/2 (London, 1691), pp. 295–321 (omitting the miracles), and by B. J. Parkinson, 'The Life of Robert de Béthune by William de Wycombe: Translation with Introduction and Notes' (unpublished BLitt thesis, University of Oxford, 1951), the latter by Diana B. Tyson, 'A Medieval Genealogy of the Lords of Brecknock', *Nottingham Medieval Studies*, 48 (2004), 1–14.

2   William Dugdale, *Monasticon Anglicanum*, 3/2 (original edition, London, 1661), pp. 58–66; 6/1 (new edition, London, 1846), pp. 128–34, no. i; Dugdale's text was translated by Robert Atkyns, *The Ancient and Present State of Gloucestershire*, 2/1 (London, 1712), pp. 502–14.

3   Michael Richter, 'Giraldus Cambrensis and Llanthony Priory', *Studia Celtica*, 12–13 (1977–8), 118–32.

4   *History*, fol. 37; Dugdale, *Monasticon Anglicanum*, 6/1, p. 130. All translations are my own unless otherwise noted.

5   See, in general on this phenomenon, Jane Herbert, 'The Transformation of Hermitages into Augustinian Priories in Twelfth-Century England', in W. J. Sheils (ed.), *Monks, Hermits and the Ascetic Tradition*, Studies in Church History 22 (Oxford, 1985), pp. 131–45 (she mentions Gerald's account but not the *History*).

6   *History*, fol. 43v; Dugdale, *Monasticon Anglicanum*, 6/1, p. 131.

7   *History*, fol. 43v; Dugdale, *Monasticon Anglicanum*, 6/1, p. 131; Phillipians 2:15.

8   *History*, fol. 45r; Dugdale, *Monasticon Anglicanum*, 6/1, p. 132.

9   On the general history of the priory, see Arlene Hogan, *The Priory of Llanthony Prima and Secunda in Ireland, 1172–1541: Lands, Patronage and Politics* (Dublin, 2008); David H. Williams, 'Llanthony Prima Priory', *The Monmouthshire Antiquary*, 25–6 (2009–10), 13–50; Janet Burton and Karen Stöber, *Abbeys and Priories of Medieval Wales* (Cardiff, 2015), pp. 128–34, all with further bibliography.

10  See Richard Sharpe, *A Handlist of the Latin Writers of Great Britain and Ireland before 1540* (Turnhout, 1997), s.n. 'Clement.'

11  *History*, fol. 53r–v.

12  *Itinerarium*, i.3, pp. 37–47.

13  *Symbolum electorum, Epistolae*, xvi–xvii, pp. 245–8.

14  *Speculum duorum, Epistolae*, vii, p. 258; it is not clear whether Llanthony Prima or Secunda is meant, since the reference is to the office of Geoffrey of Henlawe, who was prior before the two houses were formally separated in 1205.

15  Michael Richter, *Giraldus Cambrensis: The Growth of the Welsh Nation* (Aberystwyth, 1972), pp. 67, 79–80, 83, n. 7; Yves Lefèvre and R. B. C. Huygens (eds), Brian Dawson (trans.) and Michael Richter (gen. ed.), *Giraldus Cambrensis: Speculum Duorum, or A Mirror of Two Men, Preserved in the Vatican Library in Rome, Cod. Reg. Lat. 470* (Cardiff, 1974), pp. lvi–lvii; Richter, 'Giraldus Cambrensis and Llanthony Priory'.

16  *Speculum ecclesiae*, ii.26, pp. 81–4.

17  *Speculum duorum*, p. lvi.

18  *Speculum duorum*, p. lvi, n. 155.

19   Richter, 'Giraldus Cambrensis and Llanthony Priory', 124.

20   *Topographia*, iii.29–30, pp. 175–7.

21   *De rebus*, ii.14, pp. 69–71.

22   Augustine, *Epistola* 60, in A. Goldbacher (ed.), *Augustinus, Epistulae 31–123*, Corpus Scriptorum Ecclesiasticorum Latinorum, 34/2 (Vienna, 1898), p. 221; Emil Friedberg (ed.), *Corpus Iuris Canonici, Pars Prior: Decretum Magistri Gratiani* (2nd edition, Graz, 1959), 2.16.1.36, col. 770.

23   *Symbolum electorum, Epistolae*, vii, p. 224.

24   *De invectionibus*, v.6, p. 187.

25   Oxford, Bodleian Library, MS Twyne 22, pp. 162–7, cited in N. R. Ker, *Medieval Libraries of Great Britain* (2nd edition, London, 1964), p. 112.

26   *History*, fol. 52v; *De iure*, vii, p. 355; quoting Cicero, *De senectute*, 18.66, in William Armistead Falconer (ed. and trans.), *De senecutute, De amicitia, De divinatione*, Loeb Classical Library 154 (Cambridge, 1923).

27   *De iure*, vii, pp. 354–5.

28   David Knowles, C. N. L. Brooke and Vera C. M. London (eds), *The Heads of Religious Houses: England and Wales, 1 (940–1216)* (2nd edition, Cambridge, 2001), p. 172.

29   *History*, fol. 53r–v.

30   *De rebus*, i.7, p. 40.

31   Richter, 'Giraldus Cambrensis and Llanthony Priory', 120.

32   *Itinerarium*, i.3, p. 37; Dugdale, *Monasticon Anglicanum*, 6/1, p. 129.

33   *Itinerarium*, i.3, pp. 38–40, at 38.

34   *History*, fol. 46v; Dugdale, *Monasticon Anglicanum*, 6/1, p. 133.

35   *History*, fol. 46v.

36   *Itinerarium*, i.3, pp. 46–7.

37   *Speculum ecclesiae*, iii.19, p. 244.

38   'Giraldus Cambrensis and Llanthony Priory', 123.

39   'I have published this little work at the request of certain (of the) brethren' ('hoc opusculum rogatu quorundam fratrum edidi'), *History*, fol. 31v.

40   Gerald says he writes the Life of St David 'conquered by the insistence of my brethren and fellow-canons' ('fratrum tamen et concanonicorum uictus instantia'), and the Life of St Ethelbert, patron of Hereford, 'at the insistence of our fellow canons' ('concanonicorum nostrorum instantia'): *Vita Davidis*, 'Praefatio', p. 377; *Vita Ethelberti*, §19 (xviii), p. 236.

41   *History*, fol. 31; Horace, *Ars poetica*, lines 175–6, in H. Rushton Fairclough (ed. and trans.), *Horace. Satires, Epistles and Ars Poetica* (Cambridge, 1978), pp. 464–5.

42   *Itinerarium*, i.8, p. 74.

43   The Brepols Cross Database Searchtool lists only Horace, Gerald and the *History*.

44   *History*, fol. 31r.

45   Horace, *Epistolae*, ii.1.92: 'legeret tereretque viritim publicus usus', in Fairclough (ed. and trans.), *Horace*, p. 404.

46   *Topographia*, ii, 'Praefatio', p. 76; *Expugnatio*, 'Introitus', p. 8 n.; *Symbolum electorum*, Cambridge, Trinity College MS R. 7. 11, fols 75, 77; *Gemma ecclesiastica*, 'Praefatio', p. 5; *Epistola ad capitulum*, i.409–19, p. 419.

47   Again, the Brepols Cross Database Searchtool lists only Horace, Gerald and the *History*.

48   *History*, fol. 31r.

49   *History*, fol. 31r; *Vita Davidis*, 'Praefatio', p. 377.

50   *History*, fol. 31v.

51   *History*, fol. 31v.

52   *History*, fols 37v–41.

53   *History*, fol. 38; *Itinerarium*, i.4, p. 50: 'ridendo dicere verum quis vetat?'; compare Horace, *Saturae*, i.1.24: 'quamquam ridentem dicere verum quid vetat?' ('what is to prevent one from telling the truth as he laughs?') in Fairclough (ed. and trans.), *Horace*, pp. 6–7.

54   *History*, fols 40v–41r.

55   See Brian Golding, 'Gerald of Wales and the Monks', *Thirteenth-Century England*, 5 (1993), 53–64; 'Gerald of Wales and the Cistercians', *Reading Medieval Studies*, 21 (1995), 5–30.

56   For example, *Speculum ecclesiae*, ii.31, 34; iii.13, pp. 98–100, 113, 208–19.

57   *Speculum ecclesiae*, ii.31, p. 99.

58   *History*, fol. 32r.

59   The dating is based upon the opinion of Ludwig Bieler: Richter, 'Giraldus Cambrensis and Llanthony Priory', 118, n. 3.

60   H. T. Riley (ed.), *Gesta abbatum monasterii sancti Albani*, 3 vols (London, 1867–9); on the composition of the text see John Taylor, *English Historical Literature in the Fourteenth Century* (Oxford, 1987), pp. 70–3.

61   *History*, fol. 49v.

62   *History*, fol. 51r.

63   *Epistola ad capitulum*.

64   W. P. W. Phillimore and F. N. Davis (eds), *Rotuli Hugonis de Welles episcopi Lincolniensis, A.D. MCCIX–MCCXXXV*, 4/2 (London, 1907), pp. 9–10.

❖

# SIX

# The Early Manuscripts of Gerald of Wales

Catherine Rooney
*University of Cambridge*

I N MY PHD DISSERTATION, I identified 100 manuscripts containing works of Gerald of Wales, including extracts, translations, and incomplete and mutilated copies.[1] Of these, twenty-two manuscripts are datable, on palaeographical grounds, within Gerald's lifetime.[2] Moreover, several of these manuscripts, it has been suggested, were produced and kept close to Gerald himself.[3] I will look at aspects of the manuscripts that might connect them either to each other or to Gerald, to see what conclusions may be drawn about the production and early transmission of Gerald's works. There are a number of other features in the early manuscripts that may point to connections between them. I shall first consider the varied forms of decoration, and then look at details of text and layout, finishing with the script itself.

Two manuscripts contain a series of marginal illustrations to *Topographia Hibernica*: London, British Library, Royal MS 13 B. viii[4] and Dublin, National Library of Ireland, MS 700.[5] The illustrations in both manuscripts are very similar and are thought to have derived from the same original series.[6] Nigel Morgan has wondered whether the illustrations in NLI 700 were 'possibly from the same workshop [as Royal 13 B. viii] but a slightly later product';[7] A. B. Scott has gone further and asserted 'It seems clear that those in I [NLI 700] are crude copies of the originals in R [Royal 13 B. viii] . . . In general the execution of the pictures in R is vastly superior to what we see in I, particularly as regards their firmness of line.'[8] However, Michelle Brown has asserted that the illustrations in NLI 700 represent an earlier phase in the development of the programme of illustration than those in Royal 13 B. viii.[9]

As to whether the illustrations can be connected to Gerald himself, according to A. B. Scott,

> the illustrations are most definitely the work of someone who knew Ireland, and the dress and appearance of the Irish, or else had them described to him in some detail. For there is nothing in the text of the *Expugnatio* or the *Topographia* to suggest to the illustrator what kind of dress was worn in Ireland.[10]

Nigel Morgan has also suggested that 'very possibly the original versions of the subjects were sketches by Giraldus himself'.[11]

Some of the early manuscripts contain another type of decoration in the form of a map. Cambridge, Corpus Christi College MS 400 [B] (on the verso of the leaf preceding fol. 1),[12] London, British Library, Additional MS 33991 (26r), London, British Library, Arundel MS 14 (27v) and Paris, Bibliothèque nationale de France, MS lat. 4846[13] (63r) each contain a map of the British Isles; all these maps follow exactly the same form. East is at the top and Britain, Ireland and the Orkneys are shown in green with a red or brown border. Britain is carrot-shaped, Ireland is kidney-shaped and the Orkneys are round or oval. The words BRITANNIA, HYBERNIA and ORCADES are in red or blue capitals; AUSTER is to the bottom-right of Britain, and between Britain and Ireland and to the top-left of the Orkneys is AQUILO. The similarity between the four copies of this map is so great that there can be little doubt that they were copied either from the same original or from each other.

There is also a more detailed map of Europe in NLI 700 (48r), which was discussed by Thomas O'Loughlin.[14] He thinks this map originated in Gerald's circle and that he was involved in its production. Certainly we know that Gerald was interested in maps, as in one of his letters he describes a map of Wales, 'constructed with a wealth of detail and craftsmanship' ('copiosa pariter et artificiosa sumptuositate constructis'), which was attached to a copy of *Descriptio Kambriae*: 'It was confined to a single folio, and although the details were very minutely planned and in the most narrow space, yet they were distinct and clear' ('arcto folio, strictoque ualde locello et spatio breuissimo, distincte tamen et aperte declaraui').[15] Sadly there is no such map surviving among the early manuscripts. Although the crude maps accompanying copies of *Topographia Hibernica* do not much resemble this description, it at least suggests that Gerald is a possible source of maps in the early manuscripts.[16]

In most of the early manuscripts, major sections of the text begin with initials decorated with flourishes. These can be either red and green or red and blue, with the initial in one colour and the flourishes in the other. However, there is a group of six manuscripts with a richer style of decoration: initials set in square frames, in gold leaf, pink, blue and white, and either historiated or decorated with scrolls and zoomorphic ornament.[17] Of particular note in this group are CCCC 400 [B] and Oxford, Bodleian Library, MS Rawlinson B. 483, both containing the second edition of *Topographia Hibernica*.[18] Unfortunately all but two of the major initials are now missing from Rawlinson B. 483, but the **D** at the beginning of Book III (17v: Fig. 1b) bears a very close resemblance to the corresponding initial in CCCC 400 [B] (31v). In both manuscripts it contains a picture of people in a boat, with the person at the front of the boat stepping out of it and pointing, and the person at the back wearing a hood. These people were presumably meant to represent the inhabitants of Ireland whose history and customs are discussed in Book III. In BNF lat. 4846 the initials are decorated with scrolls, either zoomorphic or decorated with leaf-like shapes. In CCCC 390[19] and 425[20] the initials are decorated with pictures of the men whose history is recounted in the text (Archbishop Geoffrey of York and various bishops of Lincoln).

Gold-leaf decoration was expensive, technically demanding and unusual in manuscripts of this type of work. I have not seen any contemporary manuscripts of the works of, for example, William of Malmesbury, Geoffrey of Monmouth or Henry of Huntingdon that are so richly decorated. Maps and marginal illustrations were also rare.[21] Gerald dedicated certain editions of his works to bishops (William de Longchamp, William de Vere, Hugh of Avalon), archbishops (Baldwin, Hubert Walter, Stephen Langton), kings (Henry II, Richard I, John) and even a pope (Innocent III).[22] These unusually richly decorated manuscripts may have been presentation copies – which would in principle originate with the author.

I shall now move on from decorative aspects of the manuscripts to discuss aspects of the layout of the text. The texts of these manuscripts offer some small evidence of connections between them. According to James Dimock, the editor of the Rolls Series edition of *Topographia Hibernica*, the texts of two manuscripts, Oxford, Bodleian Library, MS Rawlinson B. 188 and London, British Library, Royal MS 13 B. viii, are very closely related, sharing many distinctive readings.[23] Dimock did not think that either of the two manuscripts was copied from the other,[24] but A. B. Scott, the editor of a more recent version of *Expugnatio Hibernica*, has suggested that the original text of Royal 13 B. viii (R) could have been copied from Rawlinson B. 188 (B): 'I can find nowhere in the text where B has a mistake or even a variant that is not echoed in . . . the original text of R . . . Dimock does not appear to have noticed many of these, which are made over erasures.'[25] None of the other manuscripts have been thought by editors of Gerald's works to be either exemplar or copy of another.

Several of the early manuscripts have a very consistent layout. Sections of the text are marked with a hierarchy of initials: large elaborate ones for major sections and smaller, more simply decorated or plain ones for chapters. Chapters begin with a chapter heading in red ink. In fourteen of the early manuscripts (listed in Table 1) there is also a chapter list at the beginning of the text. Michelle Brown saw this 'remarkable adherence to consistent chapter divisions and headings' as an 'indication of Gerald's personal involvement in establishing the layout of the text'.[26]

Some manuscripts have more sophisticated aids to negotiating the text. Eleven manuscripts have running titles at the top of each page (and the practice of trimming books for rebinding may mean that others originally had them, but they have been cut off). These usually take the form of a **D** (*Distinctio*) or **L** (*Liber*) on one page of an opening, and the number of the book or section on the other page. Four manuscripts (CCCC 425, NLI 700, Cambridge, Trinity College MS R. 7. 11[27] and London, Lambeth Palace Library, MS 236) have numbers beside chapter headings in the chapter list which are answered beside the same heading in the text.[28] The occurrence of these features is shown in Table 1.

These practices were not particularly common at this time – even amongst the early manuscripts of Gerald's works. Richard and Mary Rouse have said that the use of the arrangement and appearance of the page as an aid to finding particular parts of the text began in the mid- to late twelfth century: 'the need for artificial devices became crucial only with the growth of the schools and, especially, with the emerging prominence of theology at Paris in the course of the twelfth century.'[29] Gerald liked to recommend certain parts of his works, so perhaps he would have thought aids to negotiating the text useful – and he was a scholar at Paris, so he had the opportunity to acquire the habit of using them.

Thirteen of the early manuscripts contain significant additions to the text – not merely corrections of scribal errors, but alterations which advance the text from one 'edition' to another. Mostly these additions are in the margin of the page, but sometimes the additions are so large that they are on separate sheets or slips of parchment inserted into the manuscript rather than in the margins. The most extreme example of this is Rome, Biblioteca Apostolica Vaticana, MS Reg. Lat. 470, which contains numerous additions both marginal and on inserted sheets of various sizes, which in their turn have marginal additions. This has led Yves Lefèvre to describe this manuscript as the author's 'working copy' ('brouillon').[30] In all manuscripts with these additions, they were made by the same scribe who wrote the main text, or a contemporary. The additions also share some physical features: a red line, sometimes straight, sometimes wavy, along two or more sides of the block of text, and the use of a similar repertoire of *signes de renvoi*. These similarities reinforce the impression of a common origin – the most obvious origin for such additions being the author himself.

The final aspect of the early manuscripts that I shall consider, and the most significant in terms of establishing a common origin for manuscripts, is the script itself. I have identified five hands which, together, can connect nine of the early manuscripts to a common place of origin.

**Hand 1** is found in four manuscripts. In both CCCC 390 and BNF lat. 4846 it is the only hand in the main text and the additions. In TCC R. 7. 11 it is one of three hands and is found in both the main text and additions (Fig. 1a). In CCCC 400 [B] it is only found in marginal additions, on an inserted sheet, and in an addition at the end of the text (a letter to William de Vere, bishop of Hereford 1186–99, recommending certain passages of *Topographia Hibernica* for his special attention). This is a round, but rather uncertain-looking hand, as may be seen (for example) in 'broken-backed' **c** and **e**. Its distinguishing feature is the addition of small forks at the tops of ascenders – not a widening and splitting of the ascender, as commonly occurs, but two separate strokes added at the top. It also has an eight-shaped **g** with a curved tail closed with a fine straight separate stroke (e.g. BNF lat. 4846, 32r, b16, *ergo*; CCCC 400[B], 22v, lower margin, line 2, *gignitur*, Fig. 1a, line 7, *gaudens*), and has the uncrossed form of *et*-nota (e.g. Fig. 1a, line 2; CCCC 390, p. 7, b11; CCCC 400 [B], 22v, lower margin, line 3; BNF lat. 4846, 32r, b5).

**Hand 2** is found in the main text and some marginal additions in CCCC 400 [B], and is the only hand in Rawlinson B. 483 (Fig. 1b). It is a small and rather narrow hand. Its most distinctive feature is a round **d** with an extended ascender at the beginning of lines (e.g. Fig. 1b, line 10; CCCC 400 [B], 31v, a13, a15, b19 and b23); there are also extended descenders on the bottom line and extended ascenders on the top line of some pages (e.g. CCCC 400 [B], 23v, a1, *cuius*; Rawlinson B. 483, 14r, b1, *Brigida locum illustrauerat*). It also features a variant form of **a** with an extended top stroke (throughout the text, not only on the top line) (e.g. Fig. 1b, line 20, *tam*). These two manuscripts have other similarities: very similar initials (as discussed above), the same number of lines per page (thirty-six), a written space of almost exactly the same dimensions (CCCC 400 [B]: 170 x 105mm and Rawlinson B. 483: 170 x 100mm) and a large number of red and blue paraphs (¶) in their texts, a feature not extensively used in the other early manuscripts. I am almost certain that these two manuscripts were made, if not by the same person, at least in the same place.

**Hand 3** is the only hand in CCCC 425. It is also to be found on pp. 1–16 of CCCC 400 [D], and is one of many hands to be found in Biblioteca Apostolica Vaticana Reg. Lat. 470 (Fig. 2). The most distinctive feature of this hand is the *est* abbreviation (÷), which has a small dished stroke above the line instead of the usual dot, and a comma-like mark below the line (e.g. Fig. 2, line 13; CCCC 400 [D], p. 9, b3; CCCC 425, p. 46, b2). It also has **q** with 'horns' on top of the bowl (e.g. Fig. 2, line 1, *tanquam*), and a small, usually uncrossed *et*-nota (e.g. Fig. 2, line 5; CCCC 400 [D], p. 9, b3; CCCC 425, p. 46, b11). R. M. Loomis, the editor of Gerald's Life of Hugh of Avalon, noted the similarity between the hand of CCCC 425 and that in Reg. Lat. 470 (containing *Speculum duorum*): 'The script shows similarities to that in Figure 3 of the introduction to *Speculum Duorum* (*SD* lxii), and it is possible that the same scribe copied this portion of the *Speculum Duorum* (folio 69 recto) and the *Vita Sancti Hugonis*.'[31]

**Hand 4** is found in the main text of and one marginal addition to TCC R. 7. 11; in most of the additions to NLI 700 (including additions in the margin, on inserted sheets and after the end of the main text); and in both the main text of and additions to Reg. Lat. 470 (Fig. 3a). Its most distinctive features are split-topped, almost 'dished' tops to ascenders and minim-strokes (e.g. Fig. 3a, line 4, *Wallia*; NLI 700, 97r, b14, *gloriamque*); a crossed and quite large *et*-nota with a wavy headstroke (e.g. Fig. 3a, lines 2–5; NLI 700, 94r, lower margin, line 2; Reg. Lat. 470, 84r, a19–22); and an *est* abbreviation with a short horizontal stroke and a long-tailed, angular comma below it (e.g. Fig. 3a, line 9; NLI 700, 69r, a35; Reg. Lat. 470, 84r, a27).[32]

**Hand 5** is found in the main text of and one marginal addition to TCC R. 7. 11 (Fig. 3b) and in the main text of NLI 700. Its most distinctive features are the elaboration of certain letters when they occur at the beginning of a word or line, namely a horizontal 'ascender' of **d** extending into the margin – not an unusual feature in itself, but in these two manuscripts *Ad* at the beginning of a line is written with horizontal 'ascender' of **d** crossing the preceding **a** (e.g. Fig. 3b, line 11; NLI 700, 54r, b1). The letter **v** at the beginning of a line or word also has a horizontal extension to the left with an upwards flick at the end (e.g. TCC R. 7. 11, 71r, lines 28 and 31; NLI 700, 54r, a19). Other distinctive letter-forms include a tall initial **P** with a pointed top (e.g. TCC R. 7. 11, 59v, b23, *Populus*; NLI 700, 49v, b24, *Portentum*); and a 2-shaped initial **Q** (e.g. TCC R. 7. 11, 10r, b15, *Qui*; NLI 700, 62r, a24, *Quod*).

All three of these manuscripts also show similarities in their initials. There is a particular likeness between those of NLI 700 and Reg. Lat. 470: certain examples of **I** (for example NLI 700, 13r, and Reg. Lat. 470, 39v; NLI 700, 40v, and Reg. Lat. 470, 87v) are almost identical. All three manuscripts often have similar infilling of initials, for example **R** (TCC R. 7. 11, 2r), **Q** (NLI 700, 47r) and **D** (Reg. Lat. 470, 2r). The unusual infilling of the major initials in NLI 700[33] is almost exactly the same as that of **C** and **R** in TCC R. 7. 11 (2r and 72r respectively), although in the latter it is rather more crudely drawn.[34] This also suggests a common origin of these manuscripts.

**Hand 6** is found in Lambeth 236 (written in one hand; Fig. 4a) and some pages of London, British Library, Cotton MS Tiberius B. xiii (Fig. 4b). This is a round, somewhat inconsistent hand with short ascenders and descenders. Its most distinctive feature is a variant form of *et*-nota with an extended top-stroke which curls downwards at the end (e.g. Fig. 4a, line 5, and Fig. 4b, line 11). Other distinctive features are the use of both round and straight-backed **d** (e.g. Fig. 4b, line 6, *pedites*) and also a 'falling' **d** (with a long ascender turning down at the end) (e.g. Tiberius B. xiii, 72r, a22, *detestanda*; Lambeth 236, 18va27, *declarauit*); and 'broken' word-final **i** (or the second of two **i**s) with a descender (e.g. Fig. 4a, lines 11–12, *suppliciis*; Fig. 4b, line 5, *spoliati*). In both manuscripts ascenders on the top line are occasionally elongated with looped headstrokes (e.g. Lambeth 236, 121r, a1, *fastidium Drogenes*; Tiberius B. xiii, 67v, b1, *abbates bonos*).

The appearance of the same hand in different manuscripts is an almost certain sign that they were written at the same place. The appearance of several hands in so many of the early manuscripts of Gerald's works means that no less than nine of them may be connected to each other, which is best represented by means of a diagram (see Fig. 5).

Moreover, the sense of a connection between these manuscripts – and some of the other early manuscripts – is strengthened by considering the other aspects I have discussed above. The manuscripts containing marginal additions, those containing chapter numbers, those containing running titles are, for the most part, the same group of manuscripts. Put another way, if a manuscript is to be found in one of the groups with a common element, it is likely to be found in others as well. The aspects of the manuscripts I have discussed above are not particularly distinctive in themselves (and in several cases, for example the presence of a map, a chapter list, running titles, and illustrations are explainable simply by copying rather than by production in the same place). However, the presence of several common elements in the same group of manuscripts strongly suggests a common place of origin for that group. I would therefore suggest that Cotton Domitian A. v, Cotton Tiberius B. xiii, Royal 13 B. viii and Lambeth 236 were produced in the same place as the nine manuscripts which can be connected palaeographically.[35]

The most obvious source of such a large group of manuscripts datable within the author's lifetime is the author himself. However, there are other reasons for linking these manuscripts to Gerald, as I have discussed in more detail above. The possibility of the marginal illustrations in NLI 700 and Royal 13 B. viii originating with Gerald has been acknowledged. The maps, particularly the map of Europe in NLI 700, tie in with Gerald's self-confessed interest in maps. The marginal (and inserted) additions may be seen as a physical manifestation of Gerald's habit of revising and adding to his works. The use of a sophisticated system of aids to negotiate the text may have been employed to help readers find the passages that Gerald was fond of recommending.[36] Gerald could have encountered such aids in the Paris schools, where he studied and they were invented.

A. B. Scott said that 'I must avoid seeming to suggest that almost every early MS. of the two Irish works goes back to Giraldus himself', and I am also wary of doing so.[37] However, I would like, in conclusion, to go back to Gerald, to a letter he wrote to the chapter of Hereford Cathedral around 1218:

> Ad illos tutum habet accessum justa petitio, quorum non ignorantur discretio pariter et eruditio. Rogo itaque quatinus librum nostrum, sc. Ecclesiae Speculum, beato Æthelberto anno jam fere praeterito datum, mihi per hunc clericum praesentium latorem, ad corrigendum adhuc plenius et utilia quaedam locis competentibus adjiciendum, remittere velitis. Memorialem enim interim vobis *Topographiam Hibernicam*, et *Vaticinalis Hybernicae expugnationis Historiam*, opera duo sc. et diversa, sed uno volumine conserta, per eundem destinavi; quem cum melioratum susceperitis, quod in proximo fiet, et emendatum, alium, si placet, remittetis.
>
> . . .
>
> A just request has safe access to those of whom discretion as much as learning is not ignorant. Therefore I ask that you kindly send back our book, namely *Speculum ecclesiae*, to me through this cleric (the bearer of these present things), given to St Æthelbert's in the year now almost past, for correcting still more fully and to add useful things in their proper places. Meanwhile I have sent to you by the same [man] *Topographia Hibernica* and *Vaticinalis Hybernicae expugnationis Historia* in rough form [*or* as a pledge], two different works but kept in one volume, which when you have received improved and emended (which you will soon) please send back the other.[38]

If the author was prepared to go to such lengths as these to make sure that everyone was reading the most up-to-date versions of his works, then suggesting that over half of the manuscripts surviving from his lifetime originated with him does not seem so far-fetched.

❖

## Table 1: Manuscripts

| Manuscript | Gold-leaf initials | Map | Marginal/inserted additions | Chapter list | Running titles | Chapter numbers |
|---|---|---|---|---|---|---|
| **CCCC 390** | X | | X | X | X | |
| **CCCC 400 [B]** | X | X | X | X | X | |
| **CCCC 400 [D]** | X | | X | No chapters | X | |
| **CCCC 425** | X | | X | X | X | x |
| **TCC 5. 7. 11** | | | X | X | X | x |
| CUL Mm.5.30 | | | | X | | |
| Douai 887 | | | | X | | |
| **NLI 700** | | X | X | X | X | x |
| Add. 33991 | | X | | First pages lost | | |
| Add. 34762 | | | | | | |
| Add. 44922 | | | | | | |
| Arundel 14 | | X | | | | |
| Cotton Domitian A. v | | | X | No chapters | X | |
| Cotton Tiberius B. xiii | | | X | X | | A few |
| Royal 13 B. viii | | | X | X | X | |
| Lambeth 236 | | | X | X | X | x |
| Lambeth 371 | | | | X | | |
| Westminster Abbey 23 | | | | X | | |
| Rawlinson B.188 | | | | X | | |
| **Rawlinson B. 483** | X | | X | X | | |
| **BNF lat. 4846** | X | X | X | X | X | |
| **BAV Reg. Lat. 470** | | | X | X | X | |

Manuscripts in **bold** are those that are connected by the presence of one or more common hands, as shown in the diagram in Fig. 5.

## Figure 5

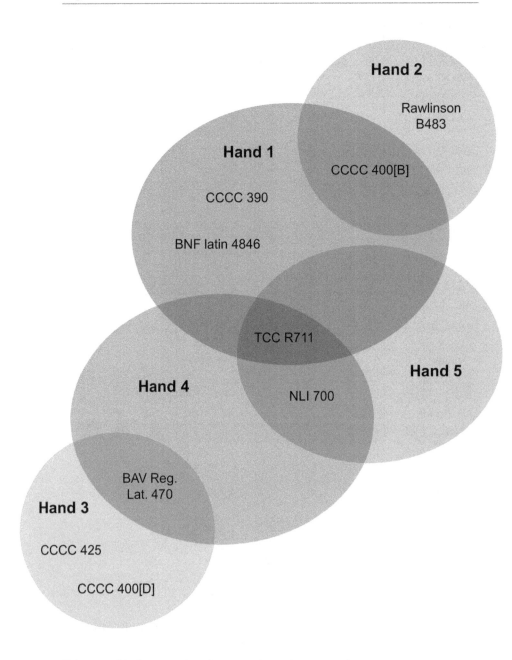

Palaeographical connections between the early manuscripts

## Appendix:
## List of the early manuscripts of the works of Gerald of Wales

1.   Cambridge, Corpus Christi College, 390 (*Vita Galfridi archiepiscopus Eboracensis*)
2.   Cambridge, Corpus Christi College, 400 [B] (*Topographia Hibernica*)
3.   Cambridge, Corpus Christi College, 400 [D] (*De iure et statu Meneuensis ecclesiae*)
4.   Cambridge, Corpus Christi College, 425 (*Vita Sancti Remigii, Vita Sancti Hugonis*)
5.   Cambridge, Trinity College, R. 7. 11 (*Symbolum electorum*)
6.   Cambridge, University Library, Mm. 5. 30 (*Topographia Hibernica*)
7.   Douai, Bibliothèque municipale, 887 (*Topographia Hibernica*)
8.   Dublin, National Library of Ireland, 700 (*Topographia Hibernica, Expugnatio Hibernica*)
9.   London, British Library, Additional 33991 (*Topographia Hibernica*)
10.  London, British Library, Additional 34762 (*Topographia Hibernica, Expugnatio Hibernica, Itinerarium Kambriae*)
11.  London, British Library, Additional 44922 (*Topographia Hibernica*)
12.  London, British Library, Arundel 14 (*Topographia Hibernica*)
13.  London, British Library, Cotton Domitian A. v (*De iure et statu Meneuensis ecclesiae*)
14.  London, British Library, Cotton Tiberius B. xiii (*Speculum ecclesiae, De rebus a se gestis*)
15.  London, British Library, Royal 13 B. viii (*Topographia Hibernica, Expugnatio Hibernica, Itinerarium Kambriae*)
16.  London, Lambeth Palace Library, 236 (*Gemma ecclesiastica*)
17.  London, Lambeth Palace Library, 371 (*Expugnatio Hibernica*)
18.  London, Westminster Abbey, 23 (*Topographia Hibernica*)
19.  Oxford, Bodleian Library, Rawlinson B. 188 (*Topographia Hibernica, Expugnatio Hibernica, Itinerarium Kambriae*)
20.  Oxford, Bodleian Library, Rawlinson B. 483 (*Topographia Hibernica*)
21.  Paris, Bibliothèque nationale de France, latin 4846 (*Topographia Hibernica*)
22.  Rome, Biblioteca Apostolica Vaticana, Reginenses Latini 470 (*De invectionibus, Speculum duorum*)

❖

# Notes

1   I would like to extend my sincerest thanks to Georgia Henley and Joey McMullen of Harvard University, the organisers of 'New Perspectives on Gerald of Wales: Texts and Contexts' (Harvard University, 10–11 April 2015), for inviting me to speak, for their excellent organisation and for their warm welcome. This paper is adapted from chapter 3 of my PhD dissertation, 'The Manuscripts of the Works of Gerald of Wales' (University of Cambridge, 2005). The dissertation is available online at *www.repository.cam.ac.uk/handle/1810/244876* (accessed 25 April 2017).

2   I considered that if a manuscript was written in Protogothic minuscule, it was datable within Gerald's lifetime, as this script was used throughout the twelfth century and was replaced by Textualis (Gothic bookhand) in the early to mid-thirteenth century. See, for example, Albert Derolez, *The Palaeography of Gothic Manuscript Books from the Twelfth to the Early Sixteenth Century* (Cambridge 2003; repr. 2006), p. 72. See Appendix above for a complete list of the early manuscripts. Several of these manuscripts are now available to view online and I have included the web addresses in the notes below.

3   See, for example, J. S. Brewer (ed.), *Giraldi Cambrensis Opera*, 8/2 (London, 1862), p. x; J. F. Dimock (ed.), *Giraldi Cambrensis Opera*, 8/7 (London, 1877), pp. ix–x; A. B. Scott and F. X. Martin (eds and trans.), *Expugnatio Hibernica: The Conquest of Ireland by Giraldus Cambrensis* (Dublin, 1978), p. xlvi.

4   See *www.bl.uk/manuscripts/FullDisplay.aspx?ref=Royal_MS_13_B_VIII* (accessed 25 April 2017): 8v–11v, 16v, 17v–18r, 19r–22r, 23r–v, 26r, 27r–29r and 30r–v.

5   See *www.isos.dias.ie/english/index.html* (accessed 25 April 2017) > Collections > National Library of Ireland > MS 700: 11v–12r, 13r–14v, 23r, 24v–26v, 27v–29v, 31r, 36r, 39r–40r and 42r.

6   There are also portraits of major figures in *Expugnatio Hibernica* in NLI 700 (on 56r, 64v, 71r, 72r, 77v, 78v, 81r and 84v), but they are unique to that manuscript.

7   Nigel Morgan, *Early Gothic Manuscripts 1190–1285*, 2/1 (London, 1982–8), p. 106, no. 59.

8   Scott and Martin (eds and trans.), *Expugnatio Hibernica*, pp. xlvi–xlvii.

9   Michelle Brown, 'Marvels of the West: Giraldus Cambrensis and the Role of the Author in the Development of Marginal Illustration', *English Manuscript Studies 1100–1700*, 10 (2002), 34–59, at 44–5. Her argument is based on a picture of a deer with gold teeth in Royal 13 B. viii, which accompanies a marginal addition; she has taken this to show that 'the cycle of illustration in this copy was being … embroidered and developed' along with the text. However, she has added in support of her argument that NLI 700 is textually earlier than Royal 13 B. viii. In fact the copies of *Topographia Hibernica* in the two manuscripts have the same complicated relationship as that described by Scott for their copies of *Expugnatio Hibernica*, with sometimes one and sometimes the other having the more advanced text.

10   Scott and Martin (eds and trans.), *Expugnatio Hibernica*, p. xliv.

11   Morgan, *Early Gothic Manuscripts*, 2/1, p. 105, no. 59a.

12   CCCC 400 is a composite codex, with five sections, all separately paginated or foliated; for ease of reference, I have called these [A], [B], [C], [D] and [E]. [B], a copy of *Topographia Hibernica*, and [D], a copy of *De iure et statu Meneuensis ecclesiae*, concern me here; [A], [C] and [E] are sixteenth century. See *https://parker.stanford. edu/parker/actions/page_turner.do?ms_no=400* (accessed 25 April 2017).

13   See *http://gallica.bnf.fr/ark:/12148/btv1b8438621m/f1.image.r=latin%204846.langFR* (accessed 25 April 2017).

14   Thomas O'Loughlin, 'An Early Thirteenth-century Map in Dublin: A Window into the World of Giraldus Cambrensis', *Imago Mundi: The International Journal for the History of Cartography*, 51 (1999), 24–39, at 32–3.

15   *Epistola ad capitulum*, pp. 414–15; J. Conway Davies, 'The Kambriae Mappa of Giraldus Cambrensis', *Journal of the Historical Society of the Church in Wales*, 2 (1950), 46–60, at 46.

16   There is also a map of the world in Oxford, Bodleian Library, MS Rawlinson B. 188 (98r); however, this map is of a very different style to the maps in the other early manuscripts, being a simple circle with some English place-names dotted around the middle, and other place-names written in semicircles around the edge. The script on the map is contemporary with, but not in the same hand as, the main text of the manuscript, and I am not sure if there was originally any connection between the manuscript and the map.

17   CCCC 400 [B]; CCCC 400 [D]; Oxford, Bodleian Library, Rawlinson B. 483; BNF lat. 4846; CCCC 390; CCCC 425; i.e. three copies of *Topographia Hibernica*, the Lives of Geoffrey, Hugh and Remigius and *De iure et statu Meneuensis ecclesiae*.

18   See J. F. Dimock (ed.), *Giraldi Cambrensis Opera*, 8/5 (London, 1867), pp. xi–xxviii and xlix–lvi for Dimock's discussion of his division of the *Topographia Hibernica* into 'editions'.

19   See *https://parker.stanford.edu/parker/actions/page_turner.do?ms_no=390* (accessed 25 April 2017): p. 7.

20   See *https://parker.stanford.edu/parker/actions/page_turner.do?ms_no=425* (accessed 25 April 2017): pp. 9, 20, 62 and 73.

21   For example, O'Loughlin, 'An Early Thirteenth-century Map', 24 states, 'no close parallels are known' to the map of Europe in NLI 700. Michelle Brown, 'Marvels of the West', 35, says that, if Gerald was the source of the illustrations in Royal 13 B. viii and NLI 700, 'he deserves to be recognised as a key figure in the perception and development of marginal space as the vehicle for new programmes of illustration: a major contribution to Gothic art' – which suggests that such illustrations were an innovation in Gerald's time.

22   He presented a copy of *Gemma ecclesiastica* to Pope Innocent III – and claimed that the pope kept it by his bedside (*De rebus*, iii.18, p. 119).

23   Dimock (ed.), *Giraldi Cambrensis Opera*, 8/5, p. xxi.

24   Dimock (ed.), *Giraldi Cambrensis Opera*, 8/5, p. xxi: 'The verbal differences . . . are amply sufficient to show that one was not copied from the other.'

25   Scott and Martin (eds and trans.), *Expugnatio Hibernica*, p. xliii.

26   Brown, 'Marvels of the West', 42.

27   See *http://sites.trin.cam.ac.uk/manuscripts/R_7_11/manuscript.php?fullpage=1&starting page=1* (accessed 25 April 2017).

28   There are also a few chapter numbers in London, British Library, Cotton MS Tiberius B. xiii. However, this manuscript is now fire-damaged so it is very difficult to know if it originally had the features mentioned here.

29   Richard H. Rouse and Mary A. Rouse, '*Statim invenire*: Schools, Preachers, and New Attitudes to the Page', in Mary A. Rouse and Richard H. Rouse (eds), *Authentic Witnesses: Approaches to Medieval Texts and Manuscripts* (Notre Dame, 1991), pp. 191–219, at 205–6.

30   Yves Lefèvre and R. B. C. Huygens (eds), Brian Dawson (trans.) and Michael Richter (gen. ed.), *Giraldus Cambrensis: Speculum Duorum, or A Mirror of Two Men, Preserved in the Vatican Library in Rome, Cod. Reg. Lat. 470* (Cardiff, 1974), p. lvii.

31   Richard M. Loomis (ed. and trans.), *The Life of St. Hugh of Avalon, Bishop of Lincoln 1186–2000* (New York, 1985), p. lii.

32   A. B. Scott thought that the additions to NLI 700 were in three different hands (Scott and Martin (eds and trans.), *Expugnatio Hibernica*, p. l), but I am almost sure that what he called I2 and I3 are actually one and the same hand.

33   1r, **C**; 2r, **P**; 3r, **S**; 5r, **P**; 17r, **N**; 32r, **D**; 49r, **Q**; 50r, **P**; 52r, **A**; 53r, **D**; 73v, **H**; 95v, **Q**.

34   See Sonia Scott-Fleming, *The Analysis of Pen Flourishing in Thirteenth-Century Manuscripts* (Leiden, 1989), pp. 44–5, 60, 65–6 and 72–3 for discussions of the features of flourishing shared by the initials in these manuscripts.

35   The position of Rawlinson B. 188 in this scheme remains problematic. Its connection to the manuscripts which I have suggested go back to Gerald depends solely on A. B. Scott's assertion that Royal 13 B. viii was copied from it, as Table 1 shows that it has hardly any of the features suggesting a common origin.

36   See also contributions by Georgia Henley and Caoimhe Whelan in this volume.

37   Scott and Martin (eds and trans.), *Expugnatio Hibernica*, p. xliv.

38   *Epistola ad capitulum*, p. 409; my translation, for which I gratefully acknowledge the help of Dr Neil Wright of the Faculty of History, University of Cambridge.

❖

# SEVEN

# Giraldian Beavers: Revision and the Making of Meaning in Gerald's Early Works

Michael Faletra
*Reed College*

T HE BEAVER CARRIED sufficient enough symbolic weight in the medieval imagination to find its way into Dante's *Commedia*. In describing Geryon, a monstrous figure representing Fraud in *Inferno* 17, Dante writes:

> e come là tra li Tedeschi lurchi
> lo bivero s'assetta a far sua guerra,
> così la fiera pessima si stava
> su l'orlo ch'è di pietra e'l sabbion serra.
>
> . . .
>
> and as among the guzzling Germans
> the beaver sets itself to catch its prey,
> so lay this worst of brutes upon the stony rim
> that makes a boundary for the sandy soil.[1]

For Dante, the beaver's amphibious nature in this simile – a trait well attested by the bestiary tradition and in more scholarly discourses – provides one among a number of literary devices that reinforce both the mimetic verisimilitude of the hybrid and liminal Geryon and, in a broader sense, the duplicity inherent to all forms of fraudulent sin. Dante would probably not be surprised to learn that the beaver had enjoyed a long, if mostly peripheral, literary life in Latin texts from at least Pliny onwards.[2] He may well have been surprised, however, to discover that a twelfth-century, half Norman half Welsh cleric – Gerald of Wales, of course – had already explored the semiotics of the beaver in depth. And although it lay beyond even the markedly self-confident Gerald's wildest ambitions to write an allegorical Christian epic of the scope of the *Commedia*, his varying deployment of accounts of beavers in several of his early works reveals a canny understanding of the ways in which 'literary' texts can be made to signify. This essay will think through the nature of Gerald's peculiar fascination with beavers – specifically as manifested in his account of the beavers that inhabited the River Teifi in Cardiganshire[3] – and will suggest some ways that this fascination sheds light on Gerald's thought process, on his development as a writer (especially during his early phase in the 1180s and early 1190s), and especially on the developing ways in which he perceived that the world could be mined for meaning. Focusing on Gerald's shifting use of the Teifi beavers in his works enables a better understanding of how the author's so-called 'naturalism' might collude with other narrative strategies in his various writings, and it will allow us to assess some of the ways in which a writer of the 'twelfth-century renaissance' and an intellectual heir of certain modes of thought that had emerged in the Paris schools earlier in that century endeavoured to make sense of the world around him.

The core of the phenomenon I want to describe is this: Gerald of Wales in three different early works – the *Topographia Hibernica* ('Topography of Ireland'), the *Itinerarium Kambriae* ('Journey Through Wales') and the *Descriptio Kambriae* ('Description of Wales') – supplies his audience with a detailed description of a colony of beavers that made its abode on the River Teifi. The versions provided in each work become increasingly longer, and they provide an excellent test-case for examining how Gerald set about revising his work. Indeed, the beaver passage may quite possibly be the text that Gerald most persistently reworked and reframed throughout his long writing career. The earliest version of Gerald's account of the Teifi beavers appears in the first recension of his *Topographia Hibernica* (c.1187).[4] Gerald extends this account slightly in the second version of the *Topographia* (c.1189). He then revises, adapts and extends it considerably in the first version of his *Itinerarium Kambriae* (1191), and these changes in turn were copied into the third and later recensions of the *Topographia*.[5] London, British Library, Royal MS 13 B. viii allows us to see this development in progress, as marginal notations there are then added into later manuscripts.[6] Gerald also extended the beaver material further for the first recension of the *Descriptio Kambriae* (about 1194) and subsequently incorporated this expanded version into the second recension of the *Itinerarium* (about 1197).

## Gerald as revisionist

This overview provides a general sense of the interest that Gerald seemed to take in this material, but a more detailed rehearsal of its developing contents is in order. Although it seems possible that the topic of beavers remained an enduring, if sporadic, interest of Gerald's throughout the latter half of his career, its textual manifestations allow one to analyse its development into four discrete phases. The first of these phases coincides with the first appearance of the material in the first recension of the *Topographia*, where it is included in Book I.26, in the midst of a longish series of chapters detailing the flora and fauna of Ireland. In a sense, this entire short chapter as it was originally conceived functions as a sort of parenthetical note, as Gerald in the previous chapter had been describing the badgers of Ireland. The original version of this brief chapter is quoted here in full, as it provides the textual basis upon which all the subsequent phases were elaborated:

> Cap. XXVI. *De castore, ejusque natura.*
> Simili naturae artificio castores utuntur; qui, dum castra sibi in fluviis construunt, sui generis servis quasi pro rheda utentes, a silvis ad aquas lignea robora miro vecturae modo contrahunt et conducunt.
>
> In utroque vero animalium genere servi notabiles sunt, tam degenerante quadam naturae deformitate, quam attrite dorsorum depilatione.
>
> Taxos Hibernia, non castores habet. Habentur tamen in Wallis, Teyvensi tantum in flumine apud Keirdigan. Habentur et in Scotia similiter rari.
>
> Notandum vero quod castores caudas habent latas, et non longas; in modum palmae humanae spissas; quibus tanquam pro remigio natando funguntur. Cumque totum corpus reliquum valde pilosum habeant, hanc partem omni pilositate carentem, in modum phocae marinae, planam habent et levigatam.
>
> Unde et in Germania, arctoisque regionibus, ubi abundant beveres, caudis hujusmodi, piscium naturam, ut aiunt, tam sapore quam colore sortitis, viri magni et religiosi jejuniorum tempore pro pisce vescuntur.
>
> . . .
>
> Ch. XXVI: *Concerning beavers and their nature.*
> Beavers use a similar contrivance of nature. When they are building homes in the rivers, they use slaves of their own kind as carts, and so by this wonderful means of transport pull and drag lengths of wood from

the forests to the waters. In both kinds of animal (beaver and badger) the slaves are distinguished by a certain inferiority of shape and a worn bare patch upon their backs.

Ireland has badgers but not beavers. In Wales beavers are to be found only in the Teifi river near Cardigan. They are, in the same way, scarce in Scotland.

One should remark that beavers have wide tails, spread out like a palm of the human hand, and not long. They use them as oars in swimming. And while the whole of the rest of their body is very furry, they are entirely free from fur on this part, and are quite bare and slippery like a seal.

Consequently in Germany and the northern regions, where beavers are plentiful, great and holy men eat the tails of beavers during fasting times – as being fish, since, as they say, they partake of the nature of fish both in taste and colour.[7]

Perhaps the most striking aspect of this brief chapter is that he includes it at all, as he notes that 'Ireland has badgers but not beavers' ('taxos Hibernia, non castores habet'). At the very least, it is clear that Gerald feels that he was bringing to light 'new' and inherently interesting information about beavers and that the novelty of his observations would justify its inclusion in a book quite obviously neither about Wales nor about British fauna more generally. He notes, for example, that they build their lodges (he uses the word *castra*, so 'forts' may actually be a better translation) in the middle of rivers; in fact, a survey of the bestiary tradition all the way back down to Pliny's *Historia naturalis* reveals that Gerald of Wales is actually the first person in the historical record to note that beavers build houses from fallen logs. Also original to Gerald is the observation that beavers use each other as a sort of vehicle for transporting these building materials. And, as mentioned above, while it is indeed odd that Gerald records as well that the beavers are, unlike badgers, *not* found in Ireland, he augments this fact with the broader observation that they are relatively scarce in Europe as a whole. Whether Gerald acquired this idea through informal investigations or through sheer inference at the paucity of references to beavers in the texts he was familiar with is impossible to say, though it is clear that he did not derive this information from any extant bestiaries or from the traditions of patristic or scholastic scholarship. Finally, his descriptions of the particular shape of beaver tails, and of the way that clergymen in Germany and other northern lands often eat beaver tails as a type of fish in order to respect various fast days in the liturgical calendar, also constitute innovative material.[9] Thus, despite the fact that the account of the beavers seems rather a misfit in the *Topographia Hibernica*, it reveals Gerald's active engagement with and observations of the natural world.

Although Gerald did add slightly to this initial description when he composed the second recension of the *Topographia* in about 1188, the next significant development of the material appears in the first recension of the *Itinerarium Kambriae* (1191). Here Gerald, no longer bound by having to transition out of a discussion of Irish fauna, writes a new introduction to the material that highlights the main points as he sees them. He has clearly been thinking about the material through a different lens. Whereas his presentation of the beavers in the *Topographia* had been relatively terse and to the point, Gerald here more clearly sees the material as carrying geographical weight and, consequently, sparking readerly interest; he thus expands it considerably. While some parts of the beaver material found in the first recension of the *Itinerarium Kambriae* are copied more or less verbatim from the *Topographia*, some of it has actually been reworded and perhaps reframed; the use of the word *Scotia* with *Albania*, for instance, is a nod to the nomenclature of Geoffrey of Monmouth's *Historia regum Britanniae* ('History of the Kings of Britain'), subtly indicating the relevance of Galfridian historiography to Gerald's account of Wales in general, but also allowing the sensitive reader a perhaps more pointed understanding of the beaver as a peculiarly 'British' phenomenon. However, much of the revised account of the beaver we witness in this second phase offers more than subtle rewording and, in fact, adds a great deal of new information. Gerald's remarks on the beaver's construction of their riparian *castra* are especially compellingly written, and they constitute the core of the new material in this second phase:

> In aliquo vero profundissimo fluvii angulo et pacifico, in castrorum constructione tanto artificio ligna connectunt, ut nec aquae stilla penetrando subintret, nec procellae vis labefactando concutiant; nec violentiam quamlibet praeter humanum, et hanc ferro munitam reformident . . . Habent autem in proxima castris ripa scrobes subterraneas, latibulaque in sicco munitissima. Ad quae venator explorans dum praeacutis sudibus desuper transpenetrare molitur, ictum audiens et violentiam timens, quam citius ad castri munimenta se bestia confert. Sed primo ad ipsum foraminis ingressum in ripa residens, aquam exsufflat, terram pedibus scalpens immiscet, et ex limpida visuique pervia turbidam reddit et coenulentam; ut sic hostis a ripa cum fuscina ferrea saltum observantis artem arte deludat.
>
> . . .
>
> There in some deep and tranquil bend of the river the beavers piece together with such skill the logs of wood which form their lodge that no drop of water can easily enter and no storm however violent do harm to

it or loosen it. They have no reason to fear any attack, except that of us human beings, and even we must bring our weapons shod with iron … Near their lodges they build underground hiding-places in the river-bank, carefully protected retreats which they dig into the dry earth. When the hunter comes to prise the beaver out and strives his hardest to poke sharpened poles down into its den, the creature hears the attack and knows that danger threatens. It retreats as fast as it can to the protection of its dam; but first, while still in the river-bank, it stirs up the water all around the entrance to its hole, scraping at the earth with its feet to form a muddy mixture, thus making the clear transparent river all thick and foul. In this way by its own stratagem it finds an answer to the wiles of its enemy, who is standing on the bank above, holding his three-pronged spear and waiting for the beaver to spring out.[10]

Urban Holmes and others have quite plausibly suggested that Gerald had been observing actual beavers at some point and was drawing on such experiences when composing these passages.[11] This may well be true, and many other of Gerald's works highlight his talents as a naturalist, but, as we shall see, to read these and other passages solely in the light of a naturalistic mimesis is to fore-close other ways in which Gerald sought to allow historical and natural 'facts' to resonate meaningfully within his works.

In this light, Gerald's account of the beaver's well-known (if apocryphal) mode of protection from hunters – another addition associated with the second phase of development of this material – emphasises the writer's original orientation toward his sources and illustrates further the ways in which he could yoke what we might now call naturalistic observation to other discursive purposes. The passage in fact represents Gerald's only explicit nod to both the bestiary and to the learned Latin *auctores* like Isidore of Seville:

In eois autem regionibus, cum canes narium sagacitate sequaces se nullatenus effugere posse praesentit, ut damno partis totum redimat, partem quam appeti naturali industria novit projiciendo in venatoris prospectu seipsam bestia castrat. Unde et a castrando Castor nomen accepit. Praeterea, si bestiam praecastratam canes iterum forte persequantur, ad eminentem statim se conferens locum, coxa in altum elevata, partem venatori quam appetit praecisam ostendit.

· · ·

In Eastern countries, when the beaver finds that it cannot evade the dogs which are following it by its scent, it saves itself by self-mutilation. By some natural instinct it knows which part of the body the hunter really wants. The creature castrates itself before the hunter's eyes and throws its testicles down. It is because of this act of self-castration that it is called 'castor' in Latin. If a beaver which has already lost its testicles is hard pressed a second time by hounds, it rushes to the top of a hillock, cocks up one of its hind legs and shows the hunter that the organs he is really after have already been cut off.[12]

The source of this fabulous story, which Gerald's more naturalistically inclined and more rigorously Aristotelian contemporary Alexander Nequam rejects out of hand, as Robert Bartlett points out,[13] is perhaps ultimately Cicero, though Gerald was doubtless also familiar with a similar comment from Juvenal and with the great *auctoritas* of Isidore of Seville, whose *Etymologies* clearly inform this passage: 'Beavers [*castores*] are so called from "castrating" [*castrare*]. Their testicles are useful for medicines, on account of which, when they anticipate a hunter, they castrate themselves and amputate their own genitals with their teeth' ('castores a castrando dicti sunt . . . nam testiculi eorum apti sunt medicaminibus, propter quos se praesensuerint venatorem, ipsi se castrant et morsibus vires suas amputant').[14] *Physiologus* follows Isidore rather closely, as does the twelfth-century bestiary tradition, which Gerald must have known to a greater or lesser extent. Willene B. Clark's edition of a second-family bestiary is probably representative of sources that Gerald would have been quite familiar with:

> Est animal quod dicitur castor mansuetum nimis, cuius testiculi medicinae sunt aptissimi. De quo dicit Physiologus, quia cum venatorem se insequentem cognoverit, morsu testiculos sibi abscidit, et in faciem venatoris eos proicit, et sic fugiens evadit . . . Sic omnis qui iuxta mandatum Dei versatur, et caste vult vivere, secat a se Omnia vitia et omnes impudicitiae actus, et proicit eos a se in faciem Diaboli . . .
>
> . . .
>
> There is a very gentle animal called the beaver, whose testicles are extremely useful for medicine. Physiologus says that when [the beaver] knows the hunter is following him, he cuts off his testicles with his teeth, and throws them before the hunter, and thus escapes . . . Thus, any man who is turned toward God's command, and wishes to live chaste, cuts himself off from all vices and all acts of lewdness, and tosses them in the Devil's face . . .[15]

Tellingly, even though he had clearly been consulting the bestiaries extensively when discussing the birds and beasts of Ireland in the *Topographia Hibernica*, Gerald does not include this at all when he treated beavers in the first phase and, when he finally does add it in the second phase, he significantly suppresses the explicitly moralising aspects of the *Physiologus*/bestiary tradition, a fact that I shall address below.

The final phases of Gerald's development of the beaver materials are rather simpler to recount. Phase three is attested in the first recension of the *Descriptio Kambriae*, composed around 1194, and was then reincorporated into the second recension of the *Itinerarium Kambriae* around 1197. In this third phase, Gerald's primary motive seems to have been to include further details, perhaps in response to positive feedback or further questions he had received from readers of the previous versions; he now describes the beaver's teeth, and he conjectures that they can breathe underwater, noting how long they appear to be able to stay submersed. He also compares the beavers with toads and seals – all, to his mind, amphibious creatures. Finally, the fourth phase emerges later in Gerald's career, probably about 1216, with the third recension of the *Itinerarium* and the second recension of the *Descriptio*. In this case, the only revisions Gerald effects are to work in two quotations from classical authors, namely Cicero and Juvenal, as well as a quotation from the *Cosmographia* of Bernardus Silvestris.[16] Though the quotations add little to the reader's understanding of beavers, they do indicate that beavers remained an active focal point in Gerald's imagination three decades after he had first conceived to write about them in the mid-1180s.

## Gerald as *literatus*

Dylan Thomas writes in *A Child's Christmas in Wales* of having once received as a Christmas present a book that told 'everything about the wasp but why'.[17] And, one fears, that may also be the situation with Gerald's beaver material: Gerald has told us much about beavers, much of it original to him and quite novel within the European literary tradition, and some of it naturalistically accurate. But it is less than obvious why these creatures seemed to exert such a fascination for him, why he thought them so repeatedly worthy of mention, even within narratives where their inclusion could be considered digressive or even completely irrelevant. One is, of course, forced to speculate about the reasons why the beaver plays such a role, but one need not speculate vainly. The texts themselves – and especially the broader context within which each successive version and phase of the beaver passage is embedded – can reveal much about the changing ways in which Gerald understood the task of the making meaning.

From its initial appearance in the *Topographia*, the account of the beaver stands out as a point of contrast to the material around it, and not only because it is occupied with a Welsh rather than an Irish beast. Looking at the wider narrative context, Gerald places it just after a series of descriptions of various animals of Ireland that he draws from either the *Physiologus* or from the wider bestiary tradition. The beavers differ from his descriptions of most of the Irish animals in two main respects. First, the beaver is described straightforwardly: a quick physical description and a brief discussion of its habits; what is missing here is precisely the explicit moral allegory that Gerald would know from his sources, as he uses it to great effect with so many of the previous animals. Following the bestiaries, Gerald's Irish crow, for instance, is a moral exemplum for how even wise men can be ensnared by folly; the Irish eagle's putative ability to gaze directly at the sun becomes an emblem, in Gerald's hands, of spiritual contemplation. Gerald would well have known Isidore's colourful etymology for *castor*, and, as we have seen, he quotes it in later phases. He would also have known, from the same bestiaries that he had evidently been consulting when discussing other animals in the *Topographia*, that, because of the beaver's apocryphal practice of self-castration, the beaver is also an allegorical figure for the clergy, who make themselves eunuchs for the sake of God. In fact, in one of the early manuscripts produced in Gerald's own scriptorium (Oxford, Bodleian Library, MS Rawlinson B. 188), the headword *castores* in this section is replaced with the word *pastores* ('priests'); this 'slip' is all the more striking because it involved changing pens and making a rather large capital.[18] Still, however obvious the connection between these two different kinds of castrators – beavers and priests – was to Gerald or to his scribes and friends, Gerald himself significantly does *not* mention it during his initial development of this material, the version that appears in the earliest recensions of the *Topographia*. The effect of this omission is considerable: it dislodges the beaver description from typical, received ways of interpreting the natural world, and, indeed, of interpreting phenomena in general, and leaves the reader to face the thing itself without any explicit, or generically expected, interpretive framework: the beaver poses a reader of the *Topographia Hibernica* with a moral puzzle, a hermeneutic mystery. One's expectation is that the beaver will, the beaver must, mean something, but the *Topographia* deliberately does not indicate what. The playing field of signification is laid wide open, and the onus of interpretation thus falls on the reader.

  The second important aspect about the beaver episode in its original manifestation is so obvious it might barely deserve mentioning, did it not open up further intriguing hermeneutic possibilities. That is the fact – a fact that Gerald openly acknowledges – that there are no beavers in Ireland: they are mostly only found in Wales. This fact likewise demands interpretive scrutiny from the reader, who surely must be scrambling to figure out why Gerald bothers to mention beavers if they are not actually Irish animals: one suspects, given Gerald's subsequent development of the beaver material, that the contrast with badgers here is merely heuristic and probably unnecessary – a bit of a transition, perhaps, though it does risk overstating the beaver's irrelevance to the topic of Irish fauna. But the reader still might wonder why beavers are even *in* the

*Topographia* in the first place. Again, the lack of explicit explanation forces the reader to pass beyond immediate narrative contingencies and to engage instead with more figurative or associative interpretive strategies. Following one possible avenue of comparison, one might note that the industrious beavers contrast sharply with the Irish themselves, whom Gerald repeatedly accuses of indigence. But the 'expatriate' beaver does also suggest an interesting parallel with the author himself, who is, after all, the Welshman in Ireland, the outsider surveying and cataloguing Irish flora, fauna, geography, history and anthropology. Not merely an indulgent authorial aside, then, the beaver material may actually serve as a metonymical insertion of the author into the text: the clever and busy beaver may well be Gerald himself.

These are at least some of the potential dynamics that emerge from the brief beaver chapter in the *Topographia Hibernica*, that is, in the first phase of the evolution outlined earlier. The next phase, inaugurated in the first recension of the *Itinerarium Kambriae*, sees Gerald developing the beaver material in a different direction according to the need and themes of the larger narrative. One of the striking aspects of this second phase – which represents the single largest expansion of the beaver material – is that the new passages focus almost exclusively on the great artistry with which the beavers build their *castra* and protect themselves from hunters. Indeed, Gerald seems deliberately here to be emphasising the ways in which the beavers resemble humans. Not only do they build *castra*, they give considerable thought to their strategic placement and they adorn their lodges with layers of redundant defensive constructs. Gerald's emphasis on the way the beaver evades a persistent enemy is telling: 'by its own stratagem it finds an answer to the wiles of its enemy' ('ut sic hostis . . . artem arte deludat'). The word *arte* ('stratagem') here is particularly striking, not only because it is chiastically emphasised, but also because it is a distinctly human-oriented word, as is the word *ingenium* ('cunning') slightly later in the chapter; within this sentence, the wiles of the beaver are declared superior to human ingenuity. Indeed, such words as 'stratagem' and 'cunning' often appear in the *Itinerarium Kambriae* in descriptions of the canny subterfuges of the Welsh. One is especially reminded of Gerald's description of the crafty Welshman who defended Dinefwr castle by deceiving and misleading Anglo-Norman scouts, effectively producing a cognitive 'smoke screen' quite comparable to the beaver's muddied water.[19] Throughout the *Itinerarium Kambriae*, Gerald repeatedly refers to the cunning and sly ingenuity of the Welsh. Is his inclusion and amplification of the beaver episode here not perhaps an indirect way of suggesting a sort of parallel between beavers and the Welsh? Both exhibit an admirable cunning when working for their own defence. The reader may find this an enticing, and perhaps persuasive, reading, but is nonetheless hard pressed to find Gerald overtly endorsing one interpretation over any other.

Another major addition to the second phase is the material, again derived from the bestiary tradition, and probably, for Gerald, from Isidore of Seville, of the story of the beavers' self-castration, now stated explicitly. We have seen that he avoids this account during the first phase as a way of distancing himself at that juncture from the allegorically moralising and thus hermeneutically over-determined bestiary tradition. Including it here, in the *Itinerarium*'s first recension, Gerald still manages to avoid all trace of allegory, and yet he also adduces the act of self-castration as yet another example of the beaver's canniness at avoiding predators. He thus amplifies the sense of personification and the notional proximity to the Welsh that the description of the defensive craft of their dams also suggests.

The third and fourth phases prove rather less complicated. Phase three probably emerged in the first draft of the *Descriptio Kambriae* and was then copied back into updated recensions of the *Topographia* and the *Itinerarium*. Here Gerald adds a few comparisons of the beaver with seals, toads and other amphibians, and also adds further naturalistic observations about beaver lodges. Yet the additional material is not merely informational but serves the *Descriptio Kambriae*'s main narrative goal, which is to highlight the marvels of Wales for Anglo-Norman audiences.[20] Phase four involves even simpler sorts of changes, consisting almost entirely of quotations added to the texts. Two of these quotations, the ones from Cicero and Juvenal, are entirely characteristic of Gerald's process of revision, especially after his retirement to Lincoln around 1203–4: they lend what Gerald saw as solemn authority and a literary flair to the text. Gerald could use quotations to great effect, as texts like the *Speculum duorum* ('A Mirror of Two Men') and the *De principis instructione* ('Instruction for a Ruler') demonstrate, and certainly Gerald's decision to include them at this point in time is deliberate, as the Cicero and Juvenal quotations could be easily found in his sources and in fact were associated with the beaver tradition as far back as Isidore of Seville. Their inclusion only now, twenty-five or more years into the 'beaver project', reveals Gerald's changing sense of how a *literatus* ought to sound – how meaning, that is, can be generated in rich resonance with earlier *auctoritates*. However, the third quotation that Gerald weaves into this final version of the beaver material, the one from Bernardus Silvestris, brings a very different sort of voice to the table. By referring to Bernardus's *Cosmographia*, Gerald perhaps also invokes that poem's supreme vision of a fecund Nature teeming with multiplicity of life, forms and meanings. And although Bernardus was himself no enemy of allegory, few of the allegories in the *Cosmographia* are straightforward, many are controversial, and many more are downright ambiguous.[21] If a single *auctor* might be said to provide Gerald with a productive hermeneutic model, Bernardus Silvestris may well be it.

Assessing phases one through four together – in other words, thinking through how the beaver material accretes throughout Giraldian works composed in the three decades between about 1186 and 1216 – one can discern some interesting patterns. First, the incremental development of the beaver material serves as a useful index for Gerald's general approaches to composition and revision over this most fertile period of his literary career; it will come as no surprise to those who have studied Gerald's works to see him puttering with this passage, retooling it, expanding it, and finally – after the turn of the thirteenth century – adorning it with quotations from learned literary *auctoritates*. Yet that stylistic trajectory alone does not sufficiently account for Gerald's continued interest in beavers. Robert Bartlett views the beaver material as paradigmatic of Gerald's more general interest in the natural world that informed his early literary career, something he turned away from when he retired from court, politically frustrated, in the mid-1190s.[22] I would like to suggest, however, that Gerald's use of the beaver material reveals that he was never content with conveying mere information about the natural world. One might say that the beaver provides Gerald with a certain centre of gravity against which he could sidestep traditional allegories or other 'authoritative' meanings. The beaver instead allows Gerald to explore *narrative meaning*, that is, the idea that phenomena too often derive their meaning contextually, as a function of their narrative placement. In one sense, the concept that varying narrative contexts produce varying interpretive resonances within a given text is nothing new under the sun: Augustine's *De doctrina christiana* ('On Christian Doctrine') promotes, *mutatis mutandis*, a broadly similar model for the dynamics of signification, and certainly the idea of narrative meaning is also something that Gerald's occasional colleague and correspondent Walter Map was also aware of and used to great effect in his *De nugis curialium* ('Courtiers' Trifles').[23] On the other hand, as someone whose earliest extant work betrays the heavily Platonising influence of the Paris schools (Gerald's early poem *Mundi Cosmographia* is practically an epitome of Bernardus Silvestris's *Cosmographia*) and who also seems to have been immersed in the moralising *Physiologus* tradition, Gerald's rejection of stable, unitary meanings seems almost revolutionary.

Untethered from such over-determined interpretive frameworks, the beavers in these texts offer various possible readings: (1) the inclusion of the industrious beavers in the *Topographia* can stand as a point of contrast to the indigence of the Irish; (2) the beavers' skill at subterfuge and self-preservation in the *Itinerarium Kambriae* can serve as a subtle parallel to the prevalence of these same qualities among the Welsh; (3) the emphasis on the beaver's unusual habits in the *Descriptio Kambriae* can provide another example of the wondrous and semi-exotic exemplarity of Wales. In all these cases, Gerald works hard – as he does often elsewhere – not to foreclose meaning, not to lean upon the traditions of straightforward moral allegory, not to allow readers the luxury of letting the author do the work for them. Beavers enabled Gerald – historian and *litterateur* – to do what he does best: to allow meaning to percolate from the world as he encountered it, and to reorient his interpretive strategies as the vicissitudes of court intrigue, ecclesiastical politics, or colonial civility might demand.

# Notes

1   Dante Alighieri, *Inferno*, XVII.21–4, in Robert Hollander and Jean Hollander (ed. and trans.), *The Inferno* (New York, 2000), pp. 312–13.

2   The informational core of the beaver tradition can be found in Pliny the Elder's *Historia naturalis*, viii.47, though Pliny himself likely drew upon a stray comment from Cicero and upon an Aesopic fable. See Willene B. Clark (ed.), *A Medieval Book of Beasts: The Second-Family Bestiary, Art, Text, and Translation* (Woodbridge, 2006), p. 130.

3   In fact, the Eurasian beaver (*castor fiber*) was on the verge of extinction in the British Isles during the period in which Gerald was writing. See Oliver Rackham, *The History of the Countryside: The Classic History of Britain's Landscape, Flora and Fauna* (London, 2000), p. 34.

4   My dating of the various recensions of Gerald of Wales's works derives primarily from Robert Bartlett, *Gerald of Wales: A Voice of the Middle Ages* (Stroud, 2006), Appendix I, pp. 174–80; I have also consulted Catherine Rooney, 'The Manuscripts of the Works of Gerald of Wales' (unpublished PhD thesis, University of Cambridge, 2005). For the dating of the *Topographia Hibernica* in particular, see also Amelia Borrego Sargent, 'Gerald of Wales's *Topographia Hibernica*: Dates, Versions, Readers', *Viator*, 43 (2012), 241–61.

5   Rooney, 'Manuscripts', 30–1, provides a useful survey of the textual history of the *Topographia Hibernica*.

6   Rooney, 'Manuscripts', 32–3. See also Rooney's contribution to this volume.

7   *Topographia*, i.26, pp. 58–9, translation from John J. O'Meara (trans.), *The History and Topography of Ireland* (Harmondsworth, 1982), pp. 48–9.

8   In fact, it was not until the twelfth century that anyone had clearly recorded the fact that beavers were even aquatic animals. The honour belongs to the remarkable Hildegard of Bingen; see J.-P. Migne (ed.), *S. Hildegardis abbatissae Opera Omnia*, Patrologia Latina 197 (Paris, 1855), col. 1329A.

9   Gerald's association of beavers with German alimentary habits was copied into the subsequent bestiary tradition and thus may have become an indirect source for Dante's 'guzzling Germans' (*Tedeschi lurchi*).

10  *Itinerarium*, ii.28, pp. 115–17; translation from Lewis Thorpe (trans.), *Gerald of Wales, The Journey through Wales and The Description of Wales* (Harmondsworth, 1978), pp. 174–6.

11  Urban Holmes, 'Gerald the Naturalist', *Speculum*, 11 (1936), 110–21, especially 120; Bartlett, *Gerald*, p. 119, concurs. See also Antonia Gransden, 'Realistic Observation in Twelfth-Century England', *Speculum*, 47 (1972), 29–51, especially 48–50, where she deems Gerald a staunchly reliable naturalist.

12  *Itinerarium*, ii.3, p. 117; Thorpe (trans.), *Gerald*, p. 177.

13  Bartlett, *Gerald*, p. 120.

14  W. M. Lindsay (ed.), *Isidore of Seville, Etymologiae* (Oxford, 1911), xii.2.21; Stephen A. Barney et al. (trans.), *The Etymologies of Isidore of Seville* (Cambridge, 2006), p. 252; see also Clark (ed.), *A Medieval Book of Beasts*, p. 130.

15 Clark (ed.), *A Medieval Book of Beasts*, p. 130.

16 Neither Dimock nor Thorpe were able to trace this quotation, and Thorpe even erroneously assumed it was attributed to St Bernard of Clairvaux. In fact, these verses – 'The beaver comes forth, prompt to give up from his own body those treasures which a greedy enemy pursues' ('Prodit item castor proprio de corpore velox / Reddere quas sequitur hostis avarus opes') – are from a rather different 'Bernardus': see Winthrop Wetherbee (ed. and trans.), *Bernardus Silvestris, Poetic Works* (Cambridge, 2015), pp. 46–7.

17 Dylan Thomas, *A Child's Christmas in Wales* (New York, 1954), p. 8.

18 Rooney, 'Manuscripts', 127–55, makes a very persuasive argument that this manuscript was composed in a Giraldian scriptorium. See also her contribution in this volume.

19 See *Itinerarium*, i.10, pp. 81–2.

20 For a closer examination of these dynamics, see Asa Simon Mittman, 'The Other Close at Hand: Gerald of Wales and the "Marvels of the West"', in Bettina Bildhauer and Robert Mills (eds), *The Monstrous Middle Ages* (Cardiff, 2003), pp. 97–112.

21 On the complexities of interpretation in the *Cosmographia*, see Theodore Silverstein, 'The Fabulous Cosmology of Bernardus Silvestris', *Modern Philology*, 46 (1948–9), 92–116; Peter Dronke, 'Bernard Silvestris, Natura and Personification', *The Journal of the Warburg and Courtauld Institutes*, 43 (1980), 53–73; and Winthrop Wetherbee, *Platonism and Poetry in the Twelfth Century: The Literary Influence of the School of Chartres* (Princeton, 1972).

22 Bartlett, *Gerald*, pp. 119–20.

23 M. R. James (ed. and trans.), *Walter Map: De nugis curialium. Courtiers' Trifles*, rev. C. N. L. Brooke and R. A. B. Mynors (Oxford, 1983); see also Siân Echard, 'Map's Metafiction: Author, Narrator, and Reader in *De Nugis Curialium*', *Exemplaria*, 8 (1996), 287–314.

# EIGhT

# Style, Truth and Irony: Listening to the Voice of Gerald of Wales's Writings

Simon Meecham-Jones
*University of Cambridge*

GERALD DE BARRI'S (relatively) modest worldly advancement never equalled, and could scarcely have been expected to match, the breadth of ambition revealed in his texts. Though repeatedly passed over for major appointments, by Church and state, Gerald retains a toehold in popular consciousness, and has never lost the attention of literary historians.[1] This enduring prominence can seem surprising, since scholars have struggled to explain precisely the terms in which Gerald's importance can be assayed,[2] or have evaded this taxing question. Gerald has been acclaimed on diverse fronts, for example, as 'the father of comparative philology',[3] 'the father of . . . ethnography',[4] and as an important witness about the nature of medieval music. These are appreciable claims to notice, but can still seem tangential to Gerald's avowed authorial motives, evading the question of his value and originality as a cleric, moralist and historian. Shai Burstyn draws attention to Gerald's 'prolific' output and the variety of subjects broached,[5] offering a defence which, like Michael Richter's praise of 'a man of outstanding vitality' deflects our attention from an evaluation of the elegance and acuity of Gerald's writing to the more certain ground of an appreciation of its extent and range.[6] Furthermore, it is clear that, for many critics, the process of praising Gerald's talent seems fraught with reluctance,[7] so that it can almost seem as if Gerald has obtruded himself on literary history by force of will rather than intellectual distinction.

Admittedly, this sense of reservation is often ideologically driven, particularly with regard to Gerald's work on Ireland.[8] The length of Gerald's career, and his working practices as an inveterate reviser of his own earlier work, must be allowed a role in promoting judgements like Antonia Gransden's belief that 'Gerald did not have a systematic mind'.[9] Throughout his output, unexpected ideas may appear in one manuscript, only to be expunged from latter versions, as if Gerald had thought better of his *aperçu*. Sometimes the motivation is clear,[10] but more often it is elusive, perhaps reflecting changing audiences or contexts, and almost certainly lost irrecoverably. Certainly, Gerald was not a slave to consistency. Through a long working life, there were some crucial reversals in his opinions, for example his subsequently regretted support for the Plantagenet monarchy, while his enthusiasm for involvement in the status of the see of St David peaked, then declined in his later years. Gerald's willingness to acknowledge, or even draw attention to, his changes of opinion forms an important element of his character as a writer, perhaps best evidenced in the composition of his *Retractationes* ('Retractions') near the end of his career.[11]

Such reversals are necessarily troubling for critics eager to 'place' writers within a single and consistent ideological position, providing some evidence, for example, for Gransden's conclusion that 'Gerald was not a great thinker on the conceptual level'.[12] But her four-square reading for consistency perhaps underestimates the possibility of Gerald overlaying his texts with a sheen of irony which his contemporaries would have been better placed to recognise, since many of Gerald's reversals are framed within the practice of his esteemed peers. The *Retractationes*, for example, explicitly echoes the example of Augustine. It is perhaps central to the difficulty of interpreting Gerald's work that, while his respect for literary precedent was fostered by his very extensive, and widely displayed, familiarity with a wide range of classical and medieval Latin texts, it cannot be said that he sought to conceal himself under the cloak of the textual authority of the past. Even in Gransden's dismissal of his management of sources – 'his mind was a rag-bag of diverse influences'[13] – or, in Burstyn's less than respectful description of Gerald as an 'ebullient ecclesiastic',[14] we are still reminded that Gerald's writings project a textual 'voice' which is vivid, recognisable and distinctive, no matter how inconsistent or hard to interpret its conclusions may have proved to later readers. Yet the presumption of textual presence ultimately proves frustrating, highlighting a disjunction between the emotional engagement and tendency to forthrightness certainly found in Gerald's work and the surprising difficulty critics have encountered in interpreting his purposes – from Charles Burney's pronouncement in the eighteenth century that the interpretation of Gerald's words 'will long remain an impenetrable secret' to Richter's defence of Gerald as 'often quoted but seldom understood'.[15]

The answer must surely lie in an analysis of the style of Gerald's writing, a topic generally neglected in favour of the tradition of critical engagement in his reporting and opinions rather than the literary means he used to express those convictions. For Tony Davenport, 'like old mirrors, that language has become blurred and pockmarked, leaving it by no means easy to read',[16] but the range and extent of his output qualifies Gerald as an ideal case to begin to test how far it might be possible for modern critics to recover with confidence the meaning of literature written in medieval Latin – that is, a tongue used as a trans-European medium in scholastic circles in the twelfth and thirteenth centuries,[17] but scarcely, if at all, used as a living vernacular in that time.[18]

Brian Stock has reminded us of the change of status of literacy and textuality in the twelfth century, so that 'by the mid-twelfth century, the presence of scribal culture is one of the few universalizing forces that the Western Middle Ages knows as a whole'.[19] The resultant implications of this change of status were mediated by the creation of textual communities which differed from each other in their relationship to the text.[20] Gerald's failure to attract sustained patronage from any dynastic or religious faction makes it certain that, during the different phases of his career, his texts were designed to be read by different textual communities, pursuing different principles and priorities – which may explain, in part, the addition and removal of ideas and phrases as the texts were adjusted for different audiences. One might suppose that Gerald's Welsh and Irish works attracted a courtly audience, and perhaps a secular audience in so far as such a thing existed, whereas the *Gemma ecclesiastica* and *Speculum ecclesiae* claim to have been designed for a narrower clerical audience, which perhaps explains why the religious texts survive in only a single manuscript witness each. Considering these probable differences of audience, it is interesting that critics have diagnosed little stylistic change across Gerald's career. A. A. Goddu and R. H. Rouse claim to find a consistency surprising in texts which were liable to addition and re-drafting: 'While Gerald's earliest mature works are superior in content and organization to his later ones, his basic style is generally consistent and uniform throughout his fifty-five-year literary career.'[21] They regard this consistency as being 'testimony to the solid and thorough foundation of his early training' which they characterise as 'learned'.[22] For Andrew Hughes (albeit at second-hand) that consistency has hardened into a predictability of style, leading him to conclude that 'as an author Gerald is said to have been learned but conservative, uncritical and emotional'.[23] Curiously, though Hughes does not begin to attempt to reconcile apparently opposing qualities, each head of his description proves important in explaining the expectations critics have generally brought to Gerald's texts.

'Learned' is perhaps the least surprising adjective to find used about Gerald, but it requires clarification. Goddu and Rouse's analysis concentrates on those qualities of Gerald's work which they characterise as 'formulary' to describe the way that he constructs the texture of his work by adapting the words of the 'ancient masters', adapted sometimes from the texts cited, but more often from florilegia which presented 'bleeding chunks' of classical and patristic thought, wholly divorced from the authors' personal and cultural context.[24] Demonstrating that Gerald used the *Florilegium angelicum* 'like a mine', it might seem that their analysis justifies Hughes's judgement of the style as 'learned' and 'conservative'.[25] But caution is required. Their description often reflects how Gerald might have been expected to use such a process of composition, rather than how he actually did so: 'The extracts detached from their contexts and rendered universally applicable by the compiler served Gerald as stock formulas which could be inserted interchangeably into written structures.'[26] In fact, Gerald's use was, by design or accident, less respectful and less conservative than it appears at first. J. F. Dimock had long before noted Gerald's apparent habit of quoting from memory such extracts (and sometimes the titles of the works from which they were taken), which inevitably resulted in misquotation and misappropriation: 'It would seem that he must have often quoted from memory ... More frequently, perhaps, than otherwise, he gives the words of his original more or less incorrectly; and in some cases attributes a passage to a wrong author.'[27] Dimock ascribed such waywardness (which was often erased by later copyists) to carelessness and over-confidence, but seems not to have considered the possibility that Gerald might be extracting ironic humour from the inability of words to prevent their own misappropriation. Processes of extracting, de-contextualising and occasionally re-writing gobbets of poetry from the classical masters, and sometimes even from biblical and patristic texts, were central to the composition of 'Goliardic' satirical verse by writers such as Walter of Châtillon, Peter of Blois, Hugh Primas and the Archpoet of Cologne in the twelfth century.[28] Such lyrics, often fiercely critical of authority figures in the Church, were circulated across Europe, and it is inconceivable that Gerald would have been unaware of the style. Furthermore, elements of this playful confrontation of the distance between the physicality of the word and the ease with which the word can be misappropriated surface in the work of Walter Map also.[29] There is something teasing about the relationship between these writers and Gerald – Bartlett draws together Gerald with Walter Map and Peter of Blois as examples of 'the diversity of court culture',[30] while Alan Bate compares Gerald with Walter, mostly to Gerald's disadvantage[31] – which has not been satisfactorily explained. Any comparison with Peter of Blois's work raises some historical difficulties, depending on which part of his presumed output is under discussion. If one accepts that the Peter of Blois who famously wrote letters at the court of Henry II was the same Peter of Blois who, in his youth, wrote satirical and erotic verse of disturbing originality, then, by comparison, Gerald does appear 'conservative'.[32] Despite the fragmentary survival of Walter Map's work, it is hard not to conclude that his work, also, displays an innovative questioning of form and convention quite different from Gerald's more cautious experimentation.

Comparison with Peter's later work as a prose writer proves, unexpectedly, to be more revealing. Peter's sheer facility in debating opposing premises led Richard Southern to dismiss his work as revealing 'a deep emptiness, a lack of thought, of originality, of anything but conventional feelings'.[33] But that sense of ease, of exquisite control of the medium, is by no means replicated in Gerald's more committed but less flexible reasoning. If, as Neil Cartlidge suggests, Peter's style offers 'a vehicle . . . for a teasingly evasive display of his own personality', Gerald's style is less able, or perhaps less willing, to conceal its author.[34]

Such a conclusion would probably not have surprised Gerald, though it might have troubled him. W. Llewelyn Williams noted of Gerald that 'without being Ciceronian, his Latin was far better than that of his contemporaries'.[35] Williams implicitly points out the distinction between two modes of Latin rhetoric which were available to Gerald. Throughout his career, Gerald shows he has the expertise to make use of copious rhetorical figures, but he never does so with the assurance and sheer joy in language of the Ciceronian tradition, or of the paradoxically opposed models of Walter Map and (the mature) Peter of Blois. Rather, he is drawn to the more restrained and more pragmatic tradition derived from Quintilian.[36] Quintilian has no truck with the idea that eloquence may have a life and an importance far beyond the intentions of its author – an idea that had become intoxicating and axiomatic for the Goliardic style. Rather, for Quintilian, eloquence is dependent on the pre-existing moral worth of its compositor:

> Oratorem autem instituimus illum perfectum, qui esse nisi vir bonus non potest; ideoque non dicendi modo eximiam in eo facultatem sed omnes animi virtutes exigimus. Neque enim hoc concesserim, rationem rectae honestaeque vitae (ut quidam putaverunt) ad philosophos relegandam, cum vir ille vere civilis et publicarum privatarumque rerum administrationi accommodatus, qui regere consilis urbes, fundare legibus, emendare iudiciis possit, non alius sit profecto quam orator.
>
> . . .
>
> My aim, then, is the education of the perfect orator. The first essential for such a one is that he should be a good man, and consequently we demand of him not merely the possession of exceptional gifts of speech but of all the excellences of character as well. For I will not admit that

the principles of upright and honourable living should, as some have held, be regarded as the peculiar concern of philosophy. The man who can really play his part as a citizen and is capable of meeting the demands both of public and private business, the man who can guide a state by his counsels, give it a firm basis by his legislation and purge its vices by his decisions as a judge, is assuredly no other than the orator of our quest.[37]

Quintilian's restricted view of the difficulty of deserving to be classed an orator weighs heavily on Gerald, infusing a degree of anxiety into his self-presentation. In considering Gerald's style, it is important to recognise the rigorous, if self-designed, constraints within which Gerald felt obliged to work. Derived from Quintilian's precepts, there are conflicting ideas about the proper use of language which underlie both the 'learned' and 'conservative' elements of Gerald's style, and which Gerald explored in the Prologues and Introductions to his works. In the dedication to Stephen Langton, which prefaces the *Itinerarium Kambriae*, Gerald lauds the efforts of the eloquent with an intensity that, in its repeat formulation, seems almost obsessive, though the distinction between creators and hearers is presumably intended to be comic:

> Compositores quippe tam ornati sermonis, quo tam varii casus in tanto juris corpore tam eleganti stilo complectuntur, perpetuis efferendi præconiis extant. Auctores siquidem elegantium verborum, non auditores tantum, repertores non recitatores, dixerim laude dignissimos.
>
> . . .
>
> For the composers of that polished language, in which such various cases as occur in the great body of law are treated with such an appropriate elegance of style, must ever stand forward in the first ranks of praise. I should indeed have said, that the authors of refined language, not the hearers only, the inventors, not the reciters, are most worthy of commendation.[38]

After this preamble, the work that follows is commended as being written in *scholastico stilo* ('in scholastic style'). In the introduction to the *Topographia Hibernica*, an alternative view of eloquence begins to emerge. Having posed the question whether any good might come from writing about Ireland, Gerald praises the power of eloquence to dignify an insufficient subject:

> Sugamus ergo mel de petra, et oleum de saxo: et faciamus quod oratores facere solent. Quibus in admirabili genere causæ acuenda præcipue sunt arma facundiæ, ut exilitatem materiæ gravior stilus attollat.
>
> . . .

Let us, then, endeavour to suck honey out of the rock, and draw oil from the flint. Let us follow the example of great orators, who, in an admirable manner, most polished the shafts of their eloquence, when the poverty of their subject required it to be elevated by the superiority of their style.[39]

Gerald offers a concentrated example of his rhetorical control, with its reference to familiar tropes and the punning on *stilus* as a pointed stick or weapon, a writing instrument and a word describing composition itself. But if rhetorical flourishes are required to add gravitas to an inferior subject, should that mean that such decorative elements are inappropriate for the exposition of serious matters of theology and religious practice?

If we compare the rhetorical polish of that extract with a representative sample of the spare and unadorned style of the *Gemma ecclesiastica*, it becomes clear that, in matters which have the potential to reflect on his orthodoxy, Gerald shows a preference for clarity at the expense of displaying his learning:

De sicera vero loco vini imposita hoc sciatis, quod corpus non ibi consecratur, quia nec fit conversio siceræ in sanguinem, neque etiam panis in carnem.

. . .

If cider is used in place of wine, you should know that the body of Christ does not become present in the Sacrament because there is no conversion of the cider into His blood nor of the bread into His flesh.[40]

The dry and unadorned account offers scant opportunity for ambiguity and misunderstanding, even if it seems to justify the dismissal of Gerald's work as 'uncritical' and 'conservative'. Actually, it reveals the limitations of the description 'conservative', a term which by no means encompasses the complexities and contradictions of Gerald's style of thought. Gerald was innovative in his 'topographical' works, if rarely so in his (surviving) poetry, but literary style was not his only, or even his primary, concern. More apposite is the term 'orthodox' since Gerald's 'conservatism' is more consistent doctrinally than politically. Gerald has been praised for not being cowed by authority and, as well as criticising secular rulers, he also turned his pen to castigating bishops and friars. His absolute loyalty to the institution of the Church, however, remained unquestioned. At no point in his work is found either the challenge to Church hierarchy voiced in Walter of Châtillon's satiric verse or the playful (if potentially subversive) meditation on orthodox doctrines found in poems like the lyric 'Sevit aure spiritus' by Peter of Blois.[41] We cannot guess how far Gerald's unfailing unorthodoxy was a matter of conviction and temperament or one of prudence, but it is striking in one who had received his education at the schools of Paris which in the mid-twelfth century had witnessed the unquenchable bitterness of philosophical confrontation 'resolved' by the drawing of boundaries beyond which speculation was not to be permitted. Whereas the rebellious and satirical aesthetic of Peter of Blois and Walter of Châtillon played on the capability of language and rhetoric to confront and render unstable social and philosophical presumptions, Gerald's attempt to harness a learned style to reinforce his vision of orthodoxy can be seen as an inevitable reaction to the tempting gestures towards anarchy conjured by his predecessors, a sign of the 'defensiveness' that P. J. Godman suggests infected Latin discourse in the Paris schools after the burning of Abelard's treatise on the Trinity.[42] But there were alternative strategies for managing and perhaps overcoming such defensiveness. Where Cartlidge suggests that Peter of Blois refracted the expression of his personality into a bemusing figuration which Cartlidge dubs 'multiple Peter' to address his anxiety 'about defining his own place in an environment constantly demanding a new "self-fashioning" – the court of Henry II',[43] it was precisely Gerald's unwillingness (and, probably, inability) to adapt or disguise his purpose which ensured his inability to stay within, far less prosper within, such circles, and which, in turn, dictated the radical stylistic shift between the Gerald who 'delighted in stylistic embellishments'[44] and the Gerald whose prose eschews all such distractions, creating a marked discontinuity of styles not from work to work, but rather within the texture of individual works.

This careful grading of rhetorical performance was not used by Gerald only to avoid any hint of error in doctrinal matters. Similar effects can be observed in his (apparently) more rhetorically decorated works. Commenting on Gerald's re-writing of Rhygyfarch's Life of St David, Robert Bartlett notes that the process of re-composition sheds a revealing 'light thrown on Gerald's own predilections and concerns', exposing the 'antifeminist bias of his thought'.[45] This leads him to conclude that 'Nothing can explain Gerald's handling of this passage except a personal preoccupation, perhaps even a prurient or fascinated obsession, with the vexatiousness of marriage and woman's irrationality.'[46]

So, in the opening pages of the Expugnatio Hibernica, one might expect Gerald to be in his element, recounting how the conflict is initiated by the exiling of Diarmait Mac Murchada following his 'abduction' of Derbforgaill, wife of King Tigernán Ua Ruairc. But here Gerald curbs his 'predilection', and omits the expected display of anti-feminist rhetoric, not even drawing the obvious comparison with stock exemplars of women's unreliability, such as Eve and Delilah. It does not suit his purpose, of magnifying the heroism of the FitzGeralds, to draw too much attention to the origins of the dispute and to conduct which might cast some doubt on the justice of their cause in restoring the deposed Diarmait. Just enough is mentioned to deflect criticism that

Gerald has not presented all the facts, while there is perhaps a touch of humour in Gerald's choice of the apparently blameless – almost inscrutable – term *incommodum* ('unfortunate') to describe what has happened:

> Accesit et aliud incommodum. Ororicio namque Medensium rege remotas in partes expedicionis cuiusdam causa profecto, uxor ipsius, Omachlachelini filia, quam in insula quadam Medie reliquerat, a predicto Dermitio, eiusdem igne dudum accenso, captata viri absencia, rapta nimirum fuit quia et rapi voluit, et quoniam *Varium et mutabile semper femina*, ut predoni preda fierent ipsa procuravit.

> Sed quoniam mala fere cuncta maiora, tam Marco Antonio quam Troia testante.

> . . .

> There was another unfortunate factor. On an occasion when Ua Ruairc king of Meath had gone off on an expedition to far distant places, his wife, Ua Máelechlainn's daughter, whom he had left on an island in Meath, was abducted by the aforesaid Diarmait, who had long been burning with love for her and took advantage of her husband's absence. No doubt she was abducted because she wanted to be and, since 'woman is always a fickle and inconstant creature', she herself arranged that she should become the kidnapper's prize.

> Almost all the world's most notable catastrophes have been caused by women, witness Mark Antony and Troy.[47]

The supposedly verbose Gerald achieves exquisite colouring of his text through the sparseness of his one-word reference to the Fall of Troy, just enough to suggest a correspondence, without needing to insist upon the fact.

The care with which this passage is constructed should banish forever F. M. Powicke's suggestion that Gerald's 'self-esteem was never disturbed by the frustrations of what we call self-consciousness'.[48] On the contrary, the apparent absence of self-consciousness was a myth Gerald was keen to promote, and he deserves credit for how successfully he has managed to mislead generations of critics. As a man who, in his own eyes, never managed to establish the career in the Church that he felt he deserved, Gerald was inevitably always sensitive to the implication, in Quintilian's model of oratory, that the virtue and veracity of his writing would be linked to the status and reputation of the writer.

It must be considered both ironic and appropriate that Gerald's fear that the reader's preconceptions about the author would, all too often, become the measure of the work. It was a conclusion he sought to escape through his frequent use of the imagery of the mirror (as noted by Davenport[49]) in the design of works like the *Speculum ecclesiae* and the *Speculum duorum*. It is an image utilised prominently in the opening of the *Topographia Hibernica* as a justification for what is being attempted:

> Expressamque Hiberniae topographiam hoc opusculo quasi speculo quodam dilucido repraesentare, et cunctis in commune palam facere.
>
> . . .
>
> Exhibiting to him the topography of Ireland in this little work of mine, as in a clear mirror, so that its features may be open to the inspection of all the world.[50]

Gerald, though, shows no recognition that, in promoting this idea, he sets himself up as the mirror. That failure of insight has not prevented the idea of Gerald's writing as a mirror of his age becoming a critical commonplace, assumed, for example, in Powicke's account of him as 'a self-important gossip whom nothing escaped . . . a man with an intense curiosity and uncannily observant'.[51] Though he praises Gerald's 'eye for detail', it is as a recorder, rather than an interpreter, of information that Powicke concedes Gerald's importance.[52] But the imagery of observation using a mirror also implies that such observation has an impersonal and de-historicised universality – a claim that Gerald, as a clergyman, might have been expected to find problematic. However sharp his 'eye for detail', he could not fail to set such confidence against St Paul's pronouncement in the First Book of Corinthians that, compared to the future enlightenment achievable in heaven, 'now we see through a glass darkly' (1 Corinthians 13:12).[53]

But what is the nature of the darkness that obscures Gerald's art and purposes from the modern reader? If Davenport is right that Gerald's 'language has become blurred and pockmarked', we must ask how far that blurring is the result of language shift, as we have lost the knowledge and confidence to read the nuance of medieval Latin, or whether it reflects our distance from the ideologies within which writers like Gerald developed their ideas.[54] To give an example, Southern, having described Gerald as 'one of the most ambitious and experimental historical writers of the late twelfth century', notes with surprise his willingness to engage with vaticinal material: he 'went further than anyone else in seeking unknown prophecies and trying to fit them into his contemporary histories. He seems to have had the idea of making a complete fusion between contemporary history and ancient Celtic prophecy, writing what he called a *Historia Vaticinalis*.'[55] But if the choice of material did not impress Southern, it is what he presumes to be the tone of the work that concerns him most: 'It was all very solemn. He found nothing

funny in the idea that Prince John, blundering around Ireland, was fulfill-
ing the obscure predictions of Celtic bards.'[56] It is hard to be sure whether
Southern's primary objection is, like Gransden's,[57] to Gerald's apparent willingness to pay attention to material that might have seemed more plausible to
medieval audiences than to modern critics, with their distaste for 'irrational'
superstition. Or has Southern, perhaps misled by his expectations of Gerald's
style, failed to understand the nuance of the passage? Maybe there is an innate
comedy in John's progress around Ireland which requires no further highlighting, but which benefits from Gerald's restraint and refusal to make fun,
particularly since John's efforts bring him no profit. Whereas the imagery of
the clear mirror implies that interpretation of what is perceived is immediate
and universal, such (potential) differences of textual reading show the limitations of the image of the mirror as a representation of textual mediation.
There is always a consequent danger that an ironic discourse might inadvert-
ently be read as a statement of fact or expression of an opinion to be relied
on, and the probability of such misreadings must increase over time, as the
association of certain words with particular ideas shifts or becomes obscured.
Once the (presumed) difficulty of nuancing Gerald's work is acknowledged,
as it rarely has been, then some of the textual cruxes in his *oeuvre* become less
mysterious, if still not definitively capable of solution.

One passage that has long puzzled is what appears to be a proposed solution to 'the Matter of Wales', which occurs in one manuscript 'edition' of the
*Descriptio Kambriae*, only to be replaced by a very different passage in later
manuscripts:

> Unde et expulso prorsus veteri colono, aliaque ad regna translato, de Cam-
> bria coloniam princeps efficere praevalebit. Porro terram tam hispedam
> et tam inviam, tamque colonos domabiles habere nesciam, quas-desertum
> penitus bestiis relinquere, atque forestam inde facere, provido principi
> longe tutius et consultius fore, nonnulli sunt qui arbetrentur.
>
> . . .
>
> Therefore the king will be able to make Wales a colony, after he has
> expelled the old inhabitants and deported them to other kingdoms.
> Moreover, many judge that it would be safer and more advisable for
> a wise ruler to leave such a rough, trackless land, which can only have
> unruly inhabitants, as a wilderness for beasts and to make a forest of it.[58]

The passage presents difficulties of reading, as well as difficulties of interpretation, not least because it seems to complicate our understanding of Gerald's
relationship to his own sense of his 'Welshness'. Dimock reads the passage as
a straightforward expression of a practical idea – 'In this passage he coolly

recommended the English monarch to drive bodily the whole Welsh race out of Wales, and to colonize the country with other people.'[59] This literal reading of the passage was recently echoed by Michael Faletra who encourages his readers to 'recall Gerald of Wales's suggestion, made in the 1194 edition of his *Description of Wales*, that the entire country be emptied of its native inhabitants and transformed into a game preserve' and by Bartlett who notes that 'at this period Gerald was evidently not "Gerald the Welshman"'.[60] But such readings do not do justice to Gerald's intentions, however difficult those intentions may be to recover. Gerald does not himself recommend such a policy, and to note that a king might do something oppressive is far from egging him on to do so. Crucially, it is not Gerald who suggests that Wales would serve better as a royal forest – this is the opinion of nameless others, and the respect their suggestion deserves is perhaps hinted at by the fact that it is conveyed through the use of a passive voice. Ironically, the one part of Wales where such a process had been (at least partially) undertaken on a large scale was in Gerald's beloved south Pembrokeshire, but even there the policy of excluding the Welsh had been, at best, uneven, a fact demonstrated by the residence there of Gerald's grandmother, the Princess Nest.

Perhaps the most plausible reading of the passage is to assume that the nameless 'others' advocating the ethnic cleansing of Wales represent a real strand of opinion at the Angevin court. William of Newburgh, John of Salisbury and others had been active in promoting the idea of the physical inaccessibility and difficulty of the Welsh terrain,[61] an idea that seemed always to overlook the fertile pastures of Glamorgan, Monmouth, Carmarthen and Clwyd, while King John regularly frequented his favourite hunting sites in the region of the Wye Valley. In reporting their absurd suggestion, maybe Gerald presented it ironically as a *reductio ad absurdum* of an idea which, applied to specific lands or places, had been used to dispossess the Welsh and deny their legal title to property for a number of generations. But, if the suggestion bore any relation to notions that had been whispered around the court, then Gerald may, to his surprise, have found readers who not merely missed the irony and (like Dimock and Faletra) read it as a sincere plan of action, but actually thought it presented a sensible idea. In such circumstances, Gerald may have felt obliged to cancel the passage.

But, the idea that Gerald might have intended the passage ironically has not been seriously entertained by critics, perhaps because of the persistence of contrary expectations concerning the writer and his work. Discussing another scene notoriously difficult to interpret in Gerald's output, Julia Crick notes the rejection of ironic readings by Bartlett and Richter before reaching the conclusion that 'there is a fourth reason to credit Gerald's seriousness, as R. R. Davies has pointed out to me: irony was not his style'.[62]

But Gerald's presumed rejection of irony sits strangely with other expectations of a writer trained in the Paris schools, at a highpoint of Latin eloquence,
and it is not hard to find other examples of a more playful irony in his work.
The *Gemma ecclesiastica* has been described as Gerald's favourite amongst his
own works, and offers an elegant and extensive testament to his erudition and
powers of persuasion. It opens with a rhetorical preface in which the writer
offers an apology for his rough speech and lack of craft:

> Scio tamen quod eruditis auribus delicatisque quibus trita sunt ista lec-
> toribus vel tædiosus esse videbor in hoc opusculo vel superfluus. Sed
> sciant illi quod Walliæ nostræ soli scripta sunt ista, publicis admodum
> et planis absque ornatu, tam verbis quam sententiis rudibus, solum ad
> intelligendum exposita.

> Quod si forte mandati fines excedentia Marchiæ nostræ metas transvol-
> averunt et in majorum manus quandoque dilapsa eruditorum oculis se
> præsumptuose subjecerint, sciant et hoc illi quoniam ipsis malo propin-
> are superflua quam nostris subtrahere necessaria.
>
> . . .
>
> I know that to learned readers and delicate ears to whom these matters
> are commonplace I will appear either wearisome or superfluous. But let
> them know that this work is written exclusively for our own country
> of Wales and is set forth as much in plain and ordinary language with-
> out ornament as in commonplace judgments, in order that it may be
> understood.

> If perchance this book, going beyond the limits intended for it, should fly
> across the borders of our Marches and, having fallen into the hands of the
> great, should presumptuously submit itself to the eyes of the learned, let
> them know that I prefer to set before them these superfluous things than
> to withhold from our countrymen those things which are necessary.[63]

Offering such a disclaimer as a preface is a standard rhetorical ploy, and Gerald's
use of the device offers a graceful curtsey to tradition. It should be seen as an
example of the *trope occupatio* (or *occultatio*): '[*Occultatio*] occurs when we say that
we are passing by, or do not know, or refuse to say that which precisely now we
are saying' ('Occultatio est cum dicimus nos praeterire aut non scire aut nolle
dicere id quod nunc maxime dicimus').[64]

While apparently acknowledging the provinciality of his work, Gerald's true intention, through the skilful use of sophisticated figures of rhetoric, is precisely to prove the opposite – that the text which follows is far too

accomplished to have been written exclusively for Wales. There are tell-tale signs in the passage to warn us of its ironic intent, from the word-play on limits/borders/March to the curious use of *Walliae*, a term Gerald considered demeaning, rather than his preferred alternative *Cambriae* to designate Wales. This substitution is the more striking when we note that in the passage which supposedly advocated the depopulation of Wales, it is the preferred Giraldian form *Cambria* which appears. Nonetheless, J. S. Brewer read the preface not as a rhetorical ploy but as a statement of truth, deploring the 'barbarous and uncivilized condition of Wales' and the perceived absence of books there – even though, when Gerald wrote the *Gemma*, he was no longer resident in Wales.[65]

In art, as (apparently) in life, Gerald seems little prone to apology so, when he appears to be willing to do so, it seems wise to treat his offer with scepticism, and to ask what he is really attempting. Throughout his work, Gerald attempts to bring together a pressing need to be heard with a desire to have his opinions rest on a foundation broader than his shoulders alone. Hearing Gerald's voice poses a considerable challenge for critics not because he aspires to obscurity, but because the voice is a complex one, its assertiveness balanced and modulated by more reflective and self-questioning colours, that is, by expressions of Gerald that history has not yet been interested in listening to.

# Notes

1   Gerald's works on Wales, in particular, have remained continuously in print, creating a familiarity. To give an example, 'Y Gerallt Gymro' is the name given to the railway service connecting north Wales with Cardiff, while 'Gerald of Wales' remains a profitable marketing brand for accessories from pencil cases and maps to jewellery and scarves, to an extent not matched by, for example, John of Salisbury or Peter of Blois.

2   For example, Richter, having denied Gerald's work 'the depth of John of Salisbury's ethics, or either the wide range of the subject matter of Peter of Blois' correspondence or the technical, financial, and judicial expertise of Richard fitzNigel's [works]', falls back on praising his author through the imprecise commendation of Gerald's works' 'own special merits'. See Michael Richter, 'Gerald of Wales: A Reassessment on the 750th Anniversary of his Death', *Traditio*, 29 (1973), 379–90, at 379.

3   Edward Augustus Freeman, *The Norman Conquest*, 6/5 (Oxford, 1876), p. 579.

4   Henry Mayr-Harting, *Religion, Politics and Society in Britain, 1066–1277* (Harlow, 2011), p. 228.

5   Shai Burstyn, 'Is Gerald of Wales a Credible Musical Witness?', *The Musical Quarterly*, 72/2 (1986), 155–69, writes, 'Gerald was a prolific writer. His extant oeuvre, comprising at least seventeen titles, centers on a few fields of inquiry. But as he possessed exceptional intellectual curiosity, his writings are a gold mine of first-hand information to medieval scholars in specialities as diverse as ecclesiastical and intellectual history, historiography, folklore, geography, nature, nascent nationalism, and, of course, musical history' (156). The term 'prolific' is adopted also by Robert Bartlett, 'Reading Saints' Lives: The Case of Gerald of Wales', *Speculum*, 58 (1983), 598–613, at 599.

6   Richter, 'Gerald of Wales', 379.

7   For example, Bartlett, 'Saints' Lives', 606, voices concern that Gerald's *renovatio* of Rhygyfarch's Life of St David is by no means simply a process of improvement, as Gerald claims: 'In instances such as these, the difference in style between Rhygyfarch and Gerald seems to reflect Gerald's greater concern with style – a concern that was not necessarily accompanied by greater skill as a stylist.'

8   Thus F. X. Martin, 'Gerald of Wales, Norman Reporter on Ireland', *Studies: An Irish Quarterly Review*, 58/231 (1969), 272–92, at 272, concedes that 'it is safe to state that his book, *The Conquest of Ireland*, is our main source of information about the Norman invasion. It may be seized upon, arraigned for trial, condemned and gibbeted in public, but it cannot be disregarded. It is too carefully constructed and cleverly argued.'

9   Antonia Gransden, review of Robert Bartlett, *Gerald of Wales 1146–1223* and Brynley F. Roberts, *Gerald of Wales, English Historical Review*, 100/4 (1985), 159–61.

10  Dimock notes the changes in Gerald's accounts of Walter de Braose's involvement in a massacre of Welsh leaders during Walter's life and after his death; J. F. Dimock (ed.), *Giraldi Cambrensis Opera*, 8/6 (London, 1868), pp. xiv–xv.

11   J. S. Brewer (ed.), *Giraldi Cambrensis Opera*, 8/1 (London, 1861), pp. 425–7.

12   Gransden, review of Bartlett and Roberts, 160.

13   Gransden, review of Bartlett and Roberts, 160.

14   Burstyn, 'Is Gerald of Wales a Credible Musical Witness?', 155.

15   Charles Burney, *The General History of Music from the Earliest Ages to the Present Period*, 4/2 (2nd edition, London, 1789), p. 109; Michael Richter, *Giraldus Cambrensis: The Growth of the Welsh Nation* (Aberystwyth, 1972), p. 8.

16   Tony Davenport, 'Sex, Ghosts and Dreams: Walter Map (1135?–1210?) and Gerald of Wales (1146–1223)', in Ruth Kennedy and Simon Meecham-Jones (eds), *Writers of the Reign of Henry II: Twelve Essays* (New York, 2006), pp. 133–50, at 148.

17   E. R. Curtius and Willard R. Trask (trans.), *European Literature and the Latin Middle Ages* (London, 1979).

18   Clearly such an ambitious project is beyond the scope of this paper, which seeks rather to offer some initial directions for future research.

19   Brian Stock, *The Implications of Literacy* (Princeton, 1983), pp. 17–18.

20   Stock, *The Implications of Literacy*, pp. 90–2.

21   A. A. Goddu and R. H. Rouse, 'Gerald of Wales and the *Florilegium Angelicum*', *Speculum*, 52/3 (1977), 488–521, at 516–17.

22   Goddu and Rouse, 'Gerald of Wales and the *Florilegium Angelicum*', 517.

23   Andrew Hughes, 'Giraldus Cambrensis', in Stanley Sadie (ed.), *The New Grove Dictionary of Music and Musicians*, 20/7 (London, 1980), p. 404.

24   Goddu and Rouse, 'Gerald of Wales and the *Florilegium Angelicum*', 513.

25   Goddu and Rouse, 'Gerald of Wales and the *Florilegium Angelicum*', 514.

26   Goddu and Rouse, 'Gerald of Wales and the *Florilegium Angelicum*', 514.

27   Dimock (ed.), *Giraldi Cambrensis Opera*, 8/6, p. lxv.

28   See, for example, Paul Gerhard Schmidt, 'The Quotation in Goliardic Poetry: The Feast of Fools and the Goliardic Strophe *cum auctoritate*', in Oswyn Murray and Peter Godman (eds), *Latin Poetry and the Classical Tradition* (Oxford, 1990), pp. 39–55; Jill Mann, 'Satiric Subject and Satiric Object in Goliardic Literature', *Mittellateinisches Jahrbuch*, 15 (1980), 63–86; Simon Meecham-Jones, '"I will not stay silent": Sovereignty and Textual Identity in Walter of Châtillon's "Propter Sion non Tacebo"', in Kennedy and Meecham-Jones (eds), *Writers of the Reign of Henry II*, pp. 109–32.

29   See Robert R. Edwards, 'Walter Map: Authorship and the Space of Writing', *New Literary History*, 38/2 (2007), 273–92.

30   Robert Bartlett, *Gerald of Wales: A Voice of the Middle Ages* (Stroud, 2006), p. 13. He continues that 'Gerald was not simply a court littérateur', which seems to suggest that Gerald's other work (perhaps represented with a hint of scepticism) – 'he regarded himself as a historian' – deserves more respect.

31   Alan Keith Bate, 'Walter Map and Giraldus Cambrensis', *Latomus*, 31 (1972), 860–75.

32   Peter Dronke, 'Peter of Blois and Poetry at the Court of Henry II', *Mediaeval Studies*, 28 (1976), 185–235; repr. in Dronke, *The Medieval Poet and his World* (Rome, 1984), pp. 281–339. The theory of distinguishing two contemporary Peters from

Blois was developed by R. W. Southern, 'The Necessity for Two Peters of Blois', in Lesley Smith and Benedicta Ward (eds), *Intellectual Life in the Middle Ages: Essays Presented to Margaret Gibson* (London, 1992), pp. 103–18. The issue has been reconsidered in Simon Meecham-Jones, 'Sex in the Sight of God: Theology and the Erotic in Peter of Blois' "Grates ago Veneri"', in Amanda Hopkins and Cory Rushton (eds), *The Erotic in Medieval Literature* (Woodbridge, 2007), pp. 142–54.

33   R. W. Southern, *Medieval Humanism and Other Studies* (Oxford, 1970), p. 107.

34   Neil Cartlidge, 'An Intruder at the Feast? Anxiety and Debate in the Letters of Peter of Blois', in Kennedy and Meecham-Jones (eds), *Writers of the Reign of Henry II*, pp. 79–108, at 79.

35   W. Llewelyn Williams (ed. and trans.), *The Description of Wales* (London, 1908), p. xii.

36   John of Salisbury's *Metalogicon* provides evidence on how high Quintilian's reputation stood in the minds of twelfth-century educators. James J. Murphy argues that 'About 1225, Quintilian slipped into obscurity, this time for a century and a half', though it could be argued that his influence was perpetuated indirectly through the pre-eminence of those, like John, who had been trained using his precepts. See James J. Murphy and Cleve Wiese (eds and trans.), *Quintilian on the Teaching of Speaking and Writing: Translations from Books One, Two, and Ten of the Institutio Oratoria* (2nd edition, Carbondale, 2016), p. xxxvi.

37   Quintilian, *Institutio Oratoria*, I.9–10, in H. E. Butler (trans.), *The Institutio Oratio: Books I–III* (Cambridge, 1969), pp. 8–11.

38   *Itinerarium*, 'Praefatio prima', p. 6; Williams (ed. and trans.), *Description of Wales*, p. 5.

39   *Topographia*, 'Introitus', p. 6, Thomas Forester (trans.) and Thomas Wright (ed. and rev.), *The Historical Works of Giraldus Cambrensis* (London, 1863), p. 6.

40   *Gemma ecclesiastica*, i.46, p. 124; John J. Hagen (trans.), *The Jewel of the Church: A Translation of Gemma ecclesiastica by Giraldus Cambrensis* (Leiden, 1979), p. 95.

41   Versions of 'Sevit aure spiritus' are found in the *Carmina Burana* and the Arundel lyrics. For editions, see A. Hilka, O. Schumann and B. Bischoff (eds), *Carmina Burana: Die Lieder der Benediktbeurer Handschrift* (Munich, 1979); C. J. McDonough (ed.), *The Oxford Poems of Hugh Primas and the Arundel Lyrics* (Toronto, 1984). A full text and translation of the poem (titled 'Wild whistles the wind') is found in Peter Godman, 'Literary Classicism and Latin Erotic Poetry of the Twelfth Century and the Renaissance', in Peter Godman and Oswyn Murray (eds), *Latin Poetry and the Classical Tradition: Essays in Medieval and Renaissance Literature* (Oxford, 1990), pp. 142–82. See also Simon Meecham-Jones, 'Resisting Utopia: Temptation and Assertion in the Latin Lyrics of Walter of Chatillon and Peter of Blois', in Françoise Le Saux and Neil Thomas (eds), *Utopias* (Durham, 2000), pp. 77–100.

42   P. J. Godman, *The Silent Masters: Latin Literature and its Censors in the High Middle Ages* (Princeton, 2000), p. 344.

43   Cartlidge, 'An Intruder at the Feast?', p. 88.

44   Burstyn, 'Is Gerald of Wales a Credible Musical Witness?', 161.

45   Bartlett, 'Saints' Lives', 602–3.

46    Bartlett, 'Saints' Lives', 603.

47    *Expugnatio*, i.1; A. B. Scott and F. X. Martin (eds and trans.), *Expugnatio Hibernica: The Conquest of Ireland by Giraldus Cambrensis* (Dublin, 1978), pp. 24–5.

48    F. M. Powicke, *Gerald of Wales* (Manchester, 1928), p. 4.

49    Davenport, 'Sex, Ghosts and Dreams', p. 148.

50    *Topographia*, 'Introitus', p. 7; Forester (trans.), *Historical Works*, p. 7.

51    Powicke, *Gerald*, p. 4.

52    Powicke, *Gerald*, p. 10.

53    Powicke, *Gerald*, p. 10.

54    Davenport, 'Sex, Ghosts and Dreams', p. 148.

55    R. W. Southern, 'Aspects of the European Tradition of Historical Writing 3: History as Prophecy', in Robert J. Bartlett (ed.), *History and Historians: Selected Papers of R. W. Southern* (Oxford, 2004), pp. 48–65, at 56.

56    Southern, 'Aspects of the European Tradition', p. 56.

57    Gransden, review of Bartlett and Roberts, writes 'Although his literary style was humanistic, the content of his work shows many features of medieval thought – belief in divine causation, in miracles and portents, in the theory of the Four Elements, in folklore, and the like' (160).

58    Dimock (ed.), *Giraldi Cambrensis Opera*, 8/6, p. 225, n. 4; Bartlett (trans.), *Gerald*, p. 21.

59    Dimock (ed.), *Giraldi Cambrensis Opera*, 8/6, pp. xxx–xxxi.

60    Michael A. Faletra, *Wales and the Medieval Colonial Imagination: The Matters of Britain in the Twelfth Century* (New York, 2014); Bartlett, *Gerald of Wales*, p. 21.

61    Simon Meecham-Jones, 'Where was Wales? The Erasure of Wales in Medieval English Culture', in Ruth Kennedy and Simon Meecham-Jones (eds), *Authority and Subjugation in Writing of Medieval Wales* (New York, 2008), pp. 27–55, at 40–1.

62    Julia C. Crick, 'The British Past and the Welsh Future: Gerald of Wales, Geoffrey of Monmouth and Arthur of Britain', *Celtica*, 23 (1999), 60–75, at 66, n. 48.

63    *Gemma ecclesiastica*, 'Proemium', pp. 6–7; Hagen (trans.), *The Jewel of the Church*, pp. 3–4.

64    Pseudo-Cicero, *Rhetorica ad Herennium*, IV.xxvii.37, in Harry Caplan (trans.), *Rhetorica ad Herennium*, Loeb Classical Library 403 (Cambridge, 1954), pp. 320–1.

65    Brewer (ed.), *Giraldi Cambrensis Opera*, pp. xii–xiii: 'How indeed, could it be otherwise, when our author should have thought it incumbent to give them instructions on the most obvious points of their clerical duties, and deem it needful to apologize to the rest of the world for descending to a style of writing and a selection of topics he would have adopted towards ordinary readers?'

❖